The Two Isabellas
of King John

The Two Isabellas of King John

Kristen McQuinn

PEN & SWORD HISTORY

First published in Great Britain in 2021 by
Pen & Sword History
An imprint of
Pen & Sword Books Ltd
Yorkshire – Philadelphia

ISBN 978 1 52676 164 4

Typeset by Mac Style
Printed and bound by CPI Group (UK) Ltd, Croydon, CR0 4YY

Pen & Sword Books Limited incorporates the imprints of Atlas,
Archaeology, Aviation, Discovery, Family History, Fiction, History,
Maritime, Military, Military Classics, Politics, Select, Transport,
True Crime, Air World, Frontline Publishing, Leo Cooper, Remember
When, Seaforth Publishing, The Praetorian Press, Wharncliffe
Local History, Wharncliffe Transport, Wharncliffe True Crime
and White Owl.

For a complete list of Pen & Sword titles please contact

PEN & SWORD BOOKS LIMITED
47 Church Street, Barnsley, South Yorkshire, S70 2AS, England
E-mail: enquiries@pen-and-sword.co.uk
Website: www.pen-and-sword.co.uk

Or

PEN AND SWORD BOOKS
1950 Lawrence Rd, Havertown, PA 19083, USA
E-mail: Uspen-and-sword@casematepublishers.com
Website: www.penandswordbooks.com

To Shannon
I pinky promise…

Contents

Chapter 1

Introduction

So much of history is written for us. It is written by battles and disease and death. It is mostly written by men. The women of history are frequently lost in the shadows and forgotten. Many women, like Isabella of Gloucester, remain unknown figures, even when they were married to royalty. Others, like Isabelle of Angoulême, have their histories imposed upon them – by men, by society, by the distance of time.

But what these women have left behind goes beyond what we know or what is written. Their impact, while often unseen and unheard in their time, is nevertheless long-lasting and subtle. They created kings and nations through marriage, through childbirth, through their support or their antagonism. Their voices, heard or silenced, are the hidden force behind the thrones of kings.

Between 1135 and 1153, England was torn asunder by civil war and crises of succession. During this time, the only surviving legitimate child of Henry I, Matilda, fought her cousin, Stephen of Blois, for the throne. Noblemen chose sides, changed sides, turned their coats, and the country suffered. So great and widespread was the wretchedness of the people that the Peterborough chronicler famously wrote that Christ and His saints were sleeping. This time was known as The Anarchy.

After The Anarchy, Henry, Duke of Normandy and future Henry II, the son of Matilda, emerged victorious, having been named as Stephen's heir and eventually succeeding Stephen to the throne in a peaceful transfer of power. Thus begins the Plantagenet dynasty, also called the Angevin empire. From the Plantagenets, we have Henry II and Eleanor of Aquitaine, the power couple of the twelfth century; their son the warrior-king, Richard the Lionheart; and his younger brother, John 'Lackland', the eventual King John I. Many of us know King John primarily from Robin Hood tales but lack an understanding of the real man behind the stories. Buried further still are the stories and roles of his wives, the women behind the throne – Isabella of Gloucester and Isabelle of Angoulême. The role of these women has been largely overlooked, marginalised, and lost to historical record. However, the role women and especially queens have played throughout history cannot be overstated. Through queens, policies have been implemented, churches and colleges founded, and citizens given solace. And also through queens, kings are formed. No less is true for John and his wives, and their influence upon him has been just as profound.

Bringing these women out of the mists of history highlights the roles they played in their own time as well as bringing to the fore the notion that many of their contemporary issues remain relevant today. The strength of women has carried history and kings forward, often at the expense of their own reputations, happiness, or choice. Writing about medieval women is often a tremendous challenge, sometimes surprisingly so. There are several reasons for this, but largely it boils down to a couple of main issues. The historical record tends to favour heavily the public realms – politics, religion, warfare – and avoids the private realms, to where the vast majority of women have been relegated.[1] Records, not surprisingly, favour events that are more exciting or of greater social significance than the private lives of the citizenry, even of royals, and almost always favour the nobility and ruling classes. This general lack of personal documentation is partly why the letters of the fifteenth century Paston family are so widely studied; they give an unprecedented glimpse into the daily life of a non-noble medieval family.

Additionally, medieval convention considered reading and writing to be separate skills; if a person could read, it did not necessarily follow that they could also write. Even kings had scribes to whom they commonly dictated their correspondence. Compounding the convention separating reading from writing, 'authorship usually was restricted to those who held social authority, particularly the university-trained male clergy. Women, furthermore, except for some nuns, were excluded from learning Latin, the lingua franca of intellectual life'.[2] It was rare for women, even many nuns, to be well educated in Latin or writing. Since women throughout history were usually viewed as second-class citizens, few chroniclers bothered recording the details of their lives, adding to the further erasure of women in history.

Unfortunately, this is true even for queens and women married to future monarchs. Isabella of Gloucester is almost entirely absent from the historical record, despite her marriage of ten years to John. Isabelle of Angoulême has more written about her; however, much of it was recorded by men who hated her and so her record must be viewed with a healthy dose of skepticism.

Even their names are sometimes in dispute. Isabella of Gloucester has been documented in her time variously as Isabel, Isabella, Isabelle, Hawise, and Avice. Hawise, at least, may be an understandable mistake made by the chronicler Roger of Howden, who first referred to her as Hawise, for that actually was her mother's name.[3] Thanks to the extensive research of previous scholars, particularly Richard Price, it has been determined that the Close Rolls of John's reign refer to her as Countess Isabella and Isabella, daughter of Count William. Similarly, Isabelle of Angoulême has been called Isabelle, Isabel, Ysabel, and Isabella, depending on which chronicle one consults. For the purposes of this text, I shall refer to the lady of Gloucester as Isabella and the lady of Angoulême as Isabelle.

In popular culture, the Tudors reign supreme, if you will pardon the pun. People are drawn to the images of the glittering court, the garb, the political intrigue, and the sexual scandals. However, the Plantagenets, who lived and ruled from Henry II in 1154 to Richard III in 1485, made the Tudors look like rank amateurs in terms of sex scandals, political machinations, and in-fighting. Of course, the Plantagenet women are not as well documented as their men, unless they did something the chroniclers found particularly titillating. Despite that, we can piece together a decent understanding of their lives by examining the lives of other women of similar rank and the various literature of their time.

Chapter 2

Childhood and Education

Isabella of Gloucester and Isabelle of Angoulême were the first and second wife, respectively, of King John, the youngest and much favoured son of King Henry II and Eleanor of Aquitaine. Very little history is known about these women other than the strategic advantage their marriages served to the royal dynasty in England. Isabella of Gloucester was the daughter of a nobleman, William FitzRobert, the second Earl of Gloucester. Her marriage to King John in 1189 granted him rights over her substantial property as he was positioning himself as heir to Richard I 'The Lionheart'. Isabelle of Angoulême was the only child of Aymer of Angoulême and the great-granddaughter of King Louis VI of France, whose vast land holdings in France also made her an attractive asset. Isabella and Isabelle are among the lost women of history. Significantly, their value in the historical record is reduced to their ability to produce heirs, so there is very little direct evidence of the formative lives of these two queens of England.

When we think of kings and queens today, we tend to assume that a great deal is known about them. They did, after all, rule over nations, wage wars, and create treaties that have, in some cases, lasted for centuries and influenced more modern policies. They were important people, so naturally we think their lives have been chronicled in detail. We have numerous and thorough records of men and women from the age of Antiquity, so a person could be forgiven in thinking the same holds true for the medieval period.

Unfortunately, this is not always the case, especially for children. There are many reasons why we might not have much information about a person. Destruction of records during wars or fires, loss or degradation of the written record, or even political reasons could prevent information about a person from being recorded. Under certain circumstances, the recording of women's lives was viewed as generally unimportant, even if the woman in question was a noblewoman or married to a king.

The issue of missing information is compounded when related to children. Children very rarely left written records of their own, and adult references to children are often absent as well. The assumption is often that the duties and obligations towards children were so well known that no one bothered writing them down, viewing them as normal daily life.[1] So how do we know what the childhoods of Isabella and Isabelle were like? Given the lack of records about their formative years, studying the childhoods of other women of similar rank is necessary to form an understanding of what these two women's lives were like. It is through this somewhat murky lens that we need to focus our attention.

Concept of Childhood

An issue to consider when contemplating the childhood education of medieval noblewomen is the concept of childhood itself. How has the concept of childhood changed in the intervening centuries? Did medieval society even have a concept of childhood? How would the location of one's upbringing influence their views on the roles they hold in adulthood? The medieval notion of childhood may have been quite different from what we currently tend to think. It is tempting to assume that medieval society had similar views on childhood as modern society, but in fact, the concept of childhood varies greatly across time and cultures. As Willem Frijhoff notes, 'childhood is as much a *fact* of a biological and psychological nature as it is a cultural *notion* that through the centuries has been the object of ever-changing perceptions and definitions, images, approaches and emotions'.[2] There is a widespread notion, both in popular culture and in some academic circles, that medieval society viewed children as essentially small adults for whom childhood was merely a short timeframe to get past so as to proceed with the activities of adult life. This perception is sometimes supported because of the 'existence of child monks and nuns, called oblates, [which] would seem to support the viewpoint of children as miniature adults, and bely a psychological appreciation of children'.[3] Oblates were common throughout Europe from the Anglo-Saxon era forward, with some chronicles recording oblates as young as 3 in some monasteries.[4] However, there is other evidence which suggests that these young oblates were not treated as small adults but were understood to be children and were treated as such. For example, Asser, the biographer of

King Alfred the Great, noted that oblates were too young to choose to do good or evil, which actually aligns with some modern scholarship as well. Children who cannot yet think about good or evil are too young to make a lifelong commitment to a religious life, which Asser seems to have been noting. In fact, this sentiment fits with some modern schools of thought, where it is irksome to hear a child labeled with the religion of their parents, such as Catholic child, Muslim child, and so forth. 'Such phrases,' states Richard Dawkins, 'can be heard used of children too young to talk, let alone to hold religious opinions'.[5] While Alfred the Great and Asser lived about 150 years before the Norman Conquest, the thought of children as small adults was not one that was prevalent in the Middle Ages.

The way in which childhood is viewed throughout the centuries is fluid, based on a multitude of factors. Adding to the burden of discovering a true medieval concept of childhood is the fact that the children themselves are virtually mute voices in the historical record. Contributing to the lack of children's voices in documented history is the notion of 'childhood amnesia',[6] wherein children forget the details of their younger selves' experiences; not until adolescence do most children begin to reflect on themselves and who they are, creating themselves in the process and becoming in their way agents of history.[7] So-called childhood amnesia is undoubtedly a large part of the reason why so few records from children themselves exist, as well as the fact that most children are not self-reflective in the necessary way to leave a written record of their thoughts. Our Isabellas appear to have been no different in this and did not leave any written account of their childhood.

Moreover, many early societies may not have viewed children as independent people with an existence outside the realm of what adults oversaw. Uncovering definitions of childhood varies with culture and ages are often broken into socially influenced ranges. For example, in the Middle Ages stages of life were often divided into 'childhood until the age of 10, youth until 20, and so on, until death at age 80 or 100'.[8] Other examples of the stages of life show that some societies, such as sixteenth-century Dutch physician Levinus Lemnius, ranged later, with youth described as age 25 to 35, at which point a person could enter political office.[9] A society in which one's majority was reached at a younger age would likely impact the way childhood was viewed and represented. At various points in history, including the Middle Ages, childhood and adolescence were periods when a person transitioned out of dependence upon parents or guardians and into a more independent adulthood, often upon the event of leaving a home to go to work.[10] Twelfth-century Cluniac orders determined adolescence to be at age 15 for boys, and puberty in girls that would signal her physical readiness to bear a man heirs would have been a determining factor in her adulthood. With that mindset, 'sexual maturation stood as a proxy for true age in this society'.[11]

The legal definition of childhood is similarly complex. In the Middle Ages, the definition of childhood was rooted in the law, and varied depending on a person's age, social rank, and sex. For example, for much of the period covered in this book, a boy could make a legally recognised will and marry at age 14 and generally could inherit at 21, but girls could make a legal will and marry at 12 and were considered to have reached their majority at 12 if she was married and 14 if she was not.[12] How society dealt with child criminals would be different based on age, sex, and social class as well.

How people, parents in particular, viewed children has varied over time. Some schools of historical research claim that medieval parents were not attached to their children because there were so many ways for a young child to die. Many children died before they even reached adolescence, whether by illness, injury, or some other reason. 'Protecting themselves from a life of grief, parents could and would care for their children but without emotional involvement. Consequently, after the very first years of physical care directed at the pure survival of the child, education itself remained loose, amorphous, and largely unspoken'.[13] The idea that medieval parents did not love their children persists in part because of a paper published in the 1960s by Philippe Ariès, who claimed that there was no place for childhood in the medieval world.[14] His thesis was supported by a chronicle from the fifteenth century which states, 'The want of affection in the English is strongly manifested towards their children, for after having them at home until they reach the age of seven or nine, they board them out to service in the homes of other people.'[15]

Because of the dearth of documentation about children in the historical record, ideas such as this have persisted well into modern scholarship. However, more recent scholarship has offered a different perspective. Now, it is generally accepted that the Middle Ages did have a distinct view of childhood and treated children as such, and that they received ample attention and affection. Nicholas Orme, who has closely studied medieval childhood says that 'it cannot be over-emphasised that there is nothing to be said for Ariès's view of childhood in the middle ages … [His] views were mistaken: not simply in detail but in substance. It is time to lay them to rest.'[16] Regardless of the difficulties of any given era, or the higher risk of childhood death, believing that parents love their children any less than modern parents do is a thought worthy of a good deal of skepticism. However, imposing modern sentiments onto a distant culture is a slippery slope and in truth, there is not enough evidence to prove medieval sentiment one way or the other.

In modern Western society, it is common to view childhood as a lengthy period ranging from birth to anywhere between 16 and 21. A female child in medieval society generally stayed with her mother and other female relatives until age 7 or 8. At that point, depending on her social status, a girl might either stay with her mother and begin learning skills appropriate to her station, be sent to another home for fostering and further education, or possibly to a convent school. A boy would leave his mother's exclusive care at the same age and either begin learning his father's trade, be apprenticed to a trade master, or be fostered at a noble house to begin squiring for a knight or lord. While the act of fostering may seem to support the notion that medieval parents did not have much love for their children, in truth they highlight a social activity designed to foster necessary skills and knowledge to children. It is akin to sending a child to school, except that medieval school was often somewhere other than home. These customs gave children the best chance of living a successful life, which may not necessarily have been through remaining with their parents or taking up their craft.

Education of Non-Noble Children

In the middle to late twelfth century, as with many eras throughout history, the childhood of a noble was significantly different from their lower-ranked contemporaries. Peasants or other non-noble members of society might have had an education consisting of essential skills for their lives; trades, including apprentice and journeyman phases; the running of a household; or basic medical care to aid the inevitable fevers, cuts, births, or illnesses to which people were susceptible. It is possible that children of peasants were fostered away from home to learn skills, but there is not much evidence to support it one way or the other. Fostering may have occurred and it simply was not noted in the historical record since they were not of a sufficiently high rank, or they may not have had the material means to do so. Most of the chronicles we have today are about the more affluent classes, where fostering did often occur.

Education of Noble Classes

A person of rank – nobility or royalty – would have a different education entirely. Many medieval noble women would have received much of their education at a nunnery. In addition to household skills such as weaving and spinning, noble women would have learned to read and possibly write, using the major texts of the day. It is possible that some medieval fathers would have taught their daughters about various influential authors as well, even if by virtue of reading them in front of their children. Eleanor of Aquitaine, for example, was educated by her father and very likely had knowledge of Greek and Roman authors, many of whom had widespread influence upon medieval thought.

While the records of Isabella of Gloucester's and Isabelle of Angoulême's early lives and education are essentially nonexistent, it is reasonable to assume their childhood and early education would have been similar to that of other young noblewomen and that they were at least somewhat familiar with the foundational thinkers of their society. There are many medieval texts which 'lead us to believe that every household of substance maintained its own domestic or family school'.[17] The social structure of being schooled at home served for both boys and girls, although it was more common for boys to receive private tutoring from either a university student, a private chaplain, or a local priest. Whereas boys were often sent to the homes of other families of the same social class for fostering and education, girls did not typically attend schools outside the home, and thus tutoring at home or at a nunnery school was more common, with lessons including Latin, reading, memorization, and learning how to manage a household or court. The most famous example of a woman receiving education via a private tutor is, of course, Heloise, student and then lover of Peter Abelard, who was one of the most renowned teachers in Paris in the twelfth century. Eleanor of Aquitaine's own father tutored her in her early childhood education, so this may also have been a common practice for educating young noblewomen, one carried on for her two daughters-in-law, Isabella of Gloucester and Isabelle of Angoulême.

For wealthy or noble classes, sending girls to a nunnery school was one of the best options for female education. Their days would have been taken up with a variety of tasks ranging from attending several services each day; reading, writing, and illuminating various religious texts and devotionals; giving out alms, clothes, and food items to the poor; and needlework for textiles used in church ceremonies. Many nuns were also healers and tended to the sick or could be hired as tutors to local children. For these reasons, nuns were often more visible and active within their communities than some monks were. While there is no evidence that either Isabella or Isabelle attended a nunnery school, if they had, they would likely have been educated to perform the duties expected of them as part of the nobility and ruling class, especially since virtue, chastity, and charity were a daily part of life in a nunnery.

It is likely that both Isabella of Gloucester and Isabelle of Angoulême would have been educated either at home by their mothers and/or hired tutors. It is also possible that they could have been educated by their fathers or other male relatives, as Heloise had been by her uncle until he fatefully hired Abelard. Given their social status, the lack of documentation about them, and the general practices at the time for their respective locations, it is probable that the childhood education of these two women would have been handled at home. If they had attended a convent school, possible locations include Fontevraud Abbey near Chinon for Isabelle and either Worcester Cathedral or Hereford Cathedral School for Isabella.

Whether educated at home or at a convent school, girls of the noble or royal classes would be instructed in areas such as reading, most likely some languages such as Latin, needlework, perhaps playing an instrument, and the diplomacy needed to run a large household or court. Skills in diplomacy would be important for girls of high rank, since women often married for political reasons or to secure a peace treaty between two rival families. These women were known as peaceweavers. In England, though the ruling classes were by this point Norman and had been since 1066, it may be possible that girls like Isabella of Gloucester learned to use these historical roles to help smooth over any ruffled feathers or bruised egos caused by the political machinations of the men in her home, in an unconscious mirroring of older queenly practices. Queens in Anglo-Saxon England often acted as 'peaceweavers' in another way, easing tensions by subtly and carefully showing favour to male nobles who might have been overlooked or undervalued by her husband. In this way, women could quietly influence the politics of her day. While none of the Norman nobles would consider actively using the Anglo-Saxon peaceweaving in their politics, nevertheless, it still occurred. Peaceweaving practices could extend to strengthening the ties between countries as well as between families.[18]

However, neither Isabella of Gloucester or Isabelle of Angoulême were of Saxon descent. The English nobles by the late thirteenth century were solidly Norman, French-speaking, and French culturally. Isabella of Gloucester's father, William FitzRobert, 2nd Earl of Gloucester, was a great-grandson of William the Conqueror, illegitimate son of King Henry I, cousin to King Stephen, and nephew of Empress Maud. Isabelle of Angoulême only came to England upon her marriage to John, and even after that spent the majority of her life in what would be modern-day France. Her father was Aymer of Angoulême, a middle son of Count William VI. Aymer was the last of the Taillefer house, which had ruled Angoulême since the days of the Carolingian Empire of the late-seventh to early twelfth centuries. Isabelle's mother was Alice of Courtenay, granddaughter of Louis VI of France and sister to Peter II of Courtenay, the Latin emperor of Constantinople. It stands to reason, then, that the education for Isabelle of Angoulême, as well as for Isabella of Gloucester, would certainly have been different from the older Saxon culture in their expected or permitted roles as noble brides. Their Norman heritage was by far the most influential on their upbringing as anything from geographic history may have been.

Educational Texts

Neoplatonism

The influence of the Greek philosopher Plato's seminal concept of the Ideal has been picked up and passed on in many eras. It heavily influenced many aspects of medieval culture including education. The specific term 'Neoplatonism' was not first used until 1832,[19] but since it has been used in modern scholarship on medieval society, we will continue its use here. The term makes sense because many noble households would have been very familiar with the works of Plotinus, Porphyry, and Pseudo-Dionysius, which shaped medieval thought for centuries. In fact, 'medieval Christian thought reveals from its inception in foundational authors like Augustine and Boethius an inherent engagement with Neoplatonism'.[20] The twelfth century in particular saw heightened intellectualism, and it was during this period that 'the impact of indirect and direct (Neo)Platonic influence on medieval authors crested in a flourishing of Christian-Platonic cosmology'.[21] Beyond this, Neoplatonism deeply influenced medieval education, becoming entwined with the educational climate that medieval society would use to inform their own understanding of culture.

Two men in particular held notable sway over medieval pedagogical theory: Hugh of St Victor (c. 1096–1141) and John of Salisbury (c. 1120–1180). Their programmes for education were intended for university, a realm not permitted to women, but they likely would have felt the impact of these men on their own education, especially if they received education from a private tutor or their fathers.

Hugh of St. Victor and John of Salisbury

Neoplatonic influence is keenly sensed in the structure and order, often hierarchical, that formed medieval thought. Both Hugh of St. Victor and John of Salisbury 'understood the need for systematic statements about what learning should be and how it should be done'.[22] They encouraged reflection on liberal arts and the place of pagan schools of thought in medieval Christian society. Hugh's major work, *Didascalion*, focuses much of its length on how to read, emphasising that reading is the beginning of education but not the completion of it. Hugh believed that students must know what to read, in what order it should be read, and how to read it. Hugh's basis for such order in education was a belief that all knowledge is unified and that a thorough understanding of the liberal arts was entwined with an understanding of the divine.[23] A major influence on Hugh's thoughts came from St. Augustine's *De Doctrina Christiania*, which determined that Christian education was for the purpose of Scriptural exegesis. Generally, John and Hugh were in agreement on the overall goal of wisdom, but John was strongly of the opinion that there must be 'mutual interaction of talent and instruction: nature needs to be cultivated or it will deteriorate'.[24] His position arises from certain criticism of teaching specific verbal arts; some of his contemporaries believed that the ability to reason and be articulate were natural skills and could not be improved upon by teaching. John believed in the intersection of native skill and formal education, as well as on practicing what was taught. In short, he was pragmatic in his approach to education and preferred to focus on the usefulness of the arts as related to life rather than their subtlety. As FitzGerald notes, 'In this regard, a key feature of John's pedagogical theory is the role of the Aristotelian *habitus*: knowledge is not truly possessed until it becomes fixed through regular practice.'[25]

A great deal of medieval education was done through learning by rote and repetition, further evidence of the lingering impact of John of Salisbury's theories on the subject. Both Hugh and John agreed that the fallen state of mankind did not limit its capacity for knowledge, which was a prevalent belief stemming from Augustine. John's position was somewhat more secular than Hugh's or Augustine's. He also paid a lot of attention to the manner in which education could be used to improve society. John viewed knowledge as a means to build up human happiness and community, and that the way a person studied was an indication of their moral development.[26] Studying and learning do not make people good, they help people 'to receive and to impart knowledge' which is the predecessor to virtue.[27]

John of Salisbury also wrote what is considered to be the first complete political theory text of the Middle Ages – the *Policraticus*. While this text does not focus on the means of education, it does discuss in detail the connections between education and public life. Given its general importance in medieval education, this treatise likely had strong influence over King John as well as the education his wives may have received in their childhood. The *Policraticus* denotes a separation between Church and State, arguing that because the spiritual is of higher importance, the Church must help the community to focus on the salvation of its members; however, a secular ruler 'has an independent purpose, to cultivate human society through the renewal of a just community on earth'.[28] The leader, according to John, must maintain a healthy balance between all the parts, which include the ruling class, clergy, and the peasantry, who he says are the ones who sustain society and move it forward.[29] John also singles out flattery as the most dangerous vice to a ruler. As he explains, the ruler who is flattered is unable to properly assess the relationship between pretty words and real life. John's pedagogical sentiments regarding the connection between education and politics would have been a part of the education of many noble sons, and possibly daughters as well, guiding them as they came into power and began to rule in their own rights. For both Hugh and John, the process of education is a model for how a person lives.

Boethius

Another work that profoundly influenced medieval thought is *De consolatione philosophiae* (*The Consolation of Philosophy*), written by Boethius in roughly the year 524 BCE, and is considered to be 'a cornerstone of medieval humanism'.[30] Boethius penned *The Consolation of Philosophy* (henceforth *Consolation*) while he was in prison, awaiting trial and execution for treason against Theodoric the Great. The premise of the work is framed as a conversation between Boethius and Lady Philosophy about the shifting nature of fame, wealth, and fortune. Specifically, it is about achieving happiness even while enduring the suffering that is a part of every human life. Within this text, the hierarchical structure that was heavily influenced by Neoplatonism is readily apparent, since a hierarchical order connects with Boethius's thoughts on Fate and Fortune. It would be safe to assume that both Isabella of Gloucester and Isabelle of Angoulême were at least passingly familiar with Boethius, and King John himself almost certainly read *Consolation* as well, as it was a common volume in the libraries of many kings. Additionally, Boethius wrote other works about mathematics, geometry, and music that later became standard texts in medieval schools.[31]

The Consolation of Philosophy had tremendous influence upon the medieval mindset. Medieval society was heavily influenced by Neoplatonism (which includes other writers such as Saccas, Plotinus, Porphyry, and Pseudo-Dionysius), and *Consolation* was a seminal Neoplatonist text. The relevance of *Consolation* particular to medieval society hinges on the concept of Fortune, which was often depicted as a fickle woman. It was taught that everyone is subject to the whims of

Fortune, or the Wheel of Fortune (*rota fortunae*), and that the great can be brought low or the low can be raised up. Fortune was used in religious instruction, particularly to describe the downfall of the great or powerful, and fit within the accepted dogma of the Church in that it taught that everything that happens is God's will, including the vicissitudes of Fortune. In fact, 'nothing in *Consolation* is inconsistent with patristic theology; indeed, precedent for nearly every idea which Boethius proposes can be found in the work of St. Augustine'.[32] Fortune herself was made into part of Christian dogma in that she is a part of fate, and thus a part of the divine ruling of the world. Furthermore, Fortune is not able to make a person virtuous or take away their virtue, so virtue therefore is how a person can overcome her. Stressing the importance of virtue in people helps to highlight their free will, and that 'free choice is a part of man's obligation to live well'.[33] Boethius maintains that Lady Philosophy is the highest kind of natural wisdom mankind can attain, and Fortune is her rival, the manifestation of prosperity or difficulty in life that can trap the incautious.

Medieval life was often difficult, even for those in power, and the idea of Fortune shifting, making life better for some and worse for others, must have been a motivator to a society that was often ravaged by internecine war and political upheaval. Those in the lower classes could be hopeful that their own lot would improve in some way through the turning of Fortune's wheel. For the nobility, *Consolation* may have served as a sort of 'Mirror for Princes' text, instructing them on how to rule while also reminding the ruling classes that their situation might be good now, but that circumstances can swiftly change, bringing with it political strife, war, famine, or any number of other ills that could trouble a medieval ruler. Additionally, *Consolation* could have provided a context for rulers to show that, in the medieval mindset, only God is perfect and even the greatest of kings made mistakes and it was not possible to be perfectly virtuous at all times. Rather than being seen as defeatist, this view offers rulers something to aspire to and improve upon in their own lives.

Assuming that John's wives were likely familiar with *Consolation*, there may have been times when they reminded John that they were in their lofty positions entirely by God's will. Truly, the limits of Fortune's powers, in that she cannot give or take away a man's virtue, can, in certain circumstances, appear to have been written precisely for John.

Other Texts

It is worth noting that, formal education aside, books and texts were generally a large presence in the homes of nobles and royals, and there were several texts which remained influential throughout the Middle Ages. During her education, medieval noblewomen like our Isabellas would have been exposed to writers from Antiquity as well as more contemporary chronicles, romances, and poems.

One of these authors, William of Malmesbury, first recorded the expression 'An unlettered king is a crowned ass' in his *Gesta regum*. Later, in his *Policraticus*, John of Salisbury emphasised the importance that a monarch be well-read. Both of these texts were familiar at the Plantagenet courts. According to historian Nicholas Vincent, William of Malmesbury and William FitzStephen were among the first chroniclers in the post-Classical world to refer to the Platonic notion of the philosopher-king, and these men would have also been known by much of twelfth century English nobility.[34] For instance, King John's grandfather, Geoffrey, Count of Anjou, was the dedicatee of William of Conches' *Dragmaticon* and, in true philosopher-king fashion, he encouraged his sons to value studying more than dangerous activities like jousting.

King John's father, Henry II, was the patron of Wace's *Roman de Rou*, a retelling of Norman history. His mother, the formidable Eleanor of Aquitaine, was Wace's patron for his *Roman de Brut*, the story of King Arthur and early British history. Thanks to the lifelong patronage of Henry II and Eleanor, all of the Arthurian literary cycle from France can be linked to the Plantagenets. John's own collection of books ranged 'from the predictable (an Old Testament, a Pliny, a Valerius Maximus) via the theological (Origen, *Super Vetus Testamentum*; Augustine, *Epistolae*, *De Civitate Dei* and *Enarrationes in Psalmos*; Peter the Lombard's *Sentences*; Hugh of St-Victor, *De Sacramentis Christiane fidei*) to the downright esoteric (Candidus Arianus, *De Generatione divina*)'.[35] John left many of these volumes for safekeeping with the monks at Reading Abbey, one of the locations where he held other of his valuables, which could imply that the royal library was mostly left to the care of the Church. It is also likely that King John owned or had access to the letters of Seneca, who was also popular in the Middle Ages for his moral wisdom and alleged connection with St Paul.

Saints' lives/*vitae*

Saints' lives, or *vitae*, were likely also part of the education of Isabella of Gloucester and Isabelle of Angoulême. These tales typically told the stories of the lives of early Christian saints and martyrs. Saints and the stories about them played a variety of roles between roughly 1100 to 1500. Some saints were created from the well-documented lives of real people, like Thomas Becket. Others were 'pseudo-historical figures [about whom] little was known of their actual lives but their legends were full of dramatic events and emblematic elements, such as St George killing the dragon',[36] and some were entirely fictitious or based on earlier pagan deities, such as St Brigid. Although there is a historical element to some of these tales, the primary purpose of saints' lives was to teach moral values, reinforce religious devotion, and exemplify Christian virtues like charity and faith. Stories of virgin saints were frequently popular, in part because they are always martyred and then go directly to Heaven at the end of the *vita*. A common theme amongst specifically female saints' *vitae* is that they almost always lived a chaste and virtuous life and then were killed for refusing to renounce their faith, to surrender their virginity, or for resisting marriage in preference to living life as a nun. In fact, 'virgin-martyrs are used as exemplars of sexual abstinence rather than virginity per se'.[37] These *vitae* are instructive in the virtues of virginity but the matter is a little more complex than it appears at first glance. To a modern audience, a virgin is simply someone who has never had sex, whereas chaste and celibate are nearly interchangeable terms, meaning someone who is temporarily abstaining from sex. The medieval definitions are more nuanced. For example, a chaste man 'did not engage in sexual activity. ... [Chastity is] further complicated by the medieval tendency to embrace (and indeed emphasise) an individual's mental state alongside his physical experiences'.[38] This means, then, that a person was only chaste if they avoided masturbation and impure thoughts as well as not having any sexual partners.

The state of virginity is usually central to female saints. These unfortunate women tended to die in particularly gruesome ways, and usually related to their refusal to surrender their virginity. For example, Saint Agatha (c. 231 CE) swore a vow of virginity and refused the suit of a Roman governor, Quintianus; hoping to turn her away from her vow, Quintianus imprisoned her and had her tortured by cutting off her breasts with pincers. Saint Catherine (c. 287 CE) was executed for being Christian, an illegal act for most of the first through third centuries CE, by the emperor Maximian when she refused to disavow her faith and refused his marriage proposal, preferring to remain a virgin. She was to be tortured on a breaking wheel (later known as the Catherine Wheel) but it shattered at her touch and she was instead beheaded. Or Saint Agnes of Rome (c. 291 CE), who was reported to authorities by one of her many spurned suitors as practicing Christianity. She was subsequently arrested and dragged naked through the streets. Any man who tried to rape her was instantly struck blind, and when she was bound to a stake to be burnt, the wood refused to light, causing the officer in charge of her execution to behead her instead. There was a nearly universal theme of virginity in the female saints' *vitae*, partly because virginity was a specifically female state rather than male. Virginity for women was always more of an issue than it was for men, and some scholars have argued that, given the importance of virgin-martyrs to medieval religious devotion, once a woman lost her virginity, she was no longer able to be considered genuinely holy.[39] The *vitae* with their virtuous women and vivid descriptions of their violent deaths were popular in medieval society, even central to medieval piety, and would certainly have held some sway over the thoughts of the people hearing them.

The lives of male saints, in stark contrast, tended to focus more on the devout acts the man performed. While it would be inaccurate to say there were no male martyrs (there were, in abundance), it is the tales of the virgin martyrs which were more wildly popular and widespread in medieval society. Male saints' lives were more sedate in general; they commonly had a wild, wealthy, and frivolous youth which they eventually later renounced after having a 'dark night of the soul,' after which they repented (usually publicly and demonstratively), turned away from their families, and gave themselves over to God. From then on, they often performed miracles or other notable acts such as becoming an ascetic or hermit. A stereotypical male saint's life is that of late-twelfth, early-thirteenth century Francis of Assisi, who sowed his wild oats in his youth, had a dark night of the soul, loudly and publicly renounced his rich father, and then set off to found the Franciscan order. No martyrdom necessary. The emphasis placed on virginity is absent in many male saints' lives.

Even the qualities for a proper bishop-turned-saint appear to be far more lax than they would be for women, if they were permitted to become priests. A man intent on a priesthood should focus on having good morals and judgment rather than on being ascetic. The most important trait was that he be kind, and if he was also a good administrator, then that was an added bonus.[40]

The differences in the way male and female saints' lives are depicted is important, not simply because they underscore the ingrained patriarchal and misogynistic worldview of the times, but because Isabella of Gloucester and Isabelle of Angoulême may well have been shaped by such stories. Saint Etheldreda of Ely (636 CE) is an early medieval woman who may have been familiar to Isabella of Gloucester. Etheldreda is one of the most commonly discussed English saints ever. Carrying on the trope of virtuous woman, Etheldreda supposedly remained a virgin through two marriages.[41] Women were expected to lead virtuous lives, be obedient to their fathers and then husbands, and safeguard their virginity until sanctified by marriage. Etheldreda was held up as an icon of female chastity and virginity even within marriage. In Lyon, France, Blandina (c. 162 CE) was martyred for her faith during the reign of Marcus Aurelius, when she was flayed, burnt on hot grates, and thrown in a net before a wild bull. These saints, strong in their dedication to their faith, virginity, and virtues, were held up as models of feminine behaviour and it would have been understood that noble women should strive to emulate them. That all saints' lives generally adhered to a standard structure also helped to highlight the idea of conformity. Medieval society typically did not encourage individuality as modern Western society understands it. Instead, the thought was that there was an ideal form for men and a different ideal form for women, and that all should live and operate within their prescribed social set. Both of John's wives would have been familiar with the idealised comportment of female saints as well as the conformity required by society and taken those lessons with them to their marriages to John.

Courtly Love: Marie de France

Other texts that were well known in medieval society and which Isabella of Gloucester and Isabelle of Angoulême may have read included courtly love and troubadour literature. In particular, Marie de France and her *lais* were known in the Plantagenet courts and could well have been read by both of John's wives. As with so many women throughout history, little is known about the author of the *lais*. There has been much debate about her possible identity, but some of the more credible suggestions have been that she was Marie de Champagne, the daughter of Eleanor of Aquitaine with her first husband; the illegitimate daughter of Geoffrey Plantagenet; or an abbess called Mary at Reading Abbey. Marie de Champagne was a patroness of Chrétien de Troyes, which could lend slightly more credence to her identity as Marie de France. Regardless of Marie's true identity, it is widely accepted that, yes, she was a woman, and was well-educated, probably from a noble family, because she knew enough Latin to have considered translating some Latin texts into French. She was, in other words, 'fully conversant with the life and aspirations of the nobility of her time'.[42]

It is most likely that she was writing in the 1180s, evidenced by the commentary by Denis Piramus. He wrote *The Life of St Edmund the King* and, in the prologue to that text, mentioned a Dame Marie who wrote lays in verse. Denis was known only in England, so it seems clear from his reference of Marie that her works were widely popular and had travelled from the Continent to England, assuming she initially composed them outside of England. It is also apparent from Denis's comments that there was, indeed, a woman named Marie who was writing *lais* in his lifetime, that they were popular among aristocratic men and women, and that Marie had her finger on the pulse of some social issues that she addressed in the tales. Denis goes on to say, 'the lays are accustomed to please the ladies: they listen to them joyfully and willingly, for they are just what they desire'.[43] Supporting the idea that women wanted to read about love, it should be noted that it is rather surprising for Marie to have written stories about love and marriage that ended happily, considering that most marriages of the time were unlikely to be very happy ones.[44] Marie's *lais* speak to the desire for these happy marriages and her writing reflects loving and happy marriages as the ultimate goal.

Furthermore, throughout the *lais* there is evidence of a concern for children that is lacking in other similar works written by men, and young women with their frustrations and fear at being married off to much older men often are the central agents within the stories. Scholars have long accepted that there are important works written by Occitan women troubadours (called *trobairitz*, from Southern France) and women *trouvère* poets (from Northern France) which provide an alternate perspective on medieval society.[45] Courtly love romances tend to have two versions – the traditionally interpreted male-centred story with fetishised ideals of women, and a version which upends these traditions. The *lais* of Marie de France's place women as the subject of the story instead of the object and in which she either critiques her male lover's propositions or else works her way to a love match of her choosing. Most of the male authors of courtly love literature created their female characters with an eye to uphold patriarchal social structures of the time, using the placement of women within the stories to offset her legal and social independence; however, other courtly love works show female protagonists as having skills and wit that are not derived from witchcraft or magic, giving them authority that is typically reserved for learned men. The female troubadours and their protagonists 'think, speak, and act both within and against the highly prescribed social strictures that define and delimit the literary courtly lady in the medieval French and Occitan traditions'.[46] In any case, given the popularity of Marie's *lais*, it seems unlikely that they were not familiar to Isabella of Gloucester and Isabelle of Angoulême. Perhaps, as apparently other women of the time did, they saw something of themselves within the pages of the *lais*.

Arthurian Romances: Nennius and Gildas

Marie de France was not the only author of romance literature in the twelfth century by any means. As Burgess and Busby state, 'The second half of the twelfth century was in France a period of intense literary activity. ... and the literary traffic is practically one-way, from France to England, Germany, the Low Countries, Scandinavia, the Iberian peninsula and Italy.[47] Other texts that Isabella and Isabelle may well have known and read include the Arthurian romances of Chrétien de Troyes and *Chanson de Roland* (*Song of Roland*), possibly written by the French poet Turold.

Chrétien most likely wrote his romances between 1159 and 1191, based on records from his two major patrons, Marie de Champagne, a daughter of Eleanor of Aquitaine from her first marriage to Louis VII of France and half-sister to Henry II of England, and then Philip of Alsace, Count of Flanders. Chrétien had also probably spent time in England based on the descriptions of cities and land which correlate to that of Henry II's reign. There is a substantial number of surviving manuscripts which contain Chrétien's works, which shows that he was very popular, given the sheer number of manuscripts that survive in which his works exist.[48] Chrétien composed what may well be the first version in French of the Tristan and Iseult Breton legend. He was influenced by traveling Breton minstrels and Geoffrey of Monmouth, using older material and fashioning it into a new form, that of the courtly romance. He was the first to bring Guinevere, Lancelot, Camelot, and the Grail Quest into the older Arthurian tales that originated from Breton and Welsh sources. Chrétien was also influenced by the Classical poet Ovid, who was one of the most popular writers from the Classical period in the twelfth century. The courtly love ideal is brought to life in Chrétien's writing, as it is in Marie de France's, and could possibly have influenced how noble women viewed marriage. Burns explains that the courtly lady possessed 'a curiously hybrid gender' because, though the lady remains highly feminised, she essentially retains the power of a lord within the relationship.[49] This implies that, within the tradition of courtly love, falling in love does not automatically mean adhering to the gender stereotypes of society, with the man dominant over the woman. Instead, it offers an alternate scenario that challenges the bounds of heteronormative sexuality. In any case, high-born ladies like Isabella and Isabelle would not have expected real life to mirror what was reflected in literature. Given that Chrétien's writing often has elements of mimesis, one cannot help but wonder how much it might have influenced the expectations of some women, and in particular young girls such as Isabelle. This is worth noting because Chrétien's work was popular among the aristocracy of the eleventh and twelfth centuries, and more importantly, Lancelot is 'uniquely perfect' in medieval society.[50]

In his tale *Le Chevalier de la charrete* ('The Knight of the Cart'), Chrétien highlights the superlative nature of Lancelot above all other knights, including Yvain and Erec and even King Arthur himself. Readers must be forgiven for thinking that young medieval noblemen might look to Lancelot as an ideal of chivalrous knighthood they could attempt to emulate. Indeed, perhaps some of them did. But what is more intriguing is the thought that his splendid form and manners might be indicative of the ideal husband which many young noblewomen hoped to marry. Romantic fantasies of teenage girls cannot have truly changed much over time. In his character of Lancelot, Chrétien 'demonstrates that in his poetic world the courtly, chivalric, and Christian ideals are unifiable in the ideal knight'.[51] While there is a great deal of irony in viewing Lancelot perfect considering that 'The Knight of the Cart' features a love that is adulterous there is no escaping the fact that Lancelot himself was medieval masculinity embodied. He is strong, fierce in battle, wins at the tournament lists, and is chivalrous to all ladies. What lady would not dream of having a husband such as Lancelot? Realists who believe the courts of love truly did exist view Lancelot as the perfect courtly lover. None of the characters or narrator berate Lancelot for his adultery, leading readers to believe that his adultery was overlooked or even tacitly accepted as the actions of a medieval man. Those readers who fall into the idealist school of thought believe courtly love was, at best, 'a game to be taken lightly and ironically'.[52] They point to the risible figure Lancelot cuts when he fights with his sword behind his back so that he can keep Guinevere in his view as evidence that courtly love was a post-Romantic construct bearing little resemblance to reality. Furthermore, connecting 'the ideals of profane love, chivalry, and Christianity – manifestly irreconcilable – are somehow miraculously united in the perfect hero'.[53] Nevertheless, Lancelot may have been idealised and romanticised even in Chrétien's time.

However, a better role model for medieval mores and attitudes toward marriage are to be found in Chrétien's other romances, which advocate for marriage, love within marriage, and show that other types of love are at the least disadvantageous. These other texts may have informed the opinions of medieval women, including John's wives, as to the nature of marriage. Again, most medieval couples did not expect to find love within their marriages but hoping for it would be an entirely natural expectation. It is in this way that Chrétien's works may have directly influenced Isabella and Isabelle. In most courtly love literature, including the typical works of Chrétien, the tales highlight the 'high values for the normative principles of Christian marriage. [Courtly literature assumed] fruitful Christian marriage was the glue upon which social stability and cohesion depended, perhaps most especially at the courtly level.'[54]

Particularly in *Yvain*, Chrétien demonstrates the Christian virtue of *caritas*, which is focusing on love that achieves a higher purpose than the individual. Yvain is a character who demonstrates the ideal of *caritas*. In Yvain, Chrétien further develops the medieval concept of *caritas* by establishing 'a beneficial, other-directed love that carries a heavy obligation to the beloved'.[55] True love, as medieval thought puts it, requires acts of love displayed through honour, courtesy, generosity, and bravery to bring the lover to a genuine understanding of *caritas*. The obligation felt in true love, then, relates to the proper order of love, which is meant to reflect through his love for Laudine the believer's love for God. What does this have to do with showing Yvain as an ideal domestic partner?

Within the tale of *Yvain*, preference is given to domestic matters, implying that traditional knightly actions, such as going to tournaments or on quests, are too self-centred and focused on the knight himself. Rather, a knight's actions should be carried out in service to and for the benefit of others. Specifically, perfect love and domesticity are associated with a love that champions what is best for others, especially for the people one holds dear. All the tasks Yvain carries out after his mental breakdown revolve around this sort of domestic knighthood and focus on the concern for others. Yvain's character demonstrates a love that places him behind those he loves and cares for. He makes choices reflective of this sentiment, as seen when he chooses to kill the serpent rather than the lion, for he deems the lion to be the more honourable beast of the two. The lion then sets up the obligation related to true love through his selfless love of Yvain, reminding the knight of the honour and courage required of him. At the same time, Yvain's tending to the lion shows his predilection for domesticity, linking care and obligation into a visible depiction of the selfless duties of love.

Isabella and Isabelle may have read Chrétien's tales and seen in Yvain the sort of man they expected a noble to be and which would make an appealing spouse to any woman. Additionally, they may have learned from this tale that the obligation of true love should run both ways, thus teaching them that they, too, have obligations to their loved ones and that there is, perhaps, a correct and incorrect way of carrying out those duties and obligations. Within Yvain's tale, Gawain had negatively called marriage a yoke and leash, but that domesticity came to mean, to Yvain, a 'positively connected, virtuous, domestic identity rooted in *caritas*, which, Yvain comes to learn, begins at home'.[56] Isabella and Isabelle may have learned these lessons as well, both from their actual educations as well as from the texts of Chrétien de Troyes, and carried them with them to their marriages.

Other texts that John's wives may have read during their youth include several other Arthurian tales and pseudo-histories. One of the most popular at the time was written by Geoffrey of Monmouth, who most likely had access to the histories of Gildas and Nennius, both early chroniclers of Celtic and Breton legend. Gildas, the author of the chronicle *De Excidio et Conquestu Britanniae* (*On the Ruin and Conquest of Britain*), was born no later than 500 CE, and based on his own claim that he was born in the same year as the Battle of Mount Badon which was fought approximately in 500 CE. Little is known about Gildas's life or his birthplace, though the descriptions in his *De Excidio et Conquestu Britanniae* suggest that he lived in the western parts of Britain, near the Welsh border. Beyond some surviving accounts of Gildas in two ninth and twelfth century hagiographies, little else is known of him except that he left Britain for Brittany at some point to avoid the invasions by the Anglo-Saxons. In Brittany, he then established the monastery St. Gildas de Rhuys. *De Excidio* was a polemical discussion of Britain's history and also a chastisement of the British kings and clergymen of his own time.

In turn, Nennius was a Welsh monk who wrote his *Historia Brittanum* (*The History of Britain*) around 800 CE. We do not know much about Nennius either and historians have thus far been unable to compile a satisfactory biography of him. Regardless, his *History of Britain* was one of the first texts to describe a King Arthur and is an odd assortment of texts which covers the genealogies of kings, geography, and saints' lives. Nennius was one of the first chroniclers of early Welsh history and literature, and he may also have had access to a now-lost fifth-century text that supported his commentary. He also apparently was able to read Old English and Old Irish, in addition to his clerical Latin and native Welsh. However, the *History of Britain* text has been called 'unrestrainedly inventive', and there are errors Nennius made with people's names, dates, and genealogical facts, making his *History* a pseudo-historical chronicle rather than a true historical text.[57] Geoffrey of Monmouth later made extensive use of both Gildas's and Nennius's work. Lewis Thorpe points out that, given 'the great number of borrowings … [Monmouth] makes from the *De excidio Britanniae* of Gildas the *Historia Brittonum* of Nennius, his debt to these two early chroniclers is certainly a considerable one'.[58] It is likely that Isabella or Isabelle would have been aware of these works whether they read them or not.

What is likely that they read, however, is Geoffrey of Monmouth's *Historia Regum Britanniae* (*The History of the Kings of Britain*). It was among the most popular texts of the twelfth and thirteenth centuries. Completed around the year 1136, Geoffrey's highly influential book has been compared to the books of the Old Testament in terms of its importance to the British Isles.[59] Geoffrey's purpose in writing *Historia Regum Britanniae* was partly patriotic, desiring to make the argument that Britain is still the best of all nations even though its people have been divided and some moved back across the Channel. He wished to remind Britons of their mythical connections to the heroes of Troy, to Aeneas whose many-times-great grandson gave the name to the British Isle. He also had political reasons as well, likely hoping to give a precedent for the ambitions of the Norman kings and to ingratiate himself with the various dedicatees of the work.[60] We frequently do not ever know even the names of authors of medieval texts; when we do know a name, it is often the sum total of our knowledge about the author. However, historians do know a decent amount about Geoffrey of Monmouth. Based on his reference to himself as *Galfridus Monemutensis*, or Geoffrey of Monmouth, he must have had a strong connection to that place, likely through birth, making him either Welsh or an Anglo-Norman born in Wales in approximately 1095. In 1151, Geoffrey became the bishop-elect of St Ataph, was ordained and consecrated as a priest in February 1152, and signed several charters. Geoffrey was also a witness of the Treaty of Westminster in 1153, which effectively ended The Anarchy by ensuring that Stephen of Blois kept the English throne until his death and that Henry Plantagenet, Duke of Normandy and son of the Empress Matilda, would succeed him to the throne. During the period in which Geoffrey was writing, a time of roughly twenty-five years, evidence points to him living in Oxford, which would have included many exciting events during his tenure there, including the Empress Mathilda being besieged in Oxford Castle and making her famous escape to Abingdon in the dead of winter in 1142.

The sources for Geoffrey's texts, and especially for *Historia Regum Britanniae*, have been much debated. A mysterious source book is mentioned in Geoffrey's introduction to the *Historia* and a few other times throughout the work, which he claims was given to him by Walter the archdeacon and which he translated into Latin from 'the British language'.[61] A problem with this theory is that historians are not able to find the book Geoffrey claims to have used. While it is entirely possible that it has been lost in the intervening centuries, since more medieval manuscripts have been lost than have survived, there also is no Welsh text that can be viewed as a possible origin or even groundwork for the *Historia*. It is accepted now that Geoffrey had access to a manuscript similar to one currently in the British Library which contains Nennius's *Historia Brittonum*, the *Cities and Marvels of Britain*, the *Annales Cambriae*, and lists of Welsh kings' genealogies.[62] Some theories suggest that Geoffrey invented the whole text; others claim he was a shadow writer for another person, a pseudo-Geoffrey who really wrote the *Historia*. However, there is plenty of evidence to show that neither of these theories is true. The list of places and names Geoffrey gives at the end of the *Historia* are historical people and places. As Thorpe notes, 'Much of this background material is twisted almost beyond recognition; but in earliest essence it has some element of truth. Geoffrey did not invent it, nor did the pseudo-Geoffrey: *ergo* one or other of them must have taken it from somewhere.'[63]

While it is fascinating to consider the sources for Geoffrey's *Historia*, what is relevant here is that his work was widely read and popular during the twelfth and thirteenth centuries, and likely that Isabella of Gloucester and Isabelle of Angoulême would have been familiar with his works. We know Geoffrey was popular by the sheer number of manuscripts still extant which contain the *Historia*. In 1929, Acton Griscom listed 186 existing manuscripts which contain forty-eight complete texts and two fragments dating from the twelfth century, and since then, more have been discovered.[64] It appears that Geoffrey was a source of inspiration to other medieval romance writers, including Marie de France, Chrétien de Troyes, and Wolfram von Eschenbach, who wrote the Arthurian romance *Parzival* in the first part of the thirteenth century.

Twelfth- and thirteenth-century readers of Geoffrey's *Historia*, including Isabella and Isabelle, may have taken away some lessons from the text. A factor that seems to have been of great concern to Geoffrey while writing the *Historia* appears to revolve around inheritance. If Geoffrey was writing during the Anarchy, the politics involved could have influenced his writing. Greg Molchan notes that the Norman practice of exogamous marriage may have had the benefits of extending land holdings, but it could also destabilise alliances within the group as well. Furthermore, 'in spite of attempts to consolidate land holdings under a tradition of dynastic rule, succession was frequently solved through violence'.[65] Even Geoffrey's writing reflects that violence often wins the day, for Arthur himself had to secure and retain the throne through war and acts of violence. Furthering the practice of extending land holdings and alliances through exogamy, Geoffrey writes that Uther Pendragon and Ygerna had two children, a son they called Arthur and a daughter they called Anna. Uther eventually gave Anna in marriage to Loth of Lodonesia as a reward for his military skills. Geoffrey writes, 'The British army was put under the command of Loth of Lodonesia, with orders that he should keep the enemy at a distance. This man was one of the leaders, a valiant soldier, mature both in wisdom and age. As a reward for his prowess, the King had given him his daughter Anna and put him in charge of the kingdom while he himself was ill.'[66] Geoffrey demonstrates that daughters could and were given to men as reward for services to their fathers. Isabella and Isabelle both would probably have expected similar marriage arrangements.

Molchan suggests that Geoffrey crafts a situation in which a bride is given by a king to a man for providing military service, which is also very suggestive of the kinds of marriages often arranged by Norman nobles. Women, the passage implies, had exchange value for men who were bold and enterprising, traits that were highly prized in Norman society. Isabella and Isabelle both would have grown up knowing their value as commodities in the political arena that was noble and royal marriage and would have seen in Geoffrey's work their probable future – arranged marriage to a man who would bring an advantage to her family or as a reward for actions he took on behalf of a liege lord. Geoffrey's mostly-fictional work was nevertheless reflective of the time in which it was written, including marriage and coronation practices common within Norman society, and in which John's wives would have been reared.

One last person for us to explore as a potential influence on Isabella and Isabelle is Hildegard of Bingen. Hildegard (b. 1098) was a contemporary of Eleanor of Aquitaine, a woman given as a tithe to the Church when she was around 8 years old, and who later became an abbess, dietitian, composer, author, and mystic. In her own lifetime, she was known as the Sibyl of the Rhine and had benefactors – and adversaries – in some very high places. She was known to go toe to toe with men of the Church, including her own Abbott Kuno. She was championed by no less than the likes of Pope Eugenius III, Bernard of Clairvaux, and Abbot Suger. She defied a Church order from the clergymen of Mainz to exhume the body of an excommunicated man buried in her abbey's graveyard, resulting in an interdict being placed upon her and her nuns – until the archbishop of Mainz relented and let her leave the body undisturbed. Hildegard was, in so many ways, a firebrand of medieval society and remains influential even in the twenty-first century.

Her impact upon John's wives may have been most apparent through her music, of which over seventy compositions remain known to modern society. Based on some of Hildegard's letters, it is likely she had the chance to learn about and possibly even hear the songs and works of troubadours and their German equivalents, *minnesingers*. In short, she was probably very familiar with secular music and entertainment of her day. In Hildegard's theology, music is intrinsically bound with the cosmic order of the universe, a channel to understanding the nature of the world, humanity's place within it, and the divine nature of all. Based on her own correspondence, her reputation as a composer had gone as far as Paris in her own lifetime but there is no evidence otherwise to suggest that anyone other than clergy and her own nuns heard or participated in her musical performances. Her most famous extant composition is *Ordo Virtutum*, a morality play considered to be the first operatic composition in European history. Its plot is, in essence, the tale of a soul struggling between the virtues and the devil, with the primary focus on the reconnection of the soul to the creator. If this piece was known outside her convent, possibly John's wives could have been familiar with it, given the reputation of its composer. It was a work of art that was within the accepted curriculum of the day, with its primary purpose to bring souls into closer harmony with nature and God. It was, in short, a piece worthy of royalty.

While we may never know the specifics of the childhoods of Isabella of Gloucester or Isabelle of Angoulême, we can make some educated guesses about them. The early life and education of gently-born girls was not so dissimilar throughout much of history. In the twelfth and thirteenth centuries, as in the twenty-first century, there were many factors which could have influenced these women during their childhood and which, in turn, may have influenced their lives with King John. The literary creations of the period were widely read among the aristocracy and gentry, giving the women a glimpse of themselves within the pages as well as informing their thoughts on their roles as wives, mothers, and, in Isabelle's case, queens. It is to this topic that we will next turn.

Chapter 3

The Role of Women and Queens

As Isabella of Gloucester and Isabelle of Angoulême matured, they naturally would have been tutored in the duties expected of them generally as women, and specifically as women of the nobility. They would have known from their earliest education that their path in life would be marriage to a nobleman or similar rank, and possibly even to royalty. A royal marriage would have been seen as an advantageous match by medieval society. The trouble for modern scholars, though, is that until just the past few decades, 'the neglect of queens was common to all medieval historians'.[1] Scholars have largely pieced together the roles, duties, and expectations of women based on what little was documented. Many of the chronicles that have survived focus primarily on the political and public arena; the roles of women, even queens, most often fell within the private, family-oriented realm and thus outside the purview of most chroniclers. This holds true for both Isabella of Gloucester and Isabelle of Angoulême, both of whom are largely absent from historical records of their time. It may seem strange to our modern way of thinking that a woman as important as a queen might not be well documented, particularly given that they 'fulfilled traditional female family roles magnified by the status of royal dynasties and extended by the fraught politics of succession to the throne'.[2] The concept of a queen, in the abstract, was that she was highly visible and held up as a model of feminine behaviour. Through their marriages and the birth of their children, noble and royal women lived under intense scrutiny for the times, beginning with their upbringing as we have already discussed, and then through their marriages.

In the Middle Ages few people in the upper echelons of society truly expected to find love within marriage. Those who did were lucky, and if love, or at least affection, grew over time, that, too, was considered a fortuitous event and the marriage considered a good match. The purpose of marriage was, at least in the eyes of the Church, to regulate and control sexual desire and to demand conformity for all people. During this era, celibacy was exalted as the highest and most desirable state for both men and women. However, celibacy, no matter how much the medieval Church preferred it, would do nothing to ensure the procreation of children, which was the second reason for people to marry. As Saint Paul said, 'It is better to marry than to burn,' and so he decided that marriage was a tolerable second best. According to Church doctrine, sex was 'given to people solely for the purposes of reproduction and for no other reason. Christ had envisaged marriage as the normal state for people and pronounced it indissoluble, except in cases of adultery'.[3] Sex outside of marriage was universally considered sinful. Sex within marriage was acceptable only for the goal of procreation. The Church preferred that people remain celibate, but if that was not an option, then marriage was the only way in which it was acceptable to have sexual relations.

Even within marriage, some believed that sex should never be simply for pleasure; for example, Thomas Aquinas, who was born somewhat later than our Isabellas, believed that a man who slept with his wife purely for pleasure was treating her like a whore. Similarly, the fourth-century St. Jerome, translator of what would eventually become the Latin Vulgate Bible, stated that a man who loved his wife too passionately was an adulterer: 'A wise man ought to love his wife with judgment, not with passion. ... There is nothing blacker than to love a wife as if she were an adulteress.[4] Increasingly, control over marriage passed into the hands of the Church, as evidenced by ceremonies such as a priest, bishop, or archbishop blessing the marriage bed of a newly married couple before the two were put in it for the bedding ceremony.

There is some debate whether the bedding ritual associated with medieval marriage ceremonies actually occurred or whether it was a metonym for marriage as a whole. Gabriel Radle makes a compelling argument that the bedding ceremony was a literal event, not a metaphor for marriage as some argue. He posits that the medieval use of *thalamus* blessings is a literal, not a figurative, event and was generally enjoyed by society as a part of any wedding ceremony. Thalamus translates to 'an inner room' and typically refers specifically to a bedchamber. Because many of the documented blessings highlight themes of marriage and are often near other prayers for marriage, 'several scholars have concluded that these texts were intended as nuptial blessings performed at a newlywed couple's bedroom, that is, at the site of and immediately preceding consummation'.[5] Although many of the documented blessings do not explicitly refer to the marriage bed, it seems logical that prayers referring to the increase of humankind through procreation would be recited at the entrance to the bedchamber. Additionally, one of the oldest such blessings, recorded in the seventh century and later repeated in medieval texts, proclaims that the bishop, according to local custom, was invited to the entrance of the bedroom so that he could then bless the union by invoking the name of the Lord. This ritual is dated well before John or either of his wives, his parents, even his great-grandparents, were born; however, there is evidence that these thalamus blessings were still strongly in use in the mid-twelfth century.

One example is from the Sacramentary of Vich, which was written in approximately 1038. This text contains a thalamus ritual that calls specifically for the priest to enter the bridal chamber, sprinkle salt as a purifying element, and then bless the bed. It reads, in part, 'Bless this room, set aside for honest marriage, that no onslaught of evil may touch it. May it contain only the purity of marriage, and may your compassion assist its worth celebration'.[6] A later, twelfth-century manuscript from Albi records a priest entering the home and using incense to bless the bedchamber; yet another text from thirteenth-century Paris describes the priest accompanying the newly married couple to their home where he blesses them before they enter the bedroom, after they enter the bedroom, and a final time when they have sat down on the bed.

Other scholars take for granted that these marriage bed blessings or bedding ceremonies took place into the thirteenth century and beyond. Dolliann Margaret Hurtig explains, 'When the ceremonies of the day are over, the archbishop assumes an active role in the blessing of the couple and of the marriage bed, a ritual that will precede the couple's first night together'.[7] Even secular literature of the time, such as the *Roman de Mélusine*, written in the fourteenth century, describes a bedding ceremony, and a sixteenth-century manuscript, written by a Spanish attendee, recorded the bedding ceremony of Mary Tudor to Philip of Spain in 1554. It seems clear that these bedding ceremonies were not metaphorical or figurative, but literal components of medieval weddings. Moreover, their inclusion even in secular texts like the above *Roman de Mélusine* may be an indication that readers of the time expected these kinds of ceremonies and to exclude it would have been noticeable. By having these thalamus blessings within the bedchamber, priests formalised the marriage itself, as it was in the bedroom where the true marriage was supposed to take place. Emphasis was placed upon the validity of the marriage and all its attendant duties, expectations, and roles the couple, especially the bride, were to take on as they entered their new married life together. The blessings reinforced the belief that marriage – especially for nobility or royalty whose betrothals were rooted in politics, property, and dynasty – must come with the approval of the Church. Given this aspect of the bedding ceremonies, it seems inevitable that Isabella of Gloucester and Isabelle of Angoulême would both have experienced their own thalamus blessings upon their marriages to John.

Marriage was also a means for the exchange of property, at least among the upper classes, with families forging alliances or creating more wealth by linking themselves together through an arranged marriage. All royal marriages at the time were politically motivated. Therefore, 'Affection between the parties would have been a bonus, but it was not expected'.[8] Further research also supports the idea that marriage among the aristocracy had little to do with love in thirteenth century Europe. Instead, noble marriage was 'a marriage most likely without love or the power of the couple to choose or the mutual consent of the spouses [and] represents the way feudal society maintains itself'.[9] In theory, according to the canon laws codified in the twelfth century, known as *Decretum Gratiani*, marriages could not be forced upon a couple by their parents or anyone else; in practice, though, it appears to have been a different story. Often, marriages were arranged for men based on services they performed for another noble or king, as a reward. This was the case for William Marshal and his marriage to the great heiress Isabel de Clare. King Henry II, John's father, promised William he could have Isabel's hand in marriage for the duties Marshal carried out in his service, making the marriage very much a business arrangement, especially considering that Marshal was twenty-three years older than his bride and marrying her made him one of the wealthiest lords in England. Marshal's biography, written by an unknown contemporary and commissioned by Marshal's eldest son, assumes the transactional underpinning of the marriage: 'It was now that the king promised the Marshal, in return for his service, the good and beautiful damsel of Striguil. Having made the promise, he instructed Hubert Walter to see that the Marshal was given both the damsel and her lands as soon as he arrived back in England.'[10] Marshal later states that 'all that I have here is mine through her'.[11] So, it is clear, based on the (very biased) chronicle of Marshal's life that his marriage to Isabel de Clare was a business arrangement at the outset.

As a result of the social mores of the time and the fact that many marriages were arranged, it was not uncommon for marriages to be loveless, or indeed even for the couple to meet for the first time at the church door. Wealthy brides would bring with them a large dowry, making their marriage to their husband advantageous, at least for him. In some cases, the women were the sole heirs and rulers of their lands *suo jure* – in her own right – as was the case with both Eleanor of Aquitaine and Isabella of Gloucester. And although brides usually brought large dowries with them to their marriages, it was also expected that they would receive dowers from their husbands in return. Essentially, dowers were financial promises, typically in the form of lands and estates, that women could use to sustain themselves and their children in the event of widowhood. They would manage their own dower lands, which would bring them revenues upon which to live. The exchange of dowries and dowers further emphasises the business aspect of noble marriage.

Love matches were not common, in part because of this business-like approach to marriage, but also because marriages of love were dangerous to the patriarchal structure of medieval society. Strategically arranged medieval marriages within the ruling classes provided a structural basis to retain their power.[12] Basically, deciding who gets to marry whom is the foundation for the inheritance of property, and 'The prospect of individuals loving freely implies the possibility of their marrying freely; and this eventuality entails a concept of marriage in which the future of great family fortunes is increasingly removed from direct family control.'[13] Families used marriage to their benefit as much as possible, and that quite simply included marrying a son to a wealthy lady, after which her lands would pass into her husband's control.

This is what happened with the marriage of John and Isabella of Gloucester. Although she had two older sisters, they were already married when her father died in 1183; King Henry II declared Isabella the sole heir *suo jure* of the Gloucester estates, which excluded her sisters from the line of inheritance and prevented the Gloucester lands from being divided equally among them. When she married John in August of 1189, her lands then passed into John's control and he was able to enjoy a great deal of wealth and revenue from them. The point here is that marriage within the ruling classes was first about wealth and dynasty; any other considerations were largely irrelevant.

There are, however, examples of medieval marriages that seem to have been love matches or where love grew after marriage, even among the aristocracy. Some of these included Abelard and Heloise, who had a torrid affair, and then a secret, tragedy-laced marriage; probably Edward IV and Elizabeth Woodville; and by many accounts, the above-mentioned William Marshal and Isabel de Clare, which may have also become a love match over time. Admittedly, the anonymous chronicler of Marshal's life did not write an unbiased account of the knight's life. However, the chronicler is quick to point out flaws in other women, even queens, so perhaps there is truth to the matter when he writes that the countess, meaning Isabel de Clare, was overjoyed to see William upon his return after a lengthy absence, how she 'stayed ever at his side' when he was ill, and that, when Marshal died, the countess and her children 'were inconsolable'.[14] At Marshal's funeral Mass, the chronicler says that Isabel 'was struggling to support herself, her head and heart and limbs overwrought from the strain of grief and lack of sleep'.[15] Again, while Marshal's biographer is clearly biased in favour of the so-called 'Greatest Knight' and his family, as well as simply having a gendered bias about how a proper married woman should behave, his description of Isabel as a grieving widow seems an accurate and realistic portrayal of a woman who genuinely loved her husband. Perhaps it is an invention on the chronicler's part designed to please Marshal's son, who commissioned the biography, and the rest of his family, but it is a happy thought that at least a few medieval power couples might have had a genuine love for one another. There is no evidence that Isabella of Gloucester and John shared romantic passion for one another, and it is entirely open to debate how Isabelle of Angoulême and John actually felt about each other, despite many of the chroniclers of the time focusing at length upon John's obsession with his young wife.[16]

Marriage, Fertility, and Childbirth

Within the upper classes of society, and according to Church dogma, the primary reason for marriage was the procreation of children. Of course, having children certainly supported the business aspects of marriage in that legitimate heirs were needed to inherit familial titles and lands. Feudalism was in full swing in the twelfth and thirteenth centuries, and the home was generally the core of lay society. In a society ruled mainly by primogeniture – the practice of the oldest male child inheriting the bulk of a family's wealth – and which was strongly patriarchal, having male heirs was seen as the utmost duty for a wife. This was especially true for queens whose primary function was to provide male heirs to ensure the continuation of their royal dynasty. Because of the importance placed on family dynasty, the birth of babies, both boys and girls, was greeted with joy. In fact, many theologians determined that, while sexual desire was not a good reason to marry, a man's ability to inseminate his wife was a requirement of a valid marriage. A man with an inability to have sex could not have a valid marriage, some people argued, because there would be no way for him to produce offspring. The begetting of children, therefore, was always of paramount importance, especially for those of the upper classes.

Naturally, conception, pregnancy, and childbirth went in tandem with marriage and all it entails. Medieval society had its share of customs surrounding these three events as well. During pregnancy, it was often recommended that women perform certain activities or treatments which, to modern readers, might seem like madness. Even common medieval thoughts or practices such as having a wet nurse for one's child might seem today to be unimaginable parenting choices. As an example, avoiding certain foods during pregnancy is a practice still recommended in modern society, as some foods contain chemicals which can trigger early labour or cause miscarriage. The fear that certain foods may curdle a mother's milk and so should be avoided during pregnancy according to medieval obstetrics is not, however, one that is shared by modern medicine.[17] But as strange or superstitious as some of the treatments seem by modern standards, medieval prenatal care was a vital component of medicine and its practice, beginning with conception and fertility.

A woman's fertility was a primary factor in a successful medieval marriage. Again, a woman's first marital duty is to carry a child who can inherit the father's land and titles, thus ensuring that the family line will carry on. Therefore, a fertile wife is necessary to maintain the feudal system of inheritance. This was particularly true for queens and other women of the medieval elite 'whose ordained role in life was to be a wife and mother'.[18] According to the social mores of the time, women of the higher classes who gave birth outside of marriage would have been utterly dishonoured. It was simply not permitted for women to have extramarital or premarital sex. Of course, non-marital sex happened anyway, but most children born from a non-married relationship would have been considered illegitimate and not generally recognised in any line of succession; the wife or bride may also then have been abandoned by her husband or betrothed if he saw fit to do so. Rarely, illegitimate children could be legitimised by royal and papal decrees and placed in line for succession or inheritance, as was the case with the children of John of Gaunt and his long-time mistress, Katherine Swynford. Their children, though legitimised, were barred from ever inheriting the throne; there were limits even to a nobleman's ability to bend the rules. More commonly, though, legitimizing children born out of wedlock was not the typical course of action. In a textbook case of double standards, though, 'While extramarital sex is rigorously condemned for a woman, for a bachelor to enjoy sexual pleasure outside the marriage bond is an accepted social practice'.[19] It would be rare for a woman to have a child out of wedlock within the upper classes where dynasty and inheritance were paramount, and so most would not be able to prove their fertility before marriage. Men, on the other hand, often fathered illegitimate children before they married, proving their virility. Because women usually could not prove their fertility before their marriage, it was easy to blame her when a couple proved to be infertile.

It is a popular belief that infertility in a couple was always blamed on the woman, which is easy to understand given the above. However, the truth appears to have been quite a bit more complex than that. Medieval medical knowledge was largely rooted in Classical and Arabic traditions, and a lot of the surviving texts from that period reflect the diversity of sources used for the treatment and care of people. There are actually a lot of medical texts that exist from the medieval period, such as *The Trotula*, which would have been consulted during pregnancy and childbirth. There was also a rich culture of midwifery and female healing texts. One of the most famous that remains to us is 'The Sekenesse of Wymmyn', a text on women's gynaecological health written in the fifteenth century and well past the time of John's wives. However, *The Trotula*, which was compiled in the twelfth century and based on older extant texts, including an eleventh century Arabic medical text, was commonly referenced by medieval midwives and healers in the twelfth and thirteenth centuries. *The Trotula* states plainly, 'Conception is impeded as much by the fault of the man as by the fault of the woman.'[20] It also states that infertility in a woman over the age of 30 is untreatable.

In some cases of infertility, the first thing many couples did was pray. The Virgin Mary is one of the primary saints for women in general, as well as assisting with infertility issues. Similarly, St. Anne is the specific patron saint of infertility. Couples would pray to both for aid in conceiving and bearing healthy offspring. If simple prayer failed, a pilgrimage could be undertaken, visiting various shrines dedicated to the Virgin Mary or St. Anne and returning with blessed badges or souvenirs from these places. For those who could not afford to undertake a pilgrimage, secular badges and amulets featuring images of animals or wildmen were also sometimes used to focus on fertility, as these creatures were associated with carnality and fertility or virility.

Medical intervention was also used for infertility and for this, healers turned again to the texts available to them. As mentioned previously, *The Trotula* was one such text, and it was heavily influenced by Aristotelian and Hippocratic medical theories, particularly as related to conception. Aristotelian theory of conception was known as a one-seed form of conception, meaning that the mother provided unformed matter by way of her menstrual blood; the father brought heat and the power to transform that matter into a human body through his sperm.[21] The Hippocratic theory, on the other hand, adhered to a two-seed approach, and thought that 'the foetus was formed by the heat and moisture of the father's and mother's seeds, which provided warmth to the mother's womb to create a boiling sensation through which the child's materials coalesced'.[22] It makes sense that one of the first things a healer might do, and which *The Trotula* recommends, was to find out whether the menses of the woman in question were normal. The text states that 'common people call the menses "the flowers," because just as trees do not bring forth fruit without flowers, so women without their flowers are cheated of the ability to conceive'.[23] *The Trotula* compendium was often consulted in infertility cases and learning about the menses is one of the first things discussed in the treatment of infertility even today. *The Trotula* also suggests that infertility may be the fault of the would-be father, especially if his semen is too thin and slips out of the woman's body.[24]

This collection of medical works also recommends ensuring a couple's weight is correct. It states, 'There are some women who are useless for conception, either because they are too lean and thin, or because they are too fat and the flesh surrounding the orifice of the womb constricts it, and does not permit the seed of the man to enter into [the womb]'.[25] The medical treatises also provide remedies and treatments for making patients slim down if that is what is required. The consideration of the patients' weight makes sense as it is well known that diet and obesity can greatly impact fertility.[26]

However, *The Trotula* also makes strong use of the four humours prevalent in medieval medicine. Medieval science believed that the heat or cold of a woman's body – that is, according to humours, not actual temperature – had tremendous impact upon fertility. To test a woman's temperature, the healer should soak a piece of linen with pennyroyal or laurel oils, insert it into the vagina, and tie a piece of it around the woman's thigh. The idea was that, if the piece of linen was drawn up into her body, she was cold; if it was expelled, she was hot. If a woman's body was too hot, *The Trotula* author recommends fumigating her with herbs that are considered to be cold, such as roses, mallow, or violets. If she is too cold, the use of hot-natured herbs is recommended, such as clove, spikenard, or nutmeg. Fumigating apparently required that 'there be prepared a perforated chair so that all the fumes go toward the inside'.[27] The rest of this delightful treatment I shall leave to the reader's imagination.

Other treatments given in *The Trotula* for becoming pregnant include the man mixing the dried, powdered womb of a rabbit into wine and drinking it; powdering the liver and testicles of a pig and giving it 'in a potion' to either the man or the woman; and mixing the dried, powdered testicles of a pig or boar and drinking it with wine after the woman's period.[28] There is ample evidence to suggest that women across the social spectrum turned to the remedies suggested in *The Trotula*, including queens.[29] It may seem difficult to envision a queen, or really any woman, enduring some of the treatments recommended for infertility or any other condition, but it was a widely consulted text and the therapeutics given within must have been carried out with some frequency. As such, it is very likely *The Trotula* was consulted for the pregnancies and deliveries of Isabelle of Angoulême, and perhaps even for Isabella of Gloucester, though more on her will come later. As we know, queens had more reason than anyone else to wish to be fertile; dynasties could rise or fall for want of an heir. The health and fertility of queens was generally a topic of interest to much of society, for an heir to the throne meant by and large that there should be a peaceful transfer of power from one monarch to the next.

Once conception took place, there was a whole other set of practices recommended for the pregnant woman, some of which was based on the beliefs on how the foetus developed. As with the understanding of conception, medieval knowledge of pregnancy was based mostly on Ancient Greek and Near East science, particularly Aristotle and Galen. Aristotle thought that embryos developed in three stages: the first stage gave the embryo vegetable-like properties, the ability to feed itself and grow but nothing more; the second stage saw it develop animal-like properties and could move, feel, and desire; the third and final step was the development of intellect and reason, at which point the embryo had a human shape. The medieval Christian view of embryonic development was most heavily influenced by Aristotelian science and that they thought the child's soul was a gift from God which was received once the child developed into human shape. This, they believed, occurred at forty-six days if the baby was a boy and ninety if it was a girl. Additionally, the generally accepted idea was that '[i]f the resulting embryo grew on the woman's right side, it became a male; if on the left side, a female'.[30] There is no evidence of the attempts queens may have made to ensure that they conceived a son rather than daughter; however, given the time period and its social structure, it seems likely that queens and other noblewomen would have tried any number of rituals to bring about the birth of a son.

The actions of the foetus were also thought to have an impact on its future health. Movement within the uterus indicated a baby's desire to be born, but too much movement could also weaken it, which was an explanation for why some children die shortly after birth. It was also a practice not to mention any food in front of a pregnant woman that she was not allowed to have because 'if she sets her mind on it and it is not given to her, this occasions miscarriage'.[31] Instead, a pregnant woman was to be given food that was easily digestible, and to rub her belly with olive oil and violet oil when she went into labour. She was also to be fumigated with musk or ambergris. Other treatments for pregnant women included rubbing her feet with rose oil and giving her pomegranates if they were swollen.[32] Even though *The Trotula* was a commonly used source of women's medical advice during the twelfth and thirteenth centuries and included remedies that could have been used by those of lower social classes, it seems unlikely that anyone but queens or other wealthy ladies could acquire some of the items required, such as ambergris or pure rose oil, which are both still extremely expensive.

Childbirth has been a dangerous event for women for most of history, and even today it continues to be a point of contention within the medical community in terms of safety and maternal health. Current data reports that 16.9 out of every 100,000 live births results in maternal death in the United States; in the United Kingdom, the rate is 7 deaths for every 100,000 live births.[33] Britain, at least, has managed to come a long way with regard to maternal death in childbirth. However, in the Middle Ages, these rates would have been quite a bit higher given the lack of sterile techniques and more effective medicine available to modern women. Childbirth in medieval times was a dangerous process and people wanted reassurance that all would turn out well.

To effect positive outcomes, medieval people turned to a number of practices. One was to have a 'lying in' or 'confinement' period. During this time a woman near her due date would pick a room where she wanted to give birth. It was then carpeted and had cloth and tapestries hung on the walls. One window was left available for light if she desired, but otherwise the room was dark. She and her attendant ladies would enter this chamber about a month before giving birth and would stay until about six weeks after delivery. Before entering her birthing chamber, the woman would have a special rite in the chapel of the house where she planned to give birth and take communion. Taking communion was not very common for people at the time; usually they only had it at Easter and on 'occasions of great peril', which childbirth most certainly was.[34] Probably, this particular practice of lying-in was something only women of the highest social classes would have done; it seems unreasonable that a woman of a lower class would have the ability to take two or more months away from her daily duties as well as any other children she may have to tend. However, it is almost certain Isabelle of Angoulême would have had a lying-in for her births, though surviving documentation on this practice from before the middle of the fifteenth century is uncommon.

Another birthing practice was to make use of religious relics during pregnancy and childbirth. These relics could be lent to a pregnant or labouring woman by the cathedral or other religious house that housed it. Some such relics included the fingerbones of various saints, pieces of a saint's clothes or a staff to lean on. Usually, women of higher rank and wealth were the ones who had access to these relics or ones like a girdle of the Virgin Mary, housed at Westminster Abbey. The relics would be placed upon the woman's abdomen before or during birth with the hope that the associated saint would intervene on the woman's behalf.

Women who did not have access would resort to other kinds of supernatural assistance, such as having a scroll with a cross 1/15 the size of Christ's cross drawn on it being laid upon their bellis. Also, placing stones such as jasper, malachite or eaglestone, which is a kind of iron ore, on the woman's belly was another option. These stones were thought to possess certain properties which would aid in a smooth and successful delivery. Of these tactics, it is very likely that Isabelle of Angoulême would have been permitted to borrow various relics during her deliveries, as would Isabella of Gloucester had she given birth. Regardless of social class or wealth, it is documented in 'innumerable handbooks that Saint Margaret, the Virgin Mary, and Saint Anne were called on by women in childbed', the most relatable and accessible icons of religion available to any woman in labour.[35]

Of course, not all births went smoothly or successfully, no matter what social rank the mother held. In fact, many did not. The Church was aware of this and sought to make rules with regard to handling certain situations in the birthing chamber, also paving the way for women and midwives to have less control over the birthing process and moving it eventually into the hands of male physicians. Often, churches and congregations were asked to pray for all pregnant women, whether within their own parish or in all parishes. A prayer that was in use asked that God deliver both mother and baby with joy, bring the child to its christening, and for the mother to be purified again. This prayer, though, is rife with anxiety and sadness in that it asks only 'that babies may survive long enough to be baptised, in other words for just a few minutes, and their mothers long enough to be purified in church after forty days'.[36] There is an underlying awareness in these kinds of prayers that death was not an uncommon outcome of childbirth and people tried to prepare as best they could for it. This and similar prayers would probably have been familiar to most medieval people across all spectrums of life and social classes.

Normally, baptisms were performed on the day of birth or very shortly after that, from the twelfth century on. But, as we know, not all births were normal or successful. During difficult deliveries, if the baby delivered was sickly, or if a death seemed likely, the baptism would occur as soon as it was born or even during the birth process. The concern for the eternal souls of both mother and child was so strong that the Church determined that anyone could perform a baptism if no priest were available. As a result, the clergy were very careful 'to describe the procedures, and priests were urged to ensure that everyone knew them'. Such procedures for an emergency baptism included two elements. First, the child was to be 'washed ... with pure water'. This was to be followed by the person baptising saying, 'I christen thee in the name of the Father, and the Son, and the Holy Spirit'.[37] Midwives were, of course, permitted to perform emergency baptisms if a baby delivered was in mortal peril. Additionally, during labour, the midwife, her assistants, and the labouring woman were all encouraged to pray to various saints to intercede on behalf of the woman and to ensure a live birth.

Given the medieval preoccupation with the supernatural, it should come as no real surprise that midwives were also the frequent target for accusations of witchcraft; it was an explanation which would have made sense to medieval society for the sudden death of an infant or its mother, and the midwife was a convenient scapegoat. The same was true for instances of impotence, infertility, and stillbirth. *On the Properties of Things*, an early thirteenth century compendium by Bartholomeus Anglicus, describes the actions a midwife must take after the baby is delivered, including anointing the newborn with 'salt and honey (or salt and roses, pounded together) to dry him and comfort his limbs and members, [and wrapping] him in clothes. His mouth and gums should be rubbed with a finger dipped in honey to cleanse them, and to stimulate the child to suck'.[38] Such a practice begs the question of how many newborns may have died of botulism, though this would be nearly impossible to track since the botulism toxin was not even identified until the early nineteenth century.[39] Regardless, stimulating the sucking response of a newborn is a common practice even in today's medical field, being essential in assisting a newborn to thrive. All these actions would have been similarly performed for Isabelle and her infants.

After a successful birth, there were again several customs and ceremonies that medieval society expected. As mentioned above, the baptism of the newborn was a top priority. Assuming a healthy delivery with no emergency baptism was required, a normal baptism usually occurred on the day of birth or a very few days after. A boy was to have two godfathers and one godmother, and a girl, the reverse, a custom that was well established by the twelfth century. Parents themselves were not supposed to stand in during the baptism ceremony except in extreme situations, though children could act as sponsors to their newborn siblings. During the ceremony, which would begin at the door of the church, the priest would christen the baby and use salt, brought by the godparents, to help purify the soul. There would be prayers recited, differing depending on whether the child was a boy or a girl. Then the baptism party would enter the church, where the priest would anoint the baby with oil, ask its name again, and dunk it three times into the font of holy water. The basic ceremony was the same for all people, though the wealthy and higher classes would elaborate the process as much as they could. Some might hang the church door with gold cloth or use a silver baptismal font instead of the regular one.

Godparents of a royal baby were usually chosen before the birth and would stay nearby so they were at hand and ready for the birth, as was a bishop who was expected to be ready to perform the rite. Then, once the baby was born, 'it was carried to church by the chief lady present – preferably a duchess in the case of the royal family, with another duchess to carry the chrisom [baptism robes for the baby] upon her shoulder. The baby was dressed in a robe with a long train, held up (if a prince or princess) by an earl or a countess respectively'.[40] Traditionally, royal baptisms and christenings were private events and not for public viewing, so it is highly unlikely that these ceremonies for Isabelle's children would have been witnessed by many other than the godparents and a select few nobles and clergy.

One of the most anticipated of these ceremonies, at least for many women, was the 'churching' of the new mother, the ceremony by which she is purified from childbirth and able to take communion and attend mass again. According to Jewish tradition, a woman was unclean for seven days after delivering a son and it took another thirty-three for her to be purified; if she delivered a girl, she was unclean for fourteen days and only purified after an additional sixty-six days. This formula comes from Leviticus 12:1-5, which reads, 'A woman who becomes pregnant and gives birth to a son will be ceremonially unclean for seven days, just as she is unclean during her monthly period ... Then the woman must wait thirty-three days to be purified from her bleeding ... If she gives birth to a daughter, for two weeks the woman will be unclean, as during her period. Then she must wait sixty-six days to be purified from her bleeding.' By the end of the twelfth century, the time of impurity was made to be forty days for all Christians, regardless of whether the child was a boy or a girl.

During a special ceremony, a priest would purify the mother and make her spiritually clean again so that she could attend church. However, a woman could be purified or churched right away if she desired to go to church and give thanks for a successful delivery, a concession granted by Pope Gregory the Great in a letter to Augustine of Canterbury sometime around 600. Gregory stated that if a woman wanted to go to church to give thanks for a successful delivery, even right after giving birth, this was not a sin and she should be permitted to enter. This perspective was later codified in a later medieval service book known as the *Manual* which was used by clergy to minister to their parishioners at major events such as childbirth, death, or marriage. Ultimately, the purification ceremony was expected to take place at the church itself, not at home or elsewhere. The woman, along with her female friends, neighbours, and sometimes midwives, would meet the priest at the door of the church, where he would read Psalm 121, some other verses, give a prayer of thanks for the safe delivery of a new Christian into the world, and sprinkle the mother with holy water. Then the priest would lead her by the right hand into the church, where she could stay to listen to mass if she desired. This churching ceremony was deemed important in that it reintegrated the new mother back into society, but there may have been other, more practical, reasons for observing this ritual.

In preindustrial societies, the postpartum confinement period essentially enforced rest after giving birth, which may, in turn, have led to better recovery for the mother and child. Resuming any kind of very rigorous work after birth could lead to exhaustion and illness, something any new mother wants to avoid. From the perspective of duty, a queen's churching could bring her back into the public sphere where she might play important roles within the political sphere as well as provide a role model for other women. It is to these roles of women, and queens in particular, that we will now turn.

Queens as Role Models

Queens, as the highest-ranking woman of any land, naturally were held up as role models for other women. They were often as visible as anyone could be without being the actual monarch or the local religious leader. Although they rarely ruled kingdoms in their own right, queens could and did command a great deal of social influence and, in their own ways, power. Pinning down the scope of medieval women's power is, however, a tricky task. As Jacqueline Murray says, 'The paucity of sources that troubles every area of medieval scholarship presents serious difficulties for the study of gender ... There are few sources written by women and fewer still that were self-consciously written to present a woman's perspective'.[41] Moreover, it can be difficult to determine the true scope of women's roles and power because the documents that have survived were generally written by male clerics; their perspectives were largely coloured by the Mary/ Eve and the male/ female dichotomies, which were influenced by Aristotle's views on gender polarity.

Elizabeth Norton explains that since most chroniclers were men who were, because of their vocation, cut off from women in general, they were automatically going to be suspicious of them. These chroniclers were writing for a specific reason, which was usually to show an example of a notorious woman so that other women knew how not to behave. In short, the few women recorded in the surviving chronicles were there either because they did something amazing or something that was not viewed well. By the twelfth century, the male clergy doing the recording tended to view men and especially women in very binary ways – good or bad, virgins or whores, and so on. The good news is that, prior to the late 1200s when Thomas Aquinas managed to reconcile Aristotle's philosophy with Christian theology, there was a greater plurality of belief. So, what might that have looked like? How did women attain power? Did coronations and the attendant ceremonies accompanying them impart the power, or was it something more transcendental? What role models did queens themselves have for women in power? The issue of women's power and influence is, of course, highly complex and nuanced, with influences reaching across many levels of society, history, and ecclesiastical authority.

Certainly, women in religious roles could wield a great deal of power both within the religious community and sometimes in the secular world as well. Some were more authoritative than others, for a variety of reasons and in different ways. One of the most famous religious women of the medieval world was Hildegard of Bingen. She was well known throughout twelfth century Europe and who remains a source of fascination today. Born to a family of lower nobility sometime around 1098, though the exact date is not known, Hildegard was given as a tithe to the church. She went to live at the monastery of Disibodenberg with another noble born lady named Jutta who became an anchoress at the monastery. Hildegard was enclosed with her for twenty-four years. When Jutta died in 1136, Hildegard was able to come out from enclosure. At the same time, the other nuns unanimously elected Hildegard to be the convent's *magistra*.

Hildegard wanted more independence for herself and her nuns, so she founded a new convent at Rupertsberg. Through her long and storied life, Hildegard became an advocate for herself and her nuns, an advisor for many monks and other clergy, made friends (and enemies) in some very high places, corresponded with bishops, cardinals, and popes, and established two separate convents. Hildegard also managed to write several texts about her visions, health and nutrition, and compose more than seventy songs, including what is considered to be the first opera.

During her life, Hildegard was able to depart from the gender polarity that is so often associated with medieval society and instead 'sought to reconcile biological difference and spiritual equality'.[42] She thought that men and women each had their own traits that were complementary, and she urged each to try to develop characteristics of the other gender. She also decided that the unequal social status of men and women was explained because women obeyed men by choice as a way to demonstrate the virtue of obedience. Ultimately, to Hildegard, whether one was obedient to a man or a woman was beside the point since there were many circumstances in which women could, and did, have authority over men.

The abbesses were a great example of authority and indeed held a good deal of power and control, even over men in a monastery that housed both men and women such as Hildegard's, an abbess held rank over the male monks in residence. Hildegard herself grew up with such examples, so it is no real surprise that she felt obedience was dependent more upon a person's role and desire to be virtuous, not their gender. In the double monastery where she grew up, men and women both obeyed the abbot, and an abbess would have exercised command over many of the men who lived there as well as women.

Later in her life, she risked excommunication, she and her nuns being placed under interdict because as abbess, she refused to turn over the body of a man she had buried in the consecrated cemetery. He had been excommunicated and, by canon law, should not have been buried in holy ground. However, Hildegard claimed that the man had been reconciled with the Church and received the sacraments before his death, and thus deserved a burial within holy ground. Eventually, she won her argument with the local bishop of Disibodenberg and the interdict was lifted from her and her nuns in the months before her death.

Another influential woman of the Middle Ages was Heloise of the Paraclete, lover and wife of Peter Abelard. Heloise was a contemporary of Hildegard, and both were contemporaries of Eleanor of Aquitaine, that most famous medieval female firebrand. Heloise was a renowned scholar in her own right even before her star-crossed affair and marriage to Peter Abelard. She was well known for her mastery of Latin, Greek, and Hebrew, as well as for her skill in writing and general philosophy. When Abelard became her tutor, it is likely he taught her medicine and further philosophy, and, in later life, she garnered a reputation for being an adroit healer.

Like Hildegard, Heloise also became an abbess, at Abelard's Paraclete, though unwillingly, as she had not wished to join orders in the first place, nor even to marry when she was younger. All the same, Heloise appears to have been a strong and skilled leader and was respected by her nuns. Moreover, Abelard also respected her and her thoughts, treating her in many ways as his equal, both in the secular world and later in the spiritual. In one of his letters to Heloise, Abelard stated, 'Offer to God a constant sacrifice of prayer. Urge him to pardon our great and manifold sins, and to avert the dangers which threaten me ... I well know how powerful your intercession may be. I pray you, exert it in this my need ... Urge your entreaties, for it is just that you should be heard.'[43] In his letter to Heloise, Abelard is asking that she plead on his behalf with God, for it seems that he believes the prayers of women appear to hold particular sway over the Almighty. Similarly, Heloise asked Peter the Venerable, one of Abelard's last friends and protectors, to ensure that a series of masses would be said for her at Cluny when she died, that an official copy of the papal absolution given to Abelard which cleared him of heresy charges be issued, and for a Church appointment for her son. In turn, Peter advised her to continue working to be a 'mother, teacher, and warrior' for her nuns; protecting, teaching, and advocating for herself, her nuns, and the convent was a vital role of an abbess.[44]

The twelfth and thirteenth centuries became more and more misogynistic because of an increased influence of Aristotelian philosophy on ecclesiastical thought; however, there still appears to have been the idea that women were intended to pray and be intercessors for others. An example from the thirteenth-century mystic, Mechtild of Magdeburg, bears this idea out when she wrote in her book *Das fließende licht der Gottheit* (*The Flowing Light of the Godhead*) about a vision she received of a friar in trouble. He appeared to her to beg, 'Have women and priests pray for me.'[45] This sentiment, and apparent progressive feminism, should not be misunderstood to reflect more authority or enlightenment than was truly the case, however tempting. But, as Caroline Walker Bynum notes, it gives us a paradigm of two sources of authority. For priests, they had the power of their office; for women, their motherly instincts were a source of authority. Specifically, 'The vision implies that those especially endowed with clerical authority and those especially prohibited from it are equally effective in mediating remission of the suffering brought by sin. The disqualification of gender becomes itself a qualification ... Mechtild sees herself as denuded, base, suffering union with the suffering Christ, and yet also as a purged channel by which God may speak to others.'[46] Mechtild was an ideal go-between for people and the divine.

Queens as Intercessors

The connection between these religious women and queens may not be readily apparent. However, they both acted as intercessors for others, whether for a convent of nuns, parishioners, or other people of the religious life, or for their subjects and other nobles. The role of intercessor was a vital duty for many women, and in particular for a queen. Queens rarely ruled in their own right, but they could and did wield a great deal of political power because of their proximity to the king. As a king's wife, a queen had more opportunity and resources to wield authority, but medieval society often refused to let her share her husband's power. Therefore, she had to use the tools that were within her power and which complemented the king's. The main tool available to her was intercession, which was intended to make the king more lenient toward his subjects.[47] Although not a queen, the medieval anchoress Christina of Markyate was betrothed to a man called Beorhtred and, upon the wedding night, she attempted to convert him into a spiritual marriage in imitation of the life of St. Cecilia and her husband, Valerian. Perhaps Christina herself was not well known at the time or had any influence over either of John's wives, but the story of St. Cecilia could have served as a model of a wife's spiritual duty to her husband and, in fact, probably was. Certainly, St. Margaret of Scotland would have been very familiar to queens of this period, including John's wives. This eleventh-century woman was held up as a paragon of queenship throughout England, in particular her role of intercession. Clergy of the day also 'expected wives to move their husbands to good'.[48] Thomas of Chobham, writing his *Summa Confessorum* shortly after John's death, even went so far as to say wives ought to be preachers to their stubborn or wayward husbands. No doubt there were other clergy who thought similarly and who may have been in a position to influence Isabella or Isabelle with regard to this role they would be expected to perform.

This potential power and ability to intercede with the king on behalf of others traditionally began with her coronation ceremony. The coronation itself was, in part, to show the power a monarch held over all his citizens, including his queen. During the ancient coronation ceremony, which to this day contains traces of pre-Christian practices and symbols, the king was anointed with holy oil, the most important part of the coronation. This action elevated him above the rest of the citizenry or nobility and made him akin to a priest, giving him both spiritual and material authority over all in his kingdom. In addition, he promised to defend the Church with the full strength of his authority. In effect, the coronation highlighted his masculine strength as a ruler who must be obeyed.

We can even see this power dynamic constructed in many of the literary works and French romances of the time, which create the female protagonists in such a way as to highlight the heroism of her male counterpart. Some examples include 'Le Chevalier au Lion' by Chrétien de Troyes, which both Isabella of Gloucester and Isabelle of Angoulême had likely read. These tales showed the royal power dynamic and normalised it in terms of social roles, eventually ending with the masculine authority solidly intact despite some potential for women to subvert and destabilise patriarchal social structure along the way.

In counterpoint to highlighting the authority of the king, the coronation was a time to show that the queen was subordinate to him, but also that she was ready and willing to intercede with the king on behalf of his subjects. Coronation pardons were the first way in which she could test out this intercessory role; these pardons had become common, at least in England, by the thirteenth century. During the coronation, the newly crowned king could, of course, issue pardons for those who had been found guilty of wrongdoing by his predecessor. However, coronation pardons were traditionally the province of the new queen who could appeal to the king on behalf of criminals or other petitioners, on minor issues ranging from injustices done by local bailiffs or sheriffs, to trespassing in the royal forests, to pardoning more serious offences. Beginning with these coronation pardons, intercession was generally expected from English queens from the very beginning of their reign.[49] The ritual of coronation pardons was a time for people to see the queen and, more importantly, to allow her an official and public first time to influence the king in favour of leniency. Her role as intercessor was emphasised by her placement, during coronation, at the king's left hand rather than his right. Placing her to his left was indicative of her subservient role but also highlighted the acts of mercy she is supposed to bring about. A woman's role, and especially a queen's, was to help her husband by interceding with him to encourage him to be merciful, and to be his moral guide as well.

The role of queens has been debated a lot in recent years. Some scholars argue that the influence of the queens was in decline by the twelfth century based on fewer appearances in charters they signed. Others claim that the decline in queens signing charters merely indicates a shift in how her role was viewed, with new or additional roles being examined. Beginning in 1154 with the accession of Henry II, the 'strict control of queens' resources limited their independence'.[50] During this time, queens did not retain control of their own dower lands while their husbands were alive and most of their income was dependent upon the king's authorisation. Moreover, Eleanor of Aquitaine, Henry's own wife, did not witness as many charters or other official documents after 1155, which may have contributed to the further erosion of the queens' authority in the public sphere.[51] The role of queens in France was not as politically active as was customary in England, and Eleanor only rarely witnessed charters while married to Louis. Since she was accustomed to ruling Aquitaine in her own right, her role as Louis's queen may have been disappointing to her; when she married Henry, she may have, at times, been prevented from a more active role in government because of her sex. Nevertheless, she still took a prominent role as regent of England during the times Henry travelled to his lands in Normandy.[52]

Regardless of the reasons why there may have been a decline in queenly authority, the role of intercessor remained multifaceted and was an expected role for the queen because 'it played a variety of useful roles for the king. Intercession not only affirmed the gender hierarchy, it also allowed men to change their minds without appearing weak.'[53] Moreover, intercession by the queen could provide something lacking in the king – that is, mercy as opposed to a harsher justice. It also emphasised the authority of the king while still allowing the queen an acceptable method of exerting her own authority.

In France, queenly intercession seems to have been primarily a private action since she was not traditionally permitted a voice in government as she had been in England's history. However, in England at least, intercession was public, in part because of its connections to the queen's gold, a surcharge collected on all voluntary fines to the king. Because the exchequer, a public office, was involved in collecting the queen's gold, it was a public matter. Queen's gold was supposed to be a 10 percent charge on all voluntary fines and was still owed to the queen even if the king pardoned the fine. The queen, of course, could pardon the fine if she chose to. Queen's gold may also be reflective of the earlier practice of gift giving and counter-giving from Anglo-Saxon England, linking her strongly with their Anglo-Saxon counterparts. Queens and other high-born ladies would be given gifts in exchange for their intercession with the king or their lord, respectively. The queen's gold was also considered to be public because it was essentially payment for a duty she was expected to fulfil through her intercession with the king. It is also possible that the queen's gold could be given to her as a reward. There is evidence this may have been the case with Isabelle of Angoulême. In November 1207, King John informed the exchequer that the queen's gold would, going forward, again be separated from other debts. This date coincides with the birth of the future Henry III, John's heir. Prior to that date, it seems possible that, even though Isabelle was the queen consort, Eleanor of Aquitaine was still collecting it from her son in exchange for her intercessory role, rather than Isabelle.

The collection of queen's gold could also be halted by the king if he was displeased with her. We have examples of this in the reign of Henry III, Isabelle's son. He withdrew the receipt of queen's gold due to his wife, Eleanor of Provence, when she angered him by overstepping her authority. He returned the gold to her after a few weeks, but 'the lesson was a sharp one: Henry had powerfully reminded her of her dependence on him'.[54] Years earlier, Eleanor of Aquitaine appears to have lost her queen's gold, likely as a result of her supporting her sons' rebellion against her husband, Henry II. Once her son, Richard I, was on the throne, Eleanor's income from queen's gold was restored. This is an unusual occurrence because normally queen's gold was not received by queens dowager, only queens consort. As such, Richard's wife, Berengaria of Navarre, should have been the one to receive the queen's gold. However, Eleanor's 'atypical collection helps illustrate the connection between queen's gold and intercession: Eleanor received the gold because she was the intercessory female during Richard's reign'.[55]

Putting aside her rebellion, Eleanor would have been a role model, as other queens had been, to her daughters and daughters-in-law, and the role of intercessor would have been especially prominent in her case. She did, after all, intercede with basically the majority of Europe on behalf of Richard I when he was imprisoned by Leopold V, the Duke of Austria. If any one woman of the Middle Ages could be held up as a role model to her peers and those who followed in her footsteps, it would be Eleanor of Aquitaine. She would no doubt be an intimidating act to follow, and she must have made a formidable mother-in-law. One aspect of queenship Eleanor of Aquitaine may well have learned and then passed on to her daughters and daughters-in-law was that a 'powerful woman filled different roles at different stages of her life, and she learned from experience'.[56] Eleanor would have taught this and many other lessons related to the role of queenship to her daughters and probably to her daughters-in-law as well.

The queen's intercession could be used by anyone who had business at court, whether in political circles, domestic issues, or even international relations. This was important because, on the one hand, a queen as intercessor was idealised as one who ran the palace, managed the treasury, and thus oversaw the vital role of gift giving and patronage. On the other hand, a queen who was wicked, or perceived to be so, could give bad advice to the king and influence him in a way that could be disastrous to the kingdom.

Eleanor again provides an example of a bad influence when she convinced Louis to invade the Champagne region in retaliation against the Count of Champagne. Louis heeded Eleanor's advice and as a result, the townspeople of Vitry were burned to death in the church, to the horror of Louis and most of Europe. This specific event may well have influenced noblemen and the clergy against women having too much influence over their husbands or too much political involvement. Isabelle was also perceived to have undue influence over John, which was a continual source of concern to medieval men. To borrow a term from Lois Huneycutt, the argument can be made that Isabelle of Angoulême was one of those 'wicked queens' who had too much influence, and that her failure in her role as intercessor helped bring about the fall of the Angevin empire.[57] Carmi Parsons claims that 'the matrimonial careers of Richard I and John increased the queens' declining prominence'.[58]

Records about Isabelle often reflect that at least some of the nobles of England thought that she was too outspoken or had too much of a negative influence over John and that, because of pure lust, John allowed his empire to be whittled away while the royal couple stayed in bed. The chronicler Matthew Paris took a particularly harsh view of Isabelle and her acts. As Pauline Stafford is quick to point out, though, the 'reaction to power itself and to the immediate past influenced comment on royal women … Dead women may be treated differently from the living, more readily sanctified or vilified according to the needs and purposes of the writer.'[59] Isabelle was a convenient scapegoat, useful to blame for the loss of John's lands in France. However, the blame cannot rightly be attributed to Isabelle, especially given her very young age at the time John lost these lands. Matthew Paris, however, remained unsparing in his criticism of Isabelle of Angoulême, which may have contributed to her reputation throughout history as 'more Jezebel than Isabelle', as he wrote. However, his views of her are unduly based on his clerical opinion of women's authority, reflecting his own biases more than what may have been reality.

As a woman of the highest social status, a queen was held to exacting standards and as a result, may have been even more restricted than many of her contemporaries. It is also no doubt part of the reason why they may be maligned so strongly in the surviving documents. Isabella of Gloucester is rarely mentioned at all in chronicles and she seems not to have signed many charters with her husband in the ten years of their marriage. She did, however, sign a few with her second husband, Geoffrey de Mandeville, sometime after 1214. On the other hand, Isabelle of Angoulême did sign some charters with John, at least in the early years of their marriage. The author of the *History of the Dukes of Normandy*, writing contemporaneously during the time of John's reign, suggests that John was smitten with his young wife, which could imply that her role as an intercessor should have been a strong one. Isabelle was crowned at the same time as John, on 8 October 1200, which could imply that he intended for her to take a more prominent role in government. Whatever his initial intentions, though, there is little evidence that Isabelle acted in an intercessory role very often, or in any other role within government. Moreover, Isabelle seems not to have had the personality to be an effective intercessor, either for herself or anyone else. Described as having a sharp or scathing wit and abrasive temperament, Isabelle does not seem to have performed any direct intercession for others during her marriage to John, at least none that has survived in chronicles. This seems to be supported by the evidence that her mother in law, Eleanor of Aquitaine, retained the duty of intercessor during the early years of John's reign, possibly until her death in 1204.

However, as Gillian Adler notes, 'Mothers, like other intercessory female figures, attempt to intercede in governmental futures, but maternal authority is always forfeited for paternal control of political destiny.'[60] Isabelle did, indeed, attempt to negotiate with French Capetian forces after John's death on behalf of her son, the newly crowned Henry III, in an attempt to prevent them from invading Plantagenet lands. Her intercession failed, though it was primarily because John had specified that William Marshal, not Isabelle, be given the regency of England until Henry III came of age. It is possible, too, that she may have interceded during her wedding and coronation ceremonies on behalf of the musicians who performed, since it is written in the Norman Rolls for 10 October 1200 that King John was especially generous to the players and gave them 25 shillings for their performance, a huge sum for the time.[61] There is no way to know this for certain, but it seems at least within the scope of possibility that John wanted to please his new, young wife by favouring the musicians if she liked them.

Biblical Imagery

The practice of queenly intercession is strongly linked to the Marian devotion that was at its apex during the Middle Ages. Using the Virgin Mary as a model of queenly intercession may provide us with 'a valuable tool with which to approach petitioners' perceptions of the queen and her role'.[62] Adopting Marian imagery in connection to queens makes sense because Mary was worshipped as the Great Intercessor for the salvation of humanity. Throughout the Middle Ages, and in particular the thirteenth century with the reign of Isabelle of Angoulême's son, Henry III, churchmen strongly encouraged the biblical connections between queens and their scriptural role models. Even some of the ecclesiastical statuary and literary creations reflect the link between Mary, queens, and their role as intercessors. In the Arsenal Missal, for example, Christ is depicted on a throne and his mother is approaching to ask him to show mercy to his servants. Encouraging the queen's role of intercessor was, in part, a way to limit the potential power and authority a queen could have by making her not an authority figure but a merciful intercessor; this interpretation is in alignment with what some scholars view as a rising misogyny of the time. However, the association of women with the private sphere as opposed to the public should not be automatically taken to mean they lacked power, and we should keep in mind that women and queens had 'informal means of wielding public power alongside more formal institutional structures'.[63] We also must take into consideration that the queen would have made a more approachable intercessor for many, particularly those of lower classes, than the highly literate administrative officials of the court.

The Virgin Mary was a strong enough positive woman that linking her to queenly duties was usually enough to counterbalance the mistrust male clergymen and nobles generally felt for the female sex. There was also a tendency in medieval society to 'project the earthly hierarchy onto the heavenly, to legitimise the former by appeal to the latter, [so] it is understandable that imagery associated with earthly queens attached to their heavenly counterpart and vice versa'.[64] Thus, Marian imagery was relevant to women, and especially to queens.

Despite it being an attempt to limit women's power, queens in the early and high Middle Ages followed Marian tropes with regard to their intercessory roles. Part of the mindset surrounding this dynamic was the medieval Marian worship, holding the Virgin Mary up as the ultimate role model for women, and especially as the ideal for queens. In fact, when she interceded on behalf of Richard I, Eleanor not only fulfilled an intercessory role, but also a specifically Marian role as well. She placed herself, probably intentionally, in the role of *mater dolorosa*, the grieving mother. We see this grieving mother in Eleanor's portrayal of herself weeping, being heartbroken at the loss of her son, and physically in pain at the thought of his ordeal. 'At the same time, she is the patient sufferer of the cares and woes that God has imposed upon her in this life; she weeps for her son's future death knowing he will die without the intercession of his father'.[65] The father, in this case, was Celestine III, and Eleanor's use of her religious devotion is a means for her to push her agenda and intercede for Richard with the pope as well as with the man holding him ransom.

She created her letters in a way that transform her into a Marian figure, the pope becomes a fatherly/God figure, and Richard is an anointed king/Christ figure who is suffering in patient silence. She also calls to mind the tragedies and suffering she has endured throughout her life, as a mother who has lost children. Eleanor used her role as a mother, not a queen, to create this dynamic because a mother inhabits a space that creates an identity that cannot be ignored. As Rachel Stapleton notes, 'Eleanor needs a role model who can grant authority to her words ... the obvious choice for her is the Virgin Mary'.[66] Mary was perceived as a powerful woman and held many roles relevant to Eleanor's situation, who wasted no time using them to her advantage.

The connection Eleanor was making between herself as a queen mother and Mary as the Queen of Heaven would have been immediately obvious to Celestine. Mary was viewed as an intercessor between humankind and Jesus because of her role as his mother, which was a mirror for queenly behaviours as well. Mary was a figure unique among women; medieval society viewed her as the highest-ranking woman ever and held her up as supremely imitable, a person all women should try to emulate. In this way, Eleanor demonstrated how queens embodied their roles as both intercessors and mothers, basing her authority on her role as a mother like Mary.

While Isabella of Gloucester was childless and could therefore not base any authority upon her motherhood, Isabelle of Angoulême had five children by King John, including two daughters who predeceased her; she could have based much of her authority on her maternity, as Eleanor did, and as Mary did. The connection between Mary, motherhood, and grief had, by the end of the eleventh century, accreted into a specific cult of the Lady of Sorrows, and so the trope of the grieving mother in connection to Marian imagery was at its peak and widely recognised by the time Eleanor wrote to Celestine. But the connection between Marian imagery and queenly intercession emerged much earlier and was well established by the tenth century. It was a tool queens could have used to their advantage, and certainly did in many cases. The idea was that a queen, like Mary, could use their influence and proximity to the king to cause him to be merciful in ways that may not have been available to him without the influence of a woman; everyone knows, of course, that kings were for law and justice, and queens for mercy and compassion.

In addition to the views held by contemporaries of the king's wife as merciful and compassionate, there was the ideal of the chaste woman or virgin that queen were also encouraged to adhere to. This links again to the likely education women of a certain class may have received, including both of John's wives. The veneration of virgin-martyrs continued strongly in the twelfth and thirteenth centuries and would have informed the ways in which society viewed women and queens. While queens by definition could not really be virgins, given the directive for them to produce heirs for the king, virgin and chaste role models were still given to them as general guides for the correct comportment of women. Again, many of these models were biblical. The Virgin Mary is the highest ideal for women to strive for with regard to sexual purity. She was portrayed as 'one who possessed all the frailties of womanhood but who was able to overcome them'.[67] Even though she was a virgin and most queens of medieval society were not, Mary provided an example of human perfection to which other women could aspire.

For queens, it was not Mary's virginity that was commendable but rather her ability to overcome her weakness; many women would have been able to relate to her on that level and set their sights on improving and overcoming their own flaws as a result, often by praying to her for her intercession and assistance. However, since Mary's virginity and utter purity were also impossibly high standards for most women to emulate, Mary Magdalene was also seen as a feminine example, if not an ideal role model. Whereas Mary Magdalene was a prostitute, the whore of the virgin/whore dichotomy into which women were often placed, she also overcame her sinful ways and found joy and love from Christ. She is a model a lot of women would probably have been able to relate to, not because she was a prostitute, but because she was neither a virgin nor flawless, someone who symbolised the ecclesiastical concept of forgiveness and grace available to anyone. Women who were married, and mothers, may not have always identified with the virgin-martyrs or saints that were venerated as the epitome of womanhood, but they could relate to mercy and compassion.

A queen was encouraged to try to improve her husband's habits so that he may gain salvation. During the coronation ceremony, it was common for doves to be symbols of the queen for their traditional connection to mercy, linking her even more closely with the Virgin Mary. Indeed, doves have a long symbolic history that predates Christianity or Judaism, but for the purposes of medieval society, the connection between doves, the Holy Spirit, the Virgin Mary, and mercy is a vital one. The mercy of a queen mirrored the mercy encouraged by Mary, and this imagery was incorporated into medieval thought as part of the duties expected of royal women. Aside from the connections to mercy, doves had also been used as nautical guides from the ancient Near East from roughly the fifth century BCE to as recently as the nineteenth century CE. The dove as a guide would have been most familiar to medieval society from the biblical tale of Noah and the Ark from Genesis 8:8-11, in which Noah sends a dove out of the ark to see if there is land, knowing the waters have receded when it brings back an olive branch. Doves used as guides mesh well with the thought that the Virgin Mary was a guide for humanity, and that a queen should also guide her husband the king toward a better spiritual life as well as toward mercy.

Many statues of the Virgin Mary were created in such a way that they brought into a visual form the idea of a divine intercessor. Some of these statues depicted Mary on a throne and holding the Christ child in her lap. These statues, known as Throne of Wisdom statues, are linked to the Throne of Solomon. This form implies that Mary herself is 'a *Sedes Sapientiae* or Throne of Wisdom—the Mother of God, enthroned herself, who serves as a throne for the son of God turned into human flesh'.[68] The symbolism with these Throne of Wisdom statues highlights Mary's role as wise and gentle intercessor between those souls in need and her son. The throne imagery additionally can reinforce the role of the queen as intercessor between the king and his subjects since she is usually placed to the king's left in coronation ceremonies. Placing her to the king's left normally suggests her submissive role as the king's wife, preserving the social hierarchy expected from medieval society. However, placing the queen to the king's left specifically during the coronation indicated her willingness to intercede and advocate for those who come to her for aid. Even though the biblical precedent is for a queen to sit on her husband's right side, by placing her to his left during the coronation ceremony, an English queen is virtually required to provide intercession.[69] By sitting her to the left of the king, a queen is automatically associated with the rod or virge of justice and fairness he held in his left hand, as opposed to his right hand which held the sceptre of law and authority. The Throne of Wisdom statues generally show Mary holding Jesus in her lap, making her into the literal throne upon which he sits as the personification of wisdom. Mary is sometimes shown in these statues as holding Jesus on her left hip or sitting him on the left side of her lap, which can also be symbolic of his wisdom and mercy. Mary as a throne or vessel from which Christ can dispense wisdom and mercy was a powerful connection for medieval queens and their intercessory roles.

Books and book imagery are also closely linked with the Virgin Mary and, through her, queens. This link derives from the Gospel of John 1:1, which says, 'In the beginning was the Word, and the Word was with God, and the Word was God.'[70] The Word, of course, is Jesus, and the Virgin Mary is seen as a book, a vessel that brought him into the world. Paintings and statues of Mary often portray her holding a book, which is almost always taken to symbolise the Christ Child.[71] The scene depicted usually influences how she is holding the book. Annunciation images tend to describe Mary as holding an open book, ready for the Holy Spirit to imprint words upon the pages, absorbing both the word written upon the page as well as the divine word; images other than the Annunciation generally show Mary holding a closed book, symbolic of her closed, intact, virginal body. When the book is open, she is receptive to the Holy Spirit, described often as a golden mist or light. When closed, the book is a symbol that Mary is sealed and contains secrets which are undecipherable by mere mortals. She becomes a vessel to bring her child into the world, much the same as queens are expected to become vessels to bring a king's children, preferably male, into the world. The book itself shows how the Word became flesh, derived from the prophecy of Isaiah: 'And the Lord said to me: Take thee a great book, and write in it with a man's pen'.[72] Mary, and queens, become blank spaces upon which men's words were to be written, waiting to bring a child to life. A successful queen, to extend the metaphor, produced the words of her husband in terms of bearing heirs. The link between books, the Virgin Mary, and queens can be expanded further in terms of patronage.

Queens and other noblewomen were often patronesses of the arts, including literature. There are many portraits, statues, or effigies of queens holding books, implying that they may have been patronesses of literature, or that they were deliberately imitating the connection to the Virgin Mary. These visual representations of Mary not just as a reader but also as a book herself show the generative powers in the symbolism. Patronage implies creation and so the connection between queens and their support of literature is a way in which they can be the cause of another kind of creation. In a time that associated Marian imagery with a book, commissioning a work of literature, especially a gospel, afforded 'women an opportunity to engage with the divine physically, intellectually, and spiritually'.[73]

Neither of John's wives are depicted in effigy as holding a book, which may imply they had not commissioned any literary works as Eleanor of Aquitaine often did; Eleanor's effigy actually does depict her as reading an open book. Queens and other noblewomen who did commission literary works may have viewed their affinity for books as a way of imitating Mary, *imitatio Mariae*, the ideal role model for women. The metaphor of the Virgin as a book did, however, have 'the unintended effect of authorizing women to avail themselves of direct access to the word/Word in explicit imitation of the Mother of God'.[74] Women imitating the Virgin may have been a problem for some noblemen who tended to view powerful women with deep suspicion, as evidenced by miracle stories in which the Virgin punishes or refuses to favour anyone who fails to honour her properly. No queen would have deliberately manipulated her intercessory role to portray herself as a worldly counterpart to the Virgin. Rather, popular associations of the Virgin and the queen focused more on her intercession than the woman herself. In other words, 'Like familial models of marriage and motherhood … the Marian image both exalted and limited women and was susceptible to interpretation by different groups: for church and nobility, the queen as chaste and submissive mediatrix was safely secluded from authority, and those less intimate with the court could project a loving and gracious face onto the king's wife as they sought her mercy.'[75] The queen as intercessor was expected to soften the king's heart but the ways in which she did so were suspect to a patriarchal society. However, a successful intercession allowed the king to take on the appearance of a godly identity, mirroring the divine order and reinforcing the earthly social order in the process.

Medieval queens also may have followed an Esther topos as a role model for their duties of queenship and intercession. Lois Huneycutt notes that 'the manipulation of the story of Queen Esther … served as a role model for medieval queens'.[76] In the Esther story, the titular lady is married to the king of Persia but keeps her Jewish heritage secret from him. She learns that one of her husband's councillors is plotting to kill all the Jews because Esther's uncle, Mordecai, insulted him. She risks her life by entering the king's bedroom without permission and convinces him to attend a banquet, where she was able to reveal to her husband the wicked plot and save her people.[77] Decades of coronations of queens leading up to Isabella of Gloucester and Isabelle of Angoulême used the example of Esther as a way of inspiring women to behave in a similar manner. As early as the ninth century, Esther was used as a particularly appropriate model for queens, partly because she was of equal rank to an earthly queen. Using Esther as a role model justified the sumptuous lifestyle of the nobility in that it allowed for extravagance as long as it was used in an acceptable way. Additionally, Esther's beauty was overshadowed by her other virtues and, despite being a queen, she displayed her humility by being willing to abase herself to her king. These actions would have been considered seemly in a queen whose role was to be obedient yet still intercede with her husband on behalf of others. Throughout the eleventh and twelfth centuries, queens' power was becoming more remote, and so the use of persuasion and intercession were becoming potent means by which women could exercise authority. After all, a queen who was determined enough would find a way to continue influencing her kingdom. Thus, Esther is often one of the examples used by which the ideals of queenship were shaped, particularly from the late-eleventh to the mid-twelfth centuries. During this period, various literary and ecclesiastical works were written to 'show an increasing awareness of an abstract ideal of queenly behaviour'.[78]

Power and Politics

On the opposite side of the coin from venerating virginity, queens gained power through childbirth. As previously discussed, her primary role would have been to produce a legitimate heir, a prince, and preferably more than one in case disaster struck and one died. The power queens gained through birthing heirs translated into power for the king as well. Kings who had sons were far more powerful in general than kings who had no male heirs. The accumulation of power is closely connected to the concept of authority; where women derived power is from the fact that kings needed male issue to inherit the throne after they died. A king could not generate a son without a queen to birth him. If a king had no legitimate male heir, there may not be a peaceful transition of power.

The Plantagenets knew this with painful certainty, given that Henry II's mother, Empress Matilda, and her struggle to claim the English throne resulted in The Anarchy and nearly twenty years of civil war. They learned that, although a king may have desired for his daughter to rule after him, the rest of society generally did not. In this way, a vital part of the authority of a king can be argued to come from his queen, for without her to deliver male heirs for him, a king's authority stood on shaky ground. The divine right of kings was not, apparently, infallible.

Richard I, John's brother, declared that he was born with a rank that has no superiors except God, which is interesting considering that the pope was supposed to be the intercessor between God and mankind on earth. Richard also had as his personal motto *Dieu et mon droit* ('God and my right'), which to this day is the official motto of the British monarchy. Richard had declared John to be his heir after his release from captivity in 1194. In part, this was a way to show John political friendship and grant forgiveness for his attempted usurpation of the throne while Richard was imprisoned, but also it secured the line of succession since Richard did not have any children yet, and of course there was no way for him to predict that he would die childless. By securing the line of succession, Richard would have gained stronger authority as king just as if he had fathered a legitimate heir. The absence of royal sons could cause a crisis of succession, but on the flip side, a huge royal family also prompted fighting and instability in other ways. Additionally, female heirs were also viewed as a threat to the line of succession. We have seen examples of this with the Empress Matilda, while another formidable example 400 years later concerns Henry VIII and his obsession for having a son to succeed him.

The role of intercessor is subtle and yet absolutely vital to a queen or even a noblewoman. As we have seen, by the time of John's marriages, the tradition of queenly intercession was well established, a role both of his wives should have been familiar with and acting upon. Since Isabella of Gloucester was John's wife before he was king, her role as an intercessor was probably less vital. If she acted as an intercessor during her marriage to John, it seems to have gone unrecorded. As previously discussed, it is possible that Eleanor of Aquitaine retained her role as intercessor for the reigns of both Richard and John, given her ferocious personality. After Eleanor's death, though, there is little evidence to show that Isabelle of Angoulême took her place and acted as or was successful as an intercessor while she was queen. Given the tradition of a queen's role to soften the heart of the king, if she were ineffective at doing so, she would have been seen as a failure in a vital aspect of queenship. A queen's power relied more on the appearance of influence rather than on the actual practice; it could be disastrous if the perception was lost. 'The queen who had no income of her own and no influence over her husband could have no allies at court and thus little control over her own fate.'[79] This lack of influence, perceived or otherwise, may well have impacted Isabelle's ability to intercede for herself or anyone else. In her life after her marriage to John, Isabelle did attempt to intercede on behalf of her own interests to her son, Henry III, and other high-profile individuals, to only tepid success.

Queens also held power and influence literally through their marriages. Political alliances were commonly structured through marrying off the nobly born daughters and sometimes sons of wealthy lords or royals. When women married, it was often to men outside their own country. Noblewomen generally had their own estates and were assumed to have influence over their husbands. A woman's influence over her husband encompassed the role of intercessor, but it also brought challenges to her and anxiety or even resentment to the lords and clergy of her new home. Through marriage to a king from another country, a queen could sway the politics of a nation to her favour by bringing her own culturally influenced views and background into her husband's court. She had the power to encourage the king to appoint members of her own family to important positions within his court, leaving local nobles out of the circle of influence regardless of what kind of claims they may have otherwise been entitled to. Queens also had the agency to influence what clergy were appointed to what positions, her own patronage of her preferred nominees determining the course of ecclesiastical policy. Even if her new subjects were resistant to her ideas, a queen had the potential to lead society in new ways, possibly even unconsciously.

Because of the potential for foreign-born women to bring outside influences to their marital court, fostering and educating girls in the homes of their future husbands were important practices, particularly if the contracted marriage was to help ensure an alliance or to settle peace between two antagonistic families. Sometimes, a future bride was little more than a hostage, held at the home of her future husband. This happened with Margaret, the daughter of Louis VII of France, Eleanor of Aquitaine's first husband. Margaret, delivered by the French king's second wife, Constance of Castile, had been betrothed to Eleanor's son Henry (known as the Young King) in an attempt to make peace between France and England. However, Louis refused to allow his daughter to be brought up in Eleanor's court with her new husband, Henry II, and instead sent the child to be raised in the household of the chief justice of Normandy. Margaret Capet was effectively a betrothed hostage.

There are other examples of betrothed hostages in Plantagenet history. Henry II held Alice, another daughter of Louis VII, at court when she was betrothed to marry Richard; later, King John held as hostage the two daughters of King William the Lion of Scotland, with the promise that he would marry the eldest to his son, the future Henry III. That neither of those marriages took place is beside the point; some high-born girls were sometimes badly treated by those who were supposed to be her future family, and it is possible that girls were subjected to greater mistreatment if they were living in foreign courts at the time of the conflicts. Yet another similar situation arose with Isabelle's own daughter, Joan, who was raised at the court of Hugh de Lusignan X in preparation for her marriage to him. Isabelle, after the death of John, married her own daughter's fiancé and held her as hostage to coerce Henry III into giving her military and financial aid in holding her territories. However, not all noble or royal betrothed were treated as hostages before their weddings.

An important reason for sending young girls to the homes of their husbands-to-be was to educate them early on about the rules of custom and social affairs of the country they would eventually rule as queen. Most rulers did not want foreign ideas flooding their kingdoms. If a girl was raised in the country of her fiancé, then she would have assimilated the culture, language, customs, and laws. She would effectively be a native to the culture and therefore less likely to be swayed by foreign interests, allowing her 'to function in her role of queen more quickly and effectively after marriage'.[80] In this way, a future queen grew up surrounded and influenced by the culture of her husband-to-be rather than her natal culture. She would thus take her husband's culture on as her own through her upbringing. Sometimes, boys were reared at the homes of their future wives as well, though this practice may not have been quite as common.

This fostering did not always happen; Isabelle was raised in her native Angoulême prior to her marriage to John, although she was fostered for a time at the court of the Lusignans. Isabella similarly does not appear to have left her native Gloucester before she was married to John. In Isabella's case, she was English-born and thus her marriage to John may have given other nobles or clergy little cause for concern about foreign influences upon their own interests. However, Isabelle could have been viewed as a foreigner, even though John at that point still held vast lands in France and the aristocracy was largely Anglo-Norman. Her depiction in contemporary chronicles suggests that, regardless of whether she was viewed as a foreigner or not, she was generally disliked among the nobility.

A woman's power in the Middle Ages typically came through the agency of the men in her life and her social status. The issues facing queens and the impact they could have upon society were important enough that chroniclers weighed in on who they thought should be chosen for the role.[81] The chroniclers who make note of the choice of a queen had ample reason to be aware of events and to desire caution in a king's choice of bride. The politics surrounding the choice of a royal bride were often tumultuous and delicate, having the potential to disrupt society or bring about peace. If a king chose his bride from within his own country, he thus elevated her kin and changed the balance of power and status among his other nobles; if he sought a foreign bride, even if by doing so he was making a strategic alliance with a foreign power, there was the fear that she would use her influence over the king to direct wealth and favour to her own country rather than her new country-by-marriage. Part of the challenge of being a queen was negotiating 'divided loyalties', which was 'an essential aspect of queens' understanding of themselves and others' understanding of them'.[82] Queens knew that the way in which they balanced these conflicting duties and loyalties could have a drastic impact on her own use of power as well as limiting her influence depending on how she was perceived in the land.

Even something as seemingly unimportant as clothing and fashion could have an impact on politics and the perception of a queen's influence. This example helps underscore the importance aristocratic families placed on a bride being loyal to her husband's kingdom rather than her own family or country of birth. If a woman married a king but was not raised in the king's own country, she may have brought with her certain preferences in clothing styles or use of fabrics. If the marriage was intended to cement an already strong alliance between two nations or wealthy families, the ruling classes may not consider the preferences of the new bride as too interfering. If, though, she was considered foreign or was disliked by her new countrymen, her preferences could potentially disrupt politics already in place or destabilise them further, particularly if she was able to exert a strong influence over her husband. This is always the fear among the aristocrats of a country.

Trade agreements from the Middle East became more common, partly because crusaders brought exotic fabrics and styles of clothing to Western Europe. The higher social classes began incorporating these new fabrics and styles into the daily wear, and patterns and styles of clothes were beginning to get more ornate throughout the twelfth century; the wealthier classes and gentry commonly imitated the dress of their social superiors. Changing styles influenced trade and power depending on what city or country had the most sought-after materials, and most governments began to see the need to introduce laws that dictated what people could wear based upon their social status. For example, at one point, the ends of shoes became elongated so much that governments, first in Italy, began to issue sumptuary laws stating how long a shoe could be depending upon one's social class. No sumptuary laws are recorded in England, but in France they appeared in the latter part of the thirteenth century, referring almost exclusively to what women could or could not wear; men's clothing was far less regulated.[83]

Architecture, such as Gothic, also influenced fashion, as well as trade with various countries. According to the Heraldry Society, the fleur-de-lys was first used by none other than Louis VII of France, Eleanor of Aquitaine's first husband. There is little written about the impact of specific textiles on twelfth and thirteenth century politics; really, there is not a lot documented prior to the fifteenth century regarding textiles and politics, but it is interesting to consider how politics may have played out differently if French-born brides insisted upon buying specific foreign fabrics for everything after marrying into another country. Certain regions in France were prominent for their textiles, and later, Italian fabrics were considered to be the most desirable. These later changes owed largely to politics, battles won or lost, and varying influences within the public sphere, including, perhaps, the wishes of a wife with specific preferences for her clothes.

Practicing political friendship was also common for upper class women as well as noblemen, kings, and queens. This is somewhat related to the earlier practice of peace-weaving, carried out by women in Anglo-Saxon England. It was, in fact, a vital component of political language and action in twelfth-century England.[84] This concept of friendship was not personal or intimate as we understand the concept today; it was a public bond with obligations and expectations entered into usually by two men. This form of friendship encompassed rendering council and coming to one another's aid in battle as needed. Part of being a good king was being a good friend. Based on this consideration, it is fairly clear that most chroniclers did not view John as a good king because they viewed him as unable to retain his political friends, and because he tended to sew resentment among his barons more than anything. But political friendship was not limited to the male sphere. There are numerous examples of men and women making political alliances with others to their mutual benefit.

Queens were, naturally, a target for these types of friendships, primarily because of their proximity to the king and his authority, but sometimes because of their own authority. For a queen, political friendship can be seen as an offshoot of her role as intercessor. This civic relationship between people should not be conflated with our modern understanding of friendship; it was more a form of diplomacy in which each party benefitted at some point. Specifically, 'The relationship between friendship and politics in medieval Europe was articulated explicitly as a positive one. Friendship ... was regarded as integral to politics and as inherently ethically good.'[85] Political friendship was thus a strong component of what was considered to make a good monarch.

The medieval understanding of friendship was derived from the Classical thought which stated that it is a bond between two people, but also a bond that helped unite virtue with the greater good, and thus was intimately connected with the political sphere. It is linked in particular to Cicero's treatise De Amicitia, which says that friendship is 'a complete identity of feeling about all things divine and human, strengthened by mutual good will and affection'.[86] While it was certainly the case that men engaged in political friendship more than women, given women's limited role in government in the twelfth and thirteenth centuries, there is evidence that some medieval queens engaged in the practice as well. Notably, this list includes Empress Matilda, John's grandmother; Eleanor of Aquitaine, John's mother; and Eleanor of Provence, the wife of Henry III, John and Isabelle's son. Rebecca Slitt expands on the role of friendship in politics, saying that 'women participated in political friendship just as they did in all of the other political practices of the Middle Ages ... even though theorists claimed that women should be subordinate to men'.[87]

Because of the perceived subordinate status of women, chroniclers of the time were deeply suspicious of them in the political arena and their writing tends to reflect this. Chroniclers in general tended to view political friendship as a means to assess overall political ability, so they excluded women from this aspect of the public sphere since women were not, to their mind, fully active participants in politics anyway. There are several ways we can see this viewpoint in the historical record, or rather, lack of record. Most of the chronicles from the Anarchy, for example, do not discuss Empress Matilda's political friendships. Instead, they focus more on her half-brother, Robert of Gloucester, the grandfather of Isabella, and his political relationships. They describe Matilda's rival, Stephen of Blois, in terms of his own good friendship, if they supported him, or said he showed poor judgment in choosing friends, if they supported Matilda. Even with these descriptions, chroniclers mostly ignored Matilda's own friendship or how she may have gone about gaining friends to her cause. It is likely that part of the reason for this absence of women in the political arena is because 'it was more likely that a noblewoman's public political actions would be accepted as legitimate if she acted on behalf of or in lieu of her husband, supporting familial and dynastic bonds'.[88] So, in this case, even the actions of an empress are viewed through the lens of what man is siding with her.

Isabella of Gloucester herself engaged in formal political friendship, with two charters she wrote showing friendship language between 1186 and 1199; her father, on the other hand, used this language in twenty-four out of seventy-five charters that he wrote in the same time period. Isabella's mother, Hawisa, was also active in political friendship. Records show that they used nearly identical language in their charters, stating that the charter was addressed 'to all vassals and friends, French and English, present and future'.[89] A perusal through *Earldom of Gloucester Charters* shows that this language appears to be very common, not just within the Earl of Gloucester's family but also in charters by other nobles of both sexes. Countess Hawise was so active in the daily oversight of her household that she witnessed the majority of her husband's charters. Eleanor of Aquitaine also witnessed charters for other lords and ruled over court in her role as regent for Richard I while he was away.

Even with these examples, though, political friendship is not as commonly displayed in the charters issued by women in the thirteenth century as it was in ones by men, or by both sexes in the twelfth century, which aligns with the women's less active role in politics of the time.

We have been cautioned not to take women's witnessing of charters as a sign that their participation within politics was accepted, noting that even in documented instances of female political friendship, there is 'a parallel discourse of subordination'.[90] Nevertheless, women did engage in this aspect of politics, at least some of the time, and witnessing itself denotes a semblance of power held by the women who are named, and in the order in which they appear.

Similarly, if some women practiced political friendship more frequently than historians today think they did, it simply may never have been recorded; instead, it may have been practiced in person or other ways that meant it was not documented since the chroniclers did not see women as having any active part in the political landscape. The actions of women throughout history are often ignored or overlooked, even if they were commendable actions. As good kingship was associated with good friendship, good queenship was similarly based in part on a woman's ability to intercede or morally guide her husband to be better; conversely, a woman may have been seen as a bad queen if she were unable to persuade the king to mercy, or if she was not able to help smooth over ruffled feathers on his behalf.

For example, if a ruler, male or female, were greedy or stingy with giving gifts to their political friends, chronicles may reflect that they were poor leaders. Generosity and gift giving were both vital components of being good rulers and a sign of political friendship. An example of proper generosity and gift giving can be seen in the way Richard I forgave John after the younger man's betrayal. John joined forces with Philip Augustus, the French king, and attempted to usurp the English throne. He also tried to pay Henry VI, the Holy Roman Emperor, to keep Richard imprisoned rather than releasing him as he had agreed to do in his dealings with Eleanor of Aquitaine. Richard was ultimately released and was victorious in the feud with his brother. When John came before Richard to ask forgiveness, Richard was utterly magnanimous, forgiving his brother and naming him his heir presumptive.

However, not all instances of political friendship resulted in displays of good leadership, or even friendship. John himself did not seem to learn the art of generosity prior to his accession to the throne. Many of his actions and lack of grace directly contributed to the barons rebelling and forcing him to sign the Magna Carta. Similarly, Isabelle of Angoulême demonstrated a poor grasp of political friendship in some of the letters she wrote. Isabelle may have written some of her letters that survive today with the purpose of engaging in political friendship, but they primarily seem to demonstrate her making demands for a boon or assistance of some kind rather than a more diplomatic approach to an issue. The most infamous example that survives today is her letter dated from 1220 in which she tells Henry III that she had taken Guy de Lusignan as her husband. He had been betrothed to Isabelle's own eldest daughter, Joan, and is the son of Isabelle's first betrothed before she married John; she claims to have gone through with the marriage because he wanted an heir and her daughter was too young to consummate the proposed union or produce children. Isabelle then bluntly tells Henry to give her dower to her, with an implicit threat that if he did not, he would make an enemy of the de Lusignans.[91]

Comparing this letter from Isabelle with a letter written by her mother in law, Eleanor of Aquitaine to Pope Celestine III asking for his aid in the release of King Richard, it is easy to differentiate between the tone and politics behind each letter. The only real concession to diplomacy in Isabelle's letter might be that she places Henry's name and titles before hers, the correct convention for medieval letter writing. Placing her own name and titles first would have been considered to have a lower status than Henry. Other than the order of the names and titles of recipient and sender, her letter reads very much as a mother haranguing a recalcitrant child rather than as a formal petition to a monarch. In any case, Isabelle failed to demonstrate true political friendship with her letter. That Henry III eventually assisted his mother likely speaks more to his generous personality than to any acts of diplomacy or political friendship on her part.

It is clear that medieval views of queenship were varied, complex, and at times conflicted. What made a queen popular or successful depended upon many factors, as we have discussed. Following examples set down by their predecessors is one more way in which John's wives could have learned how to carry out their expected duties. Letters were used display certain aspects of queenship, such as political friendship or intercession. They would have had many previous examples to follow, not the least of which included Eleanor of Aquitaine and Empress Matilda. Both of these women were exceptional queens in their different ways and there is a good deal of medieval source material that survived about them, though not all of it is positive.

The surviving chronicles and letters about Matilda and Eleanor, though, whether portraying them in a positive light or not, depict women who were strong and unafraid to advocate for the causes they championed. In the case of Matilda, mother of Henry II and grandmother of John, her descendants had an example of fierce political actions. She is known for going to war, literally, to claim the throne of England to which her own royal father had wanted her to accede upon his death. She proved herself to be a leader of men, able to listen to her advisors and learn from them, and an unceasing advocate for her son's claim to the throne after her own claim was given up as lost. Several letters survive that are sent from and addressed to Matilda and each one demonstrates requisite elements of either political friendship, diplomacy, or intercession at play.

Dozens of letters both to and from Eleanor of Aquitaine survive, and these also give scholars a valuable glimpse into the life and career of arguably the most famous noblewoman of the Middle Ages. Eleanor left a legacy of diplomatic acumen that her daughters, daughters in law, and granddaughters could learn from. The letters Eleanor penned adhered closely to the form expected of medieval writing and showed a keen wit and insight into the social structure of the time, which she did not hesitate to use to her advantage when necessary. From letters alone, we are able to piece together some idea of the ways in which these two women may have attended to their queenly duties. Chroniclers, mainly clergymen, were not usually as cheerful about Matilda or Eleanor, but it is possible that John's wives may have still been familiar with some of what had been written about his mother and grandmother and thus been able to emulate their behaviour within the scope of their increasingly limited authority.

Just as some queens could have been held up as examples for subsequent queens to follow, others may have been used as examples of what not to do. These examples, like those above, could be drawn from history as well as biblical story. Women such as Eve, Jezebel, or Delilah were used to portray the wickedness, fickleness, or uncompassionate side of women, the opposite of what a proper queen should be.

The views of Isabella and Isabelle themselves are murky. Of Isabella, there is almost no record before her marriage to John, and not much more after it. As stated earlier, almost nothing is known about her childhood or how she was raised. There is a dearth of records of her during her marriage to John and afterwards. Therefore, we do not know much about how she may have been received by others within the nobility. We know a little more about Isabelle, but a good portion of that has to be taken with a grain of salt; much of what we know about her was written by people who did not like her, such as social or political enemies, or chroniclers who habitually ignored women or thought they were inherently sinful anyway. There is apparently no one who wrote a contemporary, friendly account of either of these women, nor did they write anything themselves that has survived, leaving us with only the comments made by enemies, ex-husbands, or people who did not know them well. But we can piece together bits about their life when they were married to John and what factors may have influenced their life with him.

Chapter 4

John Plantagenet and Married Life

While there is not a lot of hard evidence left to us that could let us conclude anything definitively about either of John's marriages, what we do know and have touched on previously is that, in the Middle Ages, women and men generally had clearly defined roles. This was especially true for nobility and royalty. Most women did not have much, if any, say in whether they married or not, who they were married to, or if they would have children or not, for there was not much in the way of reliable birth control. Having children was generally non-negotiable and if a woman did not wish to have children, there were very few viable options available to her. For most women, though, the ultimate goal was to have children, especially boys, to help with the family trade or, if they were of the noble or royal classes, to inherit the family estates or throne upon the death of their father. The increasing reliance on the rule of primogeniture – the firstborn male inheriting the lion's share of a family's wealth – meant there was greater pressure on women to produce boys. Girls were useful as a way to seal new political alliances through marriage, but having a male heir was, of course, of vital importance to royalty; not only was a male heir more likely to ensure a peaceful transition of power, but also monarchical dynasties could die out for want of a prince. For Isabella of Gloucester and Isabelle of Angoulême, there was undoubtedly intense pressure for them to give John the male heir and prince he needed to ensure the continuance of the Plantagenet rule.

Marriage to John was not likely to have resulted in much peace or happiness for either of his wives. Truly, 'Marriage and the Plantagenet temper did not go well together. The relations between his parents, Henry II and Eleanor, were so notorious as to have sparked a whole series of popular fictions. John himself may have fared little better than his father and elder brother in terms of conjugal harmony'.[1] While medieval society did not expect to find love in marriage, many marriages did seem to become love matches in time. We have discussed previously how the marriage of William Marshal and Isabel de Clare may have been one such lucky match that grew into genuine love. Initially, though, it was motivated by politics and alliance. So was the marriage of John's grandmother, Empress Matilda, to her second husband, Geoffrey Plantagenet, Count of Anjou. Unlike the marriage of William Marshal and Isabel de Clare, Empress Matilda and the Count of Anjou never seemed to develop any feelings of genuine affection. She was, in fact, enraged to be wed to a man nearly eleven years her junior, and a non-royal at that. She did bear him sons, though, the eldest of whom became Henry II of England, and he supported her claim to the throne throughout their marriage until his death in 1151. The Count of Anjou's support of Matilda's hereditary claims were not driven by any kind of true love for her, but rather for political gain and increasing lands and territories for his sons and the growing family empire.

Similarly, it seems that John's own parents, Henry II and Eleanor of Aquitaine, also had little love lost between them. While some might argue that Henry and Eleanor loved each other, and they did seem to have a passionate relationship, their marriage appears to be largely political as well. The biggest difference between theirs and other marriages of their peers was that Eleanor and Henry arranged their own marriage and did so without the consent of their liege lord, Eleanor's first husband, King Louis VII of France. There was a large disparity in their ages, with Eleanor being around nine years older than Henry. The age difference did not seem to matter to Henry, possibly because he had as his example his own parents with his mother being much older than his father. More likely, though, Henry and Eleanor both saw that the match would make them the richest and most powerful couple in medieval Europe, controlling vast stretches of land from the Pyrenees north to Normandy, and eventually including England and parts of Ireland. Such a joining of resources would have been madness to pass up.

They married a mere six weeks after Eleanor's marriage to Louis was finally annulled, and in the interim before the annulment was official, it is clear that she and Henry came to an arrangement; it does not seem realistic that their marriage was anything other than a political alliance and business agreement, although by most accounts it was fiery. Their union as a political act is borne out by the events of their married life – from the birth of their children to carry on their new empire to the rebellion some of those children led against Henry beginning in 1173. There seems to have been little love in the relationship, but rather an abundance of political machinations and jockeying for the most advantageous position. Their family was known as the Devil's Brood, so named for a demon that was allegedly one of the Plantagenet ancestors. They were constantly fighting amongst themselves for the upper hand over the others; backstabbing and betrayal were not foreign concepts in the Plantagenet sphere of influence.

Given his family's examples, experiences in marriage, and the general medieval attitude of marriage as a political arrangement, it hardly seems realistic to think that John's own views on the matter would have been romantic or that they would have strayed from the expected roles a husband and wife would play. Following in both his grandparents' and parents' footsteps, John does not seem to have had the temperament to make a happy marriage in general. It was normal, accepted, and even expected for noblemen and kings to have mistresses during this time period; how well the practice was received by the wives of men keeping mistresses must depend largely on the woman. According to *Histoire des ducs de Normandie et des rois d'Angleterre*, John's lust was even noticed by some of his Flemish mercenaries who stated that the king was very covetous of beautiful women. Historian Ralph Turner notes that the problem was not that John kept mistresses, but that some of them were noblewomen. And yet, 'Some stories of John's sexual adventures, however, appear to have been invented after the fact to explain barons' taking up arms against the king.'[2]

Turner uses the term victim in his discussion of John's mistresses. The word choice is interesting and implies that he viewed John as a predator and possibly that all of John's mistresses were unwilling. Probably some were unwilling, but we cannot assume they all were, for being a king's mistress often came with many benefits. John's improper use of noblewomen as mistresses is documented in contemporary chronicles; many of these chronicles should be taken with a grain of salt, for John was no darling to the men making the records, and their documents are the source for most of the bad reputation which has followed him throughout history. However, vilifying John for his sexual exploits should come as no surprise since the chroniclers were almost all monastic writers. He fathered several illegitimate children, at least five that we know of, and two of them were with noblewomen. From what we know, John appears to have been a loving father to all his children and he openly acknowledged the illegitimate children born to him. Only his second marriage to Isabelle of Angoulême produced the legitimate heirs he needed as a king.

To produce legitimate heirs, the couple had to be married in the eyes of the Church. A child born out of wedlock would typically have been unable to inherit, though there are some examples of illegitimate children being legitimised, such as the previously mentioned children of John of Gaunt by his long time mistress Katherine Swynford. Isabella of Gloucester, despite having been married to John for ten years, did not deliver any children for him that we know of. When she married John, she was probably around 16 years old, though some scholars such as Marc Morris argue that she was actually a good deal older than John, around 30 years old at the time of their marriage in 1189. There is still a robust debate about which age Isabella was at the time of their marriage is more accurate.

Isabelle of Angoulême is generally considered to have been around 12 when John married her; however, arguments can and have been made that she was even younger, possibly as young as 8 or 9, when she married John in 1200. Most scholars agree that she was no older than 12 at the time of her marriage to John, still very much a child even if she was of an age to consent to marriage according to canon law. If her age even at 12 is accurate, it is not very likely that Isabelle would have been physically ready to bear children for several years after her wedding took place.

The ages of John's wives are important because it naturally would have impacted their fertility. The average age of menarche for medieval girls was roughly 15-16 years old. Further, the age of women having a successful first birth may have been later than that. Fiona Shapland explains that, 'Full fertility, in terms of the likelihood of conception, carrying a healthy pregnancy to term and surviving childbirth, would only have followed several years after menarche with the completion of pelvic growth'.[3] In a different article, Shapland says that most medieval adolescents completed puberty between the ages of 15 to 19, but that nearly 30 percent of skeletons studied from London still had not completed puberty at the time of their deaths between 22-25 years old.[4] Many medieval women would not have been fertile before their early twenties, and the legal minimum age of 12 years old for marriage would not often have resulted in a live birth for several years. While naturally there are exceptions to this, such as Margaret Beaufort delivering the future Henry VII at the age of 13, the average age of first birth seems to have been later for most women, usually in their late teens or early twenties. The age of maturity for boys and girls 'is at odds with medieval canon law, where the legal age at which boys and girls could consent to marriage was 14 and 12 years, respectively'.[5] At these ages, most women would have entered puberty but it is not likely they would be fertile yet.

This information is relevant to both Isabella of Gloucester and Isabelle of Angoulême. Isabella of Gloucester was without a doubt older than Isabelle upon her marriage to John, but she never delivered any children to him. There could have been many reasons for her childlessness, ranging from infertility on her part, to undocumented miscarriages, to a simple lack of sexual activity as a couple. History has not usually been kind to Isabella, when it has noticed her at all, and most historians seem to agree that she was barren. As we shall see, an argument can be made that she was not. Isabella's failure to produce an heir to her husband's estates is probably the biggest reason why she was ignored by contemporary chroniclers, despite being the heir *suo jure* to the vast Gloucester lands and wealth. Had she given John a son, it is not as likely he would have divorced her in favour of a new, younger bride. Even if he had proceeded with getting the marriage annulled, it seems likely that the mother of what would have been John's firstborn legitimate child would have warranted more respect, or at least more than a passing footnote in the annals of history.

Isabelle of Angoulême may have been biologically unready to bear children at the start of her marriage. Even if she and John consummated their marriage immediately, which is open to debate, the chances of her conceiving and bearing a pregnancy to term would not have been likely for another few years. Moreover, for such a young girl to carry a pregnancy to term and then safely deliver the baby was rather slim. The idea of a later age for birth aligns with the dates of Isabelle's deliveries; her first child, the future Henry III, was born in October 1207, almost exactly seven years after her marriage to John. Depending on the date of her birth, generally thought to be 1186/1188, she would have been between 19 and 21 at the birth of her first child, which fits with Fiona Shapland's discussion on the typical age of fertility in medieval women.

John's two marriages influenced his behaviours and way in which he reigned, in part because of the views contemporary chroniclers and nobles held of him. Each marriage had a different impact, and the fates of his two wives must have been influenced in turn by his feelings about the women themselves.

Isabella of Gloucester

As a young child, John was betrothed to Alice of Savoy, a daughter of Humbert III, the Count of Savoy. The betrothal was made when John was around 7 years old and was, in part, an attempt by Henry II to gain some lands for his youngest son, who was commonly known as John Lackland. Alice began the journey to the court of Henry II to be raised there in accordance with the social customs of medieval nobility, but she died before arriving. Instead, Henry II arranged for John to marry Isabella of Gloucester, the youngest daughter of the Earl of Gloucester. At the time of his betrothal to Isabella, John was around 9 years old.

The manner in which their betrothal came about was a little scandalous and caused a few chroniclers some raised eyebrows in response. This was also to be the most scandal ever really associated with Isabella, for she was otherwise 'faceless, formless, and forgotten in the chronicles'.[6] The scandal of her betrothal to John is thus: Henry II had been thwarted in his desire to expand Angevin territory by the death of Alice of Savoy before she could marry John. However, he had a different opportunity to do so later. In 1166, the only son of William FitzRobert, the Earl of Gloucester, had died, which meant that the inheritance which his son, Robert, would have received would instead traditionally fall in equal parts to Isabella and her two older sisters, Amica and Mabel. Additionally, Earl William was implicated in the rebellion of John's older brothers against the king, so the earl wanted to buy his peace with the king. Since the older sisters were already married, Henry II struck a deal with the Earl of Gloucester. He betrothed Isabella to John and promised to find a suitable husband for her if the pope did not grant permission for John to marry her because they were related within the forbidden degree of consanguinity; the earl agreed at that time to make John his official heir. This effectively disinherited Isabella's two older sisters from the Gloucester lands and made Isabella the countess of Gloucester *suo jure*, in her own right. Disinheriting her sisters was an unconventional act and caused a little rumbling from Isabella's sisters and their husbands.

The Earl of Gloucester died in 1183, at which point Henry, rather than marrying Isabella to John right away, took her under his own wardship. Wardship was a common practice when a wealthy heiress or a young boy was without a male relative to care for them. By preventing John from marrying Isabella for several years, Henry could personally maintain control of those wealthy lands himself. He was thus able to enjoy the immense income from the Gloucester lands himself for as long as Isabella was his ward. There is some question of whether Henry had made the income from the Gloucester lands available to John as Isabella's future husband, but that raises the question of why he did not simply marry the two right then. Isabella would have been past the canonical age of consent to marry, so we must assume that Henry chose not to marry her off yet specifically so that he could keep the Gloucester income for his own use. Moreover, it seems that Henry may not have officially finalised the arrangements for the marriage because he wanted to keep his options open in case a better opportunity for a marriage alliance for John came along.

Leaving room to manoeuvre in case of a better match later also may have set the tone for how John later treated Isabella, using her or casting her off as best suited him. Despite the apparent indecision on Henry's part, marrying Isabella would make John one of the wealthiest lords in England. However one looked at it, it would be a good match for a youngest and landless son.

Isabella's near anonymity in the historical record is a source of frustration to many scholars. A comment from Sharon Bennett Connolly really highlights Isabella's obscurity: 'There are no pictures of her, not even a description of her personality or appearance. At one time, no one even seemed certain of her name; she has been called Isabel, Isabella, Hawise, Avise – but Isabella is how she appears in the Close Rolls.'[7] Alan Lloyd seems to take a strongly negative view of Isabella. He writes, 'Desirable, one assumes, she was not, for in all John's travels and campaigns since the marriage at Marlborough, there was no indication that he was ever accompanied by his lawful bedmate. Controversial, or even colourful, Isabel cannot have been.'[8] While Lloyd's comment about Isabella never traveling with John is inaccurate – she is documented as having issued at least one charter alongside her husband in 1190/1191 during a journey to Normandy – we truly have no idea what she might have been like either in looks or personality. Even the otherwise gossipy chroniclers had nothing much to say about her.

When Henry II died in 1189 and Richard became king, he insisted that the marriage between John and Isabella proceed. The two were wed on August 29, 1189, at Marlborough Castle. At that time, John took over the Gloucester lands in Isabella's name. It is possible that Richard was simply honouring the betrothal agreement struck by his father. He may also have forced the issue by marrying his younger brother to Isabella as a way to control him by causing John to owe him a debt of gratitude, which is what some modern historians also believe. In truth, though, it was a huge boon to John to marry Isabella. He could enjoy the immense income of the Gloucester lands and become one of the most powerful lords in England all in one fell swoop. He was able to rule his Gloucester lands however he saw fit as a semi-autonomous lord having to answer only to Richard. John, who had been known as Lackland for most of his life, was John Lackland no more.

John's marriage to Isabella of Gloucester was immediately declared invalid by the infuriated Archbishop Baldwin of Canterbury, who was appalled when he learned the two had married, because they were related within the forbidden degree of consanguinity. The archbishop warned them that they were forbidden to cohabit or have sex because of their relation to their shared great-grandfather, Henry I. He also commanded that John come before his court and laid an interdict upon him and his estates when he did not arrive as ordered. John eventually was able to have the interdict lifted when he appealed to a visiting papal delegate, Giovanni di Anagni, and obtained a provisional dispensation from him which permitted John to remain married to Isabella. 'Presumably he was able to assure the legate that a dispensation was being sought, but none was ever received. Archbishop Baldwin died shortly afterwards and no one else sought to press the matter of the flaw in the marriage bond.'[9] Neither John nor anyone else bothered to follow up with the pope for confirmation. H.G. Richardson suggests that Richard was in a hurry to get his affairs all in order so that he could go on his crusade, and that it was because of this state of urgency that no one bothered to follow up on the dispensation. Because the couple were closely related, their consanguinity would come into play later in their lives.

Isabella's Age and its Implications

Isabella's birth date is not known for certain. The dates tend to be either around 1160 or 1173, and it seems that scholars are pretty evenly divided as to which date they believe to be accurate. Sharon Bennett Connolly and Marc Morris, for example, both favour the earlier 1160 or so as her birth year; others like W.L. Warren and Dan Jones argue that Isabella was younger than that and believe that 1173, or at least some other date after 1160, is correct. Using the later date is more compelling for a few reasons. Isabella's three siblings were all older than she was; her two sisters married before she did, implying they were older than her. This alone does not mean her birth date was as late as 1173, but considering that her father, Earl William, was often away for battles, it stands to reason that there could have been fairly large age gaps in between the births of her siblings. Such gaps were not uncommon to see in crusading families, with the men gone often for years at a time. It does not appear that Earl William went on crusade but given his activities and movement during the time of Henry II's reign, there easily can be gaps in between the births of his children from his other absences.

A lack of children in between siblings also does not at all mean that there were no pregnancies or births. Most chronicles do not mention if a miscarriage occurred, or even the death of a young child who had been born. It was most likely the case that Isabella had siblings born between her and her next closest sibling simply did not survive. There were known gaps in between the births of other noble or royal babies. These include gaps in between Eleanor of Aquitaine's two children by Louis VII, who were born five years apart; her fifth and sixth children by Henry II, who were born four years apart; and Isabelle of Angoulême's third and fourth children by John, who were born four years apart. Clearly such birth gaps are not all that uncommon. Moreover, if Isabella were born closer to 1160, then she would have been around 30 years old at the time of her marriage to John, nearly a decade older than him. While this big age difference is certainly not an insurmountable problem, as evidenced by the marriage of John's own mother who was around eleven years older than his father, it could easily seem from John's perspective that marrying an older woman was risky. After all, his mother rebelled against his father and John may associate rebellious tendencies with an older wife because of that. Going further back, he may have heard tales of the unhappy marriage of his paternal grandparents, Geoffrey of Anjou and Empress Matilda, which had a similar age difference with Matilda being the older of the two; perhaps he took a page from previous family marriages as an example of why one should avoid taking a much older wife. Given what we know of his personality, it also seems unlikely that John would be drawn to a woman so much older than him, regardless of what wealth she brought to him. There would probably have been more documented about Isabella if John was vocal in his dislike for her. If Isabella really was born in 1160, then it would appear that is further evidence of John marrying her for no reason beyond politics and gaining a wealthy estate as his own. Also, her age may well have been a factor in her marriages which came after John.

Barren – Historical Discussions and Conclusions

Many – in fact, most – medieval scholars have posited that Isabella was barren. However, a strong case can be made against this position. Assuming she was born closer to 1173, Isabella would have been around 16 when she married John in 1189 and around 26 when he divorced her in 1199. During that period, the noble couple seemed to live together only infrequently, and actually spent very little of their marriage in each other's company. When they got married, they were required to obtain a dispensation from Pope Innocent III allowing them to marry in the first place since John and Isabella were closely related. Based on their close blood relationship, the archbishop of Canterbury forbade them to consummate their marriage. It is not actually clear whether or not any kind of permission was granted for John to marry Isabella, but we do know that the papal dispensation was never acquired by any party involved. One passage written by Ralph of Diceto implies that John and Isabella had, in fact, been granted permission. The chronicle reads:

> The dissolution of the marriage of King John of England and the daughter of the Count of Gloucester, was officialised in Normandy by the bishops of Lisieux, Bayeux, Avranches, and other bishops who participated. He had married her in his father's day with the Roman Church's permission, acquiring the counties of Gloucester, Somerset, Devonshire, and Cornwall, and very many other fiefs

throughout England. But he, carried away by the hope of a more illustrious marriage, drove her away, counselled by evil men, and so incurred the great indignation of the pope, that is, of Innocent III, and of the whole Roman curia, for he had audaciously presumed to dissolve, contrary to the laws and canons, that which had been joined together by their authority.[10]

However, another chronicler writing at the same time, Ralph of Coggeshall, indicates that John never actually received the pope's permission to marry Isabella at all and that he had his marriage annulled because it lacked papal approval. Coggeshall's passage reads, 'he had sent away his first wife, that is the daughter of the Count of Gloucester, on the order of the lord pope, because of the relationship of consanguinity'.[11] John married Isabella during the earliest months of Richard's reign, not in their father's reign. The inconsistency between the two documents might indicate a harsh bias against John for setting aside his wife in the first place, with Diceto being more inclined to view John's actions far less favourably; it could, however, simply refer to their betrothal taking place during Henry's reign, not the actual marriage.

Regardless of the bias that may be implicit in the chronicles, there is a question about John and Isabella's marriage at its most basic level: Did this couple ever actually consummate their marriage? Might the injunction for them not to consummate their marriage be an instance in which John actually obeyed the Church's commands? If so, granted, it would be just about the only time in his life he ever did so. But this question deserves some exploration, and it seems unfair for history to automatically assume Isabella was barren simply because she had no children. If John and Isabella never consummated their marriage, then naturally she would not have borne children. Even if they were bedmates, they lived together so infrequently that a lack of conception would not necessarily have been surprising considering that John spent the majority of their marriage in France and it is not apparent that Isabella travelled often with him. Questions of cohabiting aside, given that many women in the Middle Ages had irregular menses because of a variety of reasons, conceiving a child might have been difficult anyway. However, most scholars agree that John and Isabella do not appear to have lived together for the majority of their marriage and may have lacked the opportunity to conceive.

If Isabella was young, only 16 or so at the time of her marriage, then it is also slightly possible she was not yet fertile, even though she would probably have been menstruating for several years by that point. If she and John had sex, it does not necessarily follow that she would have gotten pregnant quickly. Many modern couples today can try for years to have a baby with no success; it is reasonable that some medieval couples also struggled to conceive, as in fact *The Trotula* suggests. As our earlier discussion on pregnancy and childbirth in the Middle Ages mentioned, fertility had a variety of treatments available at the time and women of all social classes tried them as needed. *The Trotula* provided a thorough examination of fertility problems in couples. Since John had already proven his virility by having illegitimate children with various mistresses, it is an understandable assumption to make that Isabella herself was the cause of the couple's childlessness. But, if Isabella had truly been barren, given her high social status and being married to the then-heir to the English throne, it seems like that would have been documented in a chronicle somewhere, such as the above passage from Ralph of Diceto, even as a reference in passing or mention of a series of miscarriages.

The notion that barrenness was also 'generally seen as a violation of the law of life, a denial of the Divine creative element with which woman was blessed' would have wound its way into the rhetoric of medieval society.[12] Considering that if the ability to bear children was linked to a woman's moral character, as has been suggested by some scholars as well as some texts of the time which depict barren women as promiscuous, it seems that this particular blemish on a noblewoman's character would not go unnoticed.

Even though John was not yet a king during his marriage to Isabella, he was still the presumptive heir to King Richard, who was known to be reckless in his bravery and was mostly away from his kingdom on crusade. Death could come to Richard unexpectedly, and eventually it did. Moreover, Richard himself was rarely in his own wife's company much, and they had no children of their own. Therefore, the ability of his heir's wife to have children should therefore have been of great interest to medieval chroniclers. To further stress the point, John could have used his wife's potential infertility as yet another weapon in his arsenal for having the marriage annulled if he had slept with her often and she still failed to conceive. It may be that an inability to have children was recorded in a chronicle that has not survived to us today. However, given that medieval society viewed bearing children as a wife's primary role, it seems odd that no documents we have give any reasonable explanation for Isabella being childless. A successful marriage for a woman, after all, was based largely on her giving heirs to her husband.

That the couple were not close, or at least that John apparently had very little interest in Isabella, is also apparent in his machinations with the French king. John entered into discussions with Philip Augustus to marry his sister, Alice, to whom Richard himself had once been betrothed, as early as 1192/1193. Though it was not necessarily out of the ordinary for a noble or king to put aside one wife in exchange for a better one, if John and Isabella had a truly happy marriage, it is difficult to see why he would have been actively seeking a new marriage only two or three years after marrying her. Marriage to Isabella made him very wealthy and powerful, so any potential for making a new marriage would have had to be of unparalleled benefit to John, since at that time, he was not yet king and so he would have lost all claim to Isabella's Gloucester lands if he set her aside.

Marrying Alice would have allowed John to take control of the lands that Richard held from the French Crown, or so Philip Augustus had promised, in exchange for 'doing some mischief to Richard' while he was away on crusade.[13] John's mother, Eleanor of Aquitaine, prevented him from going to France to marry Alice, saying that if he went, the English Crown would seize his lands. John stayed in England and did not marry Alice, but the situation lends a great deal of proof to the idea that, regardless of how young or wealthy Isabella was, her marriage to John was not a happy one. It seems clear that John, for whatever reason, just did not care for her, particularly since his most of 'attentions were on other ladies'.[14]

John is known to have always had a roving eye, a trait generally tolerated and even expected in noblemen as long as they were discreet with their affairs. The siring of illegitimate children was similarly tolerated. However, it is possible, even probable, that Isabella did not think too highly of John in return. H.G. Richardson certainly takes this position, claiming that it is unlikely Isabella had any affection for John or vice versa. Richardson, however, falls into the 'Isabella was barren' school of thought, which is disputed in this book. Their lack of offspring makes

The elaborate facade of a cathedral. (*Image by David Vives from Pixabay*)

Corfe Castle. (*Omanihunter, CC BY-SA 4.0 (Wikimedia Commons)*)

King John. (*Creative Commons*)

York Minster. (*Kristen McQuinn, Aug 2019*)

York castle. (*Kristen McQuinn, Aug 2019*)

York ruins. (*Kristen McQuinn, Aug 2019*)

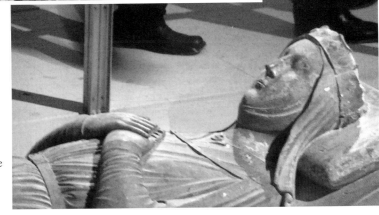

Isabelle of Angoulême effigy, Fontevraud Abbey. (*Creative Commons*)

Isabelle of Angoulême. (*Creative Commons*)

This 13th-century French manuscript shows Merlin as a bearded man in a blue robe. The seated figure is his teacher and scribe, Blaise, who records Merlin's deeds for posterity. This image illustrates *L'Histoire de Merlin* by Robert de Boron.

13th century French manuscript with Merlin. (*Kristen McQuinn, August 2019*)

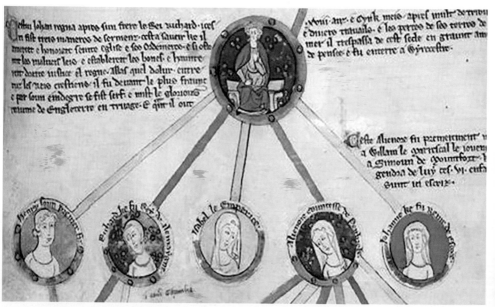

John and his legitimate children lineage. (*Creative Commons*)

Medieval medicinal herbs. (*Kristen McQuinn, August 2019*)

Chateau Gaillard, Normandy. (*Creative Commons*)

Seal of Isabelle of Angoulême. (*Creative Commons*)

King John, painted by Matthew Paris c. 1250–1259. (*Creative Commons*)

Nottingham Castle, conflict site between Richard the Lionheart and John. (*Creative Commons*)

King John silver penny. (*Creative Commons*)

The Wash. (*Creative Commons*)

Newark Castle, location of John's death from dysentery. (*Creative Commons*)

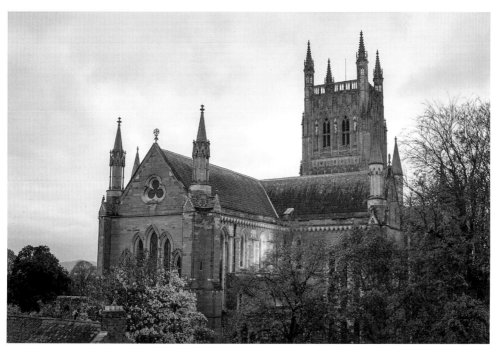

Worcester Cathedral, burial place of John. (*Creative Commons*)

Gloucester Cathedral, where Henry III was crowned. (*Creative Commons*)

Temple Church, burial site of William Marshal. (*Kristen McQuinn, August 2019*)

Another view of Temple Church, burial site of William Marshal. (*Kristen McQuinn, August 2019*)

the most sense when viewed in terms of the two disliking one another, evidenced by John wanting to make a new marriage so soon after his first one took place.

John and Isabella never seemed to have had a close relationship, and the possibility that they never shared a bed holds more weight when we consider that most of his known illegitimate children seem to have been born during his first marriage. John is known to have fathered several children outside of his marriages, two of which were by married noblewomen. It is not clear when John's affairs with the noblewomen took place, but regardless, it was not considered appropriate for nobles to have affairs with the wives or daughters of other nobles or one's own vassals. His continuing actions with regard to affairs with married noblewomen would come back to haunt him later in his reign, during his marriage to Isabelle of Angoulême. His doing so just added further bitterness and resentment among the barons; if he had taken lower class women as his mistress, no one would have cared. In any case, Nicholas Vincent explains that 'what evidence we have suggests that all of John's bastards were born before he ascended the throne, before his marriage to Isabella of Angoulême'.[15] In other words, they occurred mainly during his marriage to Isabella of Gloucester.

His affairs, while expected for a nobleman to have, may indicate that he was not best pleased with his wife and shunned her bed for the majority of their marriage, thus denying her the chance to bear him an heir. This is where the date of Isabella's birth may be most important. If she had been born around 1160, as some think, she would have been much older than John, nearly 30 at their marriage. When John was in his early twenties as he was when he married Isabella, he may have seen a much older bride as practically an old maid and simply not been interested in sleeping with her, especially when he was able to have any number of mistresses he wanted. Her age will also be important in the period of her life after her marriage to John came to an end. We do not know what Isabella looked like, but John may have been superficial enough not to want to have sex with her if he found her unattractive or old. He was known for being lustful and having many mistresses, basically a requirement for medieval nobility, but he was known to take mistresses who were thought to be pretty. If indeed he considered his first wife to be unappealing in some way, it doesn't stretch the limits of possibility that he simply looked elsewhere for sexual gratification.

Isabella's age is a factor in more than one way. If she was 16 or so when they married, John simply may have married her regardless of whether he liked her just to enjoy the income from the Gloucester estate, and because Richard forced the issue when he came to the throne. Certainly, it would not be by any means the first or the last time a couple were forced to wed for political or financial reasons. Lacking a dispensation from the pope would merely ensure that he could have the marriage annulled easily at any time he wanted to. 'The ties that bound him to Isabella were thus weak, and could easily be undone.'[16] However, if he thought she was old, that could simply have been unappealing to a young and, by some accounts, charming and handsome man. John was Henry's favourite son and probably was pampered by the standards of the day. There were plenty of chroniclers and other nobles at the time who thought John was the baby of his family and that he acted accordingly. He wanted what he wanted and, given his social status, was generally in a position to get it.

Annulment and Rationale

Whether John and Isabella ever actually consummated their marriage or not is something we will ever know for certain. Even if he had never slept with her, it is not likely John would have announced it; failure to have sex with his wife could imply there was something inadequate about him, even though he had fathered children by other women. If John had opted to take a new wife, as he did later, getting an annulment should have been relatively easy even if he had previously received a dispensation for marriage from the pope based on the rules of consanguinity.

An annulment should not come as a surprise to anyone since Isabella seems to have been absent from every aspect of John's life. For the ten years of their marriage, Isabella seems never to have had a part in his public life, despite being the heiress to one of the greatest estates in England. John appears to have kept her under tight control and did not let her manage her own estates or income. At most, she seems to have issued only one charter with John during a trip to Normandy in 1190 or 1191.[17] After that, she essentially fades from John's public life almost entirely, and it is painfully clear that John never intended for Isabella to rule alongside him.

When John acceded to the throne in May 1199, he tellingly did not have Isabella crowned with him. By the end of the year, he had managed to get the marriage annulled. The consanguinity angle worked in John's favour in this case. His failure to crown Isabella alongside him implies he had never intended to keep her as his wife, likely did so only during Richard's lifetime since he had insisted on the marriage going forward in the first place, and instead sought a marriage to another woman. By August of 1200, his desire to marry another was fulfilled when he wed Isabelle of Angoulême.

Briefly, another possibility for Isabella's lack of children, though admittedly very unlikely, is that she chose to display the ideal of medieval womanhood, which was virginity, in adoration of the various virgin saints that were popular at the time. Kim M. Phillips states that young, sexually mature but still virgin women were at the apex of medieval femininity.[18] We do not know for certain how devout Isabella was, though it is a safe assumption that she was at least as religious as was expected for the time. But if she were excessively devout or strongly influenced by the lives of various saints or virgin martyrs, could she possibly have wanted to remain chaste? If John did not find her appealing, perhaps he acquiesced to her desire because he did not care one way or the other about sleeping with her, especially since he was able to get sexual gratification elsewhere and still make use of Isabella's Gloucester lands and titles. It is not likely that Isabella had a strong devotion to virgin martyrs, especially since a woman of her status would have been expected to birth heirs. Also, virginity was the pinnacle of medieval desirability and deflowering her is probably not an opportunity John would have passed up, but it is an interesting thought experiment.

It may be easy to see why Isabella fell through the cracks of history. She was manipulated and taken advantage of for most of her life – first Henry held her for years as his ward so he could use the income from her lands, then John followed suit when he married her. He seems from a very early time to be on the lookout for a new, better wife, which no doubt influenced the way he treated Isabella in the rare times they were together. She did not appear to have objected in any way when he wanted to annul their marriage when he was crowned. H.G. Richardson notes that Isabella would probably have 'resented the breach of faith — as it might seem to her – whereby her marriage was invalidated, and that she defended the action and obstructed the proceeding'.[19] However, Richardson goes on, if she had wanted to appeal her case to the pope, her friends and advisors would have told her such was a hopeless case. There is no surviving evidence that Isabella ever appealed the decision to annul her marriage to John. Her silence and lack of objection to being cast off after ten years of marriage is probably the most vivid example of Isabella's personality. Perhaps Lloyd was correct and she was not appealing, not in the physical sense but also in her humility and meekness. John, as we shall see, kept his second wife on a short leash regarding her own lands and income just as he did his first, but Isabelle of Angoulême had a fiery spirit. Perhaps John preferred women who challenged him. What little we know about Isabella of Gloucester, she does not seem to have been any kind of firebrand. Or perhaps she is still being underestimated and no evidence of an appeal exists because Isabella deliberately did not file one; who is to say she did not choose to keep quiet so that she could be rid of a marriage she did not want to be in to begin with? There may be a great deal to conclude about Isabella's silence, but the automatic assumption of her passivity should not necessarily be at the top of the list.

Illegitimate Children and Connected Political Events

As previously noted, John's illegitimate children were mostly all born during his marriage to Isabella, as far as we are able to determine. Some events of John's life during this time could have been influenced by the birth of some of his children, or vice versa, though there is no direct connection documented one way or the other. However, it should make sense for the birth of children to impact the way in which one acts. For example, in October of 1191, when Richard I was away on crusade, John came into armed conflict with William Longchamp, one of the men appointed by the king to guard his interests in England. John had taken advantage of Longchamp's unpopularity among the nobles and clergy and set himself up as another regent in Richard's absence. After the conflict with John, Longchamp holed up in the Tower of London until the archbishop of Rouen, Walter of Coutances, returned to England on Richard's command to restore order. This conflict is a political action that probably would have occurred no matter what else was happening in John's life at the time.

However, there is some evidence that one of John's bastard children was born around 1191 or 1192. Joanna, who later wed the Welsh king Llywelyn ap Iorwerth and became known as the Lady of Wales, was born during this time. This was also roughly the time when John was in talks with Phillip of France to marry Alice and put aside Isabella of Gloucester. It is entirely possible the birth of a child had no bearing on any of John's other actions. Yet the timing of all these events raises the question of whether his children's births drove John to act in a manner that was even more brash and questionable than normal in order to raise his own political standing and thus, perhaps, to be in a better position to attend to the needs of his children. Improving his own position would result in being able to make his children's lives that much better. Possibly, John acted as he did because the birth of an illegitimate child brought attention to his lack of legitimate heir, if his children even factored in at all to his political actions.

What did possibly have an effect on John, and almost certainly did later in his own reign, was his own reputation. Much of that reputation was authored by others, including his own brother. While he was the captive of the Holy Roman Emperor, Richard was notified that John was making an attempt to seize lands from him. He responded, 'My brother is not a man to win land for himself if there is anyone to put up a mere show of resistance.' Later, upon his release, John was afraid to come to Richard because of his prior actions. The biographer of William Marshal relates a colourful image of the two brothers reuniting after Richard was released from his captivity. Richard appeared magnanimous in his forgiveness, telling him, 'Don't worry, John: you're a child and have been led astray. Those who gave you ill counsel will rue the day!'[20] Richard then proceeded to offer to serve John a large fish that had been brought in for Richard.

On the surface, this seems to be a generous position for Richard to take, considering that John was trying to steal his throne from him. But in reality, while Richard did truly seem to forgive his errant younger brother, he also delivered a stinging rebuke to him. John was no child, but a 27-year-old grown man with children of his own at that time, even if those children were illegitimate. The chroniclers wasted no time recording that interlude between the brothers, and the image of John as an undisciplined, inexperienced youth stuck with him for a good portion of his reign. In fact, even a few years into John's reign, other rulers and noblemen, including Philip Augustus, thought of John as 'a feckless young man, the baby of the family, irresponsible and troublesome to his elders'.[21] Between the chroniclers and his own poor choices of action, John's reputation was more or less solidified by the time he came to the throne.

John's reputation as an irresponsible youth began much earlier in his life, but it seems to have been cemented around the time of Richard's release from captivity. It may be possible that this humiliating defeat in his rebellion against Richard became connected in his mind to Isabella. Did he feel inadequate and project his feelings of defeat and humiliation onto her? Given what we know, John had some personality traits that have described as petty and even dangerous. It seems that John could have had the personality to associate his losses with specific individuals; certainly, he often blamed others for his own poor actions. He did so when he lost Normandy, saying that if his vassals had supported him better, he would have had enough funds for hiring mercenaries and he would not have lost his Continental lands.[22] While we will never know for certain, it seems that some of his actions were because of his sense of inadequacy, especially considering that John seems to have struggled for most of his childhood with overcoming the shadows of his older brothers. W.L. Warren notes that, even though John tried to emulate his brothers, he 'had shown only caricatures of their qualities: where the young Henry had been gay, he was frivolous, where Geoffrey had been cunning, he was sly, where Richard was bold he was merely bombastic'.[23] John's behaviour may have been a manifestation of his deep insecurities and feelings of inadequacy in comparison to his beloved and bold brothers.

Whether it was the birth of children, feeling inadequate, or simply some stunningly poor judgment, what seems clear is that John was often ruled by his emotions and the impact of events in his personal life rather than by any truly rational metric. Allowing himself to be ruled by impulse would be what brought about the beginning of the end of the Angevin empire that his mother, father, and older brothers all worked hard to protect.

Isabelle of Angoulême

Shortly after his coronation, or possibly just before it, John sought to free himself from his first marriage to Isabella of Gloucester. The question of the marriage's validity was put to two trials with three bishops each, one in Normandy and one in Aquitaine. The reasons for doing so are not entirely known for certain. However, it is likely that John wanted his annulment reviewed by several bishops in order to avoid a similar situation his contemporary, Philip Augustus of France, had to deal with. Philip brought the fury of the Church down on him by indiscreetly disposing of an unwanted wife; John, on the other hand, understood the need to get the approval of the Church.

At that early stage in his reign, keeping the Church appeased and on John's side was a prudent move to make, even though he later ruined that relationship. Possibly, he also wanted to do everything by the book to ensure that any new marriage he made would not be labelled bigamous and any future children he sired on his new wife would be viewed as legitimate. His family history was full of illegitimate children and potential heirs who could make challenges to the throne. John's own nephew was still a source of concern regarding the throne of England; therefore, avoiding confusion about the line of succession in the future was a wise path for him to tread. Ultimately, this approach worked in John's favour, as did the fact that his marriage to Isabella of Gloucester was barely legitimate to begin with. The bishops who were consulted declared the marriage void and, finally, after a ten-year marriage, John was a single man once more. As a king, just like queens, one of his most pressing duties would next be to give an heir to his fledgling reign and so he quickly turned his attention to the marriage market.

Initially, John had thought to secure a bride that would help strengthen the southern boundaries of his lands in Aquitaine. To do so, he began negotiations to marry a daughter of King Sancho of Navarre, with whom Richard had previously formed an alliance. However, Navarre was threatened by Castile and Aragon, and the rulers of those regions would likely make allies with the French king Phillip Augustus, so the negotiations came to nothing. John turned his attention to a Portuguese alliance instead, which we know about only through the chronicle of Ralph of Diceto, who records that John received a delegation from Portugal.

John may not have actually been the one who initiated the discussions of a Portuguese marriage, but regardless, ambassadors from that country had been at John's court in Normandy early in 1200 with further plans to meet again in July. However, as fate would have it, John went on progress of his southern lands and by August of 1200, John took Isabelle, the only child of Count Aymer Taillefer of Angoulême, as his new wife. There are plenty of colourful chronicles and documents which record the event and the politics leading up to his choice of new wife. Some are conflicting and some are scathing towards John, Isabelle, or both. All of them, though, portray a very dramatic period in John's reign.

As a brief summary, when John saw Isabelle, it is rumoured he was besotted with her, for she was already considered a rare beauty with long blonde hair and blue eyes; some modern historians have described her as the Helen of the Middle Ages. Most of the chroniclers at the time claimed that John fell in love with Isabelle, was utterly captivated by her beauty, and wanted her for himself. Perhaps such claims are true, but it seems equally likely, if not more so, that John was driven by political motivations and a 'hard-headed' longing to take the betrothed of Hugh de Lusignan out from under his nose and put himself in place to inherit Angoulême.[24] Some earlier scholars, such as H.G. Richardson, have argued that there is actually reason to think John was not sincere in his desire to secure a Portuguese bride for himself, despite the Portuguese envoy sent to his court to come to a marriage arrangement; this seems unlikely since, as late as June or July 1200, diplomatic envoys were out working on the marriage negotiations on his behalf. John marrying Isabelle at all, let alone so precipitously and without adhering to accepted protocol for ending an already in-process marriage negotiation, is partly what has made his seemingly abrupt marriage to her a continuing source of discussion over the years. Any lack of thought on John's part regarding his envoys is reason enough to view the union askance, for his actions could easily have placed the envoys in great danger. Protracting the discussions for a Portuguese marriage with which he had no intention of following through would only cause further troubles for John. It therefore seems likely that he was already betrothed in February 1200 when he was preparing to leave Normandy and that either the mission to Portugal had been called back or the dates were simply inaccurate in the documents.

John, as some chronicles and scholars indicate, had travelled to his Continental lands to go on progress, as was his custom. While on the Continent, he visited at the comital castle of the de Lusignans, despite being in negotiations to marry the Portuguese princess, and it was there that John met Isabelle. She was betrothed to Hugh IX 'le Brun' de Lusignan, at that time the head of that powerful family, and was living at his castle in accordance with the custom of raising young aristocratic girls in the courts of their betrothed. The history between the Plantagenets, Taillefers, and de Lusignans was complex. Count Aymer, as well as most of his forefathers, was fiercely independent and swore homage directly to the king of France, ignoring his duties to the dukes of Aquitaine. The counts of Angoulême were vassals of the dukes of Aquitaine, but in reality were mostly autonomous rulers who did not tie in strongly to the typical medieval feudal hierarchy.[25] Even Richard I, who had defeated Aymer in battle, was not able to secure for himself the count's fealty which was owed to him. Instead, Richard crafted a friendship instead with Aymer based on their shared passion for crusading, and used it to sow discord between the houses of Angoulême and de Lusignan and to prevent those families from creating a powerful alliance against the Angevin Empire. Richard had dangled before Hugh le Brun the prospect of acquiring the rich lands of La Marche to the east of Angoumois and lower Poitou. Aymer badly wanted the lands of La Marche himself, and by encouraging the historic rivalry between the Taillefers and the de Lusignans for the territory, 'Richard had achieved a balance of power in the locality, which conveniently neutralised the broader troublemaking propensities of the two families.'[26] In effect, Richard had the two families so preoccupied with their own feuding that they had no time to ally together and cause trouble for the Angevin empire, which suited Richard just fine; if the two houses were to join in an alliance, their swathes of land would cut right across the Angevin territories and would be disastrous to Richard.

When Richard died, that balance was disrupted and, to unite the de Lusignans and Taillefers in peace, Isabelle was betrothed to Hugh le Brun. Their marriage would have brought an alliance between their families and put an end to the longstanding feud between the two families that was disruptive to the politics of the entire region. The marriage of John to Isabelle upended the political machinations which Richard had so carefully orchestrated during his reign and, as a consequence, was seen by contemporary chroniclers as the death knell of the Angevin Empire which directly led to the loss of John's Continental lands. While this does appear to be the case, whether it was actually due to John and Isabelle marrying or simply John's own blundering of politics is still a matter of continuing discussion among some scholars. Solid arguments can be made for either position.

There has been some consideration about whether the betrothal of Isabelle to Hugh le Brun was an event that took place at nearly the same time as John was seeking a new wife; it is possible she had not actually been betrothed to Hugh for very long when John came calling. This idea would be supported if the death of Richard precipitated Isabelle's betrothal as an alliance to maintain peace between her family and the de Lusignans. The length of her betrothal to Hugh would have been irrelevant, though, since John should have gone through the proper channels to secure her for himself regardless. One school of thought is that John acted as an effective king by breaking up a union between two powerful families which would have been a threat to his own empire; his marriage was based purely on political need and love did not need to be a factor at all, especially considering that John had access to any number of adult mistresses whenever he wanted one. There is also some evidence to suggest that John and Isabelle were betrothed quite a bit earlier than we might think. There are documents made before 28 April 1200 that make reference to John's betrothed wife, his *uxor sua desponsata*. These are two separate charters regarding the potential inheritance of Gloucester castle to a Hugh de Bohun; John wanted to ensure that he, not Hugh de Bohun, inherited the castle.[27] This was after he had already received an annulment with Isabella of Gloucester, so we know the phrase does not refer to her. The lady mentioned in these documents is unnamed, but in light of the agreement in January 1200 between John and Hugh, it seems logical to assume she is Isabelle. Around the middle of May 1200, John entered into a peace treaty with Philip Augustus and reference was made once more to his betrothed wife, again unnamed, with a provision included stating that certain lands would pass to John's niece if John's wife did not give him a legitimate heir.[28] This date is several months before the betrothal that is generally thought to have occurred in the summer of 1200.

Several political motivations highlighted John's desire to 'bind to himself the rulers of Angoumois, La Marche and Limousin and to break any ties they might have with the king of France. The first evidence of success comes on 28 January 1200, when Hugh le Brun swore fealty to John, and John, in return, recognised Hugh's right to La Marche.'[29] It also would have made the main reason for Hugh marrying Isabelle irrelevant, since he wanted La Marche for himself; John granting him these lands anyway made a marriage alliance unnecessary. Hugh might have been persuaded to give up a betrothal to Isabelle if he was able to gain the lands he desired without her. It was a fairly beneficial move on John's part, because even though he lost direct control of La Marche by giving it to Hugh, he could potentially gain a valuable ally in the de Lusignans as well as gaining Angoumois as his own when Isabelle's father died. Some scholars have argued that this was John's intention all along and that the hostilities that erupted shortly after between John and the de Lusignans were a result of another event, an insult done to Ralph de Lusignan, rather than from John taking Isabelle for himself.[30] Given John's temperament, that scenario would not be surprising or unbelievable. Regardless, when Hugh rebelled, his claims to La Marche would have been forfeit as far as John was concerned, and he would have then taken those lands back under his own control.

He did not do so, though, until the spring of 1201, and in the meantime, the de Lusignans made use of any ammunition against John they could think of; blaming him for Hugh and Isabelle's broken betrothal was an easy choice. Chroniclers at the time may not have known all the facts, and certainly would not have had them in real-time, and so it is not unreasonable of them to assume it was because of John's marriage to Isabelle that the conflict started. However, it does not seem likely that there was some other reason for the de Lusignans' rebellion against John, and the idea that there was is not shared by a majority of scholars. It makes more sense to assume that John taking Isabelle as his wife, practically under the noses of the de Lusignans, was an insult they could not overlook.

Others argue that John's marriage to Isabelle made absolutely no political sense and that, even if he did break up the alliance between Angoulême and de Lusignan, he succeeded only in angering and insulting some powerful families, an act that would go against him badly.[31] Even the biographer of William Marshal, a man known for his unwavering loyalty to the Plantagenets, was critical of the marriage and the way it was carried out, saying that 'it wasn't a good move' and that the marriage 'was the initial cause of the disastrous war that was to cost the king his land', primarily because some players in the political arena viewed it as good news and others as bad and took advantage accordingly.[32]

W.L. Warren, Austin Lane Poole, Sydney Painter, and Alan Lloyd at least all make an argument, sometimes rather tepidly, that there is reason to believe it could have been both politics and love that drove John's actions. It is true that marrying Isabelle did prevent the alliance between La Marche and Angoulême, but John surely was able to predict how his actions would be received. One might ask what other reason could there have been for his impetuousness than that he was also smitten with the young girl? Perhaps he had ruffled enough feathers through his earlier affairs with adult, married, noblewomen that he opted not to take that route again. However, given that love was rarely a factor in the marriages of medieval aristocracy, 'the sudden infatuation of John, now approaching middle age, for a child of twelve or less, as Isabelle was … surely defies probability'.[33] Whatever his true motivations, John badly misjudged the backlash marrying Isabelle would bring.

The events leading up to John's marriage are murky. There are actually not a lot of chronicles specifying details, and many are conflicting or imprecise. But in broad strokes, John approached Isabelle's father, Count Aymer, and apparently convinced him to abduct his own daughter from Hugh de Lusignan so that John could marry her instead. It seems that Count Aymer jumped at the chance to make his daughter the queen of England, a more favourable title than being Hugh de Lusignan's countess. It is not clear how long this discussion between John and Aymer went on, nor how long it took to make arrangements for Aymer to take Isabelle back to his court. It could have taken weeks or even months. Some have argued that this scenario seems unlikely considering that John's envoys were literally in the middle of arranging his marriage to the Portuguese princess when he wed Isabelle.

However, John and Aymer may have been in discussions prior to the summer of 1200 and the envoys for his Portuguese marriage were either recalled, or the Portuguese diplomats were already on their way home, having been unsuccessful, when they were mentioned in Ralph of Diceto's chronicles; a simple misunderstanding or misinformation of the timeline and dates could explain the apparent confusion. Richardson claims that

John would have recalled his envoys unless he 'acted with an entire lack of prudence' as soon as he became betrothed to Isabelle, especially since a delay would have resulted in a different political problem for him altogether.[34] Given the mentions of John's betrothed wife in documents and treaties prior to the summer of 1200, it is probable that Diceto actually did just get the timeline wrong and that John and Isabelle were betrothed early in 1200, after the Portuguese marriage envoy had departed his court. John and Isabelle did not need to have met in person for such an arrangement to take place. As we know, many spouses met for the first time only at the church door; noble brides and bridegrooms were no exception.

After Count Aymer retrieved his daughter from Hugh le Brun's court, John then wed Isabelle in a quiet ceremony on 24 August 1200. The newlyweds stayed for about a month in John's Continental territories and then sailed for England in the first week of October. Little is known about his movements during this time, only that he stayed in his southern lands right after his marriage and then sailed in October. Instructions for the coronation were, presumably, sent to the chamberlain of London, for John and Isabelle landed in England, were at Westminster by 7 October 1200, and on 8 October 1200, Isabelle was crowned queen of England alongside John, who held a second coronation for himself. Having a second coronation was not an uncommon practice for kings at the time; it reinforced his authority over his lands and subjects. In theory, this double coronation implies that John had the intention of having Isabelle co-rule by his side, as was the tradition for Norman queens, just as his own mother had done for much of her marriage to Henry II and as regent for Richard during his own reign. In practice, Isabelle did not receive such an honour, which we will explore shortly.

Isabelle's exact date of birth is not known. However, based on the presumed date of 1186 for the marriage of her parents, many scholars place her date of birth sometime around 1188. If these dates are accurate (and there is some reason to believe they are not), she would have been only around 12 years old at the time of her marriage. Twelve is the canonical age of consent for girls to marry, and 14 for boys, though Gratian, the distinguished twelfth-century jurist, stated that a marriage was legitimate if there was meaningful consent from both parties over the age of 7. However, a young couple were not to have sexual intercourse until they reach the legal age of consent.

An argument can be made that Isabelle was even younger than the usually assumed 12 years, as young as 8 or 9; though this seems to be viewed with less likelihood than the older age of 12 or so, some evidence exists that supports Isabelle being much younger. Isabelle had been living at the court of her betrothed, Hugh de Lusignan, and because of these living arrangements, it may be understood that she was not yet considered old enough to wed him. If she was old enough, though, it begs the question of why Hugh had not yet married her. However, the swiftness with which John married her could indicate that she may have been at least very close to the Church's prescribed age of consent. Most seem to believe she was at least 12 and possibly as old as 14 when she married John, and that age would align with canon law. The dates of her parents' marriage, though, may be evidence that Isabelle was actually much younger when she wed John in 1200. Although the date of their marriage is generally considered to be around 1186, Isabelle's mother, Alice of Courtenay, was still recorded as being married to her second husband earlier in that year. Aymer and Alice were not actually mentioned in documents as being married until 1191. It is possible, of course, that they were married before that and only the records from 1191 survive, or they just had not been mentioned in any other documents prior to that year. But if they were married in 1191, then Isabelle would not have been born before that date, making her 9 years old at most at her marriage in 1200.

Bolstering the idea that Isabelle's birth year may be later than previously thought, some contemporary chroniclers also suggest a lack of certainty about her being the proper age of consent. Ralph of Coggeshall, for example, claimed that Isabelle had the appearance of being around 12 years old (specifically, *'que quasi duodenis videbatur'* – 'it seemed like she was twelve'), but there is a tone of uncertainty about his phrasing which may indicate she appeared to be younger than that. The uncertainty of her age is more clearly specified in the chronicler Roger of Howden's *Chronica*. Howden writes that Hugh de Lusignan had accepted Isabelle's *verba de presenti* vows but since she was not yet at the age of nubility, or sexual maturity, Hugh did not wish to marry her before the door of the church, the usual place for weddings. The actual phrase Howden used was *'quia ipsum nondum annos nubiles attigerat noluit eram predictus Hugo sibi in facie ecclesiae copulare'* ('because she had not reached marriageable age, Hugh refused to join her in front of the church').[35] Howden is by no means the most reliable source and some of his works have been discredited by modern scholars as inaccurate or fanciful, but the presence of at least two contemporary sources which imply Isabelle's extreme youth lends the idea further credence.

Although it was a common practice to rear young brides at the homes of their future husbands, Nicholas Vincent has made a compelling argument that Isabelle and Hugh were actually legally married but that, given her extreme youth, he had not consummated the marriage yet. According to Roger of Howden, Hugh and Isabelle gave marriage vows *in verba de presenti*, meaning that they vowed marriage in present terms, not future terms. This would have made their marriage valid in 'the full legal sense, save for his failure to consummate the union because [she] was as yet sexually immature'.[36] Even simple verbal oaths spoken in the present tense were all that was required to make a marriage legal and valid throughout medieval Europe, so if this exchange of vows had occurred, then Isabelle would have been considered a married woman even if she had not had sex with Hugh at that time. If this were the case and Isabelle and Hugh were legally wed, then she would have needed to obtain an official annulment before she could legally marry John.

It is unlikely this happened, given the apparent haste of her marriage to John, nor do we have any letters from the pope or any other paper legates stating that an annulment had been granted. However, if Isabelle was not yet at the age of consent, then her *verba de presenti* vows to Hugh could more easily be overlooked, as was the case with Isabelle's own daughter, as we shall see. It has been noted that if Isabelle had not been of age when she gave consent, then her contract with Hugh le Brun was perfectly fine to be set aside with no further ramifications. It seems that there was generally no trouble with 'setting aside an infant's betrothal, provided the concurrence of the responsible parties on either side was secured, and we may well doubt whether any words of the present tense, spoken by her or on her behalf, would have made the contract more binding upon her'.[37] Given the apparent ease with which other nobles played betrothal musical chairs with their children throughout the medieval world, it seems that these *verba de presenti* vows meant more in spirit as opposed to being the letter of the law.

There is also simply the pragmatic question of why, if Isabelle were of age, had Hugh le Brun not already married her in an official ceremony;

if she were of age, there can be few logical reasons to delay her marriage to Hugh. However, if Isabelle was not yet at the age of consent, it raises the unpleasant question that, if she were too young for Hugh to bed her, why was it acceptable for John to do so? It seems that John had gone out of his way to obtain letters from several different bishops that testified to the legitimacy of his marriage to Isabelle, but 'the suspicion remains that his bride was a pre-pubescent child in 1200, and that the king stepped in where Hugh de Lusignan, Isabella's betrothed husband, had believed it indecent to tread'.[38] The idea that John not only effectively abducted Isabelle but also that he might have been, by far more modern standards, a child molester, may well have contributed to his persistent horrible reputation through the ages. However, it seems that John and Isabelle did not live together after their joint coronation, for he left her in Marlborough, where she stayed for an extended time, and he went on a tour of his country.

John even placed her under the care of his former wife, Isabella of Gloucester, for roughly a year and possibly longer, in 1205. This could be significant and point to her being younger than 12 years old and not yet nubile, for it was another common practice for young aristocratic girls to be tended to by older women of similar social status, though perhaps not by the former wife of one's new husband. Sheltering Isabelle with his former wife and not staying long with her would also help explain the reason why John appears not to have cohabited with her much in the earlier years of their marriage; keeping a relative distance from her for a few years would indicate that he married her for political reasons and not for love or lust. If she were older and nubile, then for him not to consummate the marriage would, indeed, cast doubt upon its legitimacy.

If politics were behind John's brash decision to marry Isabelle, an abduction followed by a formal betrothal would have been just as effective at stymying the alliance between the de Lusignans and Isabelle's family, as well as being 'more decorous' because of how young she was.[39] Abductions among marriageable aristocratic women was technically not legal, either in ecclesiastical or secular courts of law, but it was not unheard of, either. In 1152, for example, John's own mother, Eleanor, evaded abduction and forced marriage herself, just after her marriage to Louis VII of France was annulled. Ironically, Geoffrey of Anjou attempted to abduct her, who was the younger brother of Henry Plantagenet, whom she did marry just a few weeks after the annulment of her first marriage. However, abducting Isabelle could have its own set of legal troubles, not necessarily because of the abduction itself, but because there was at the time a question of whether marriage was made by consent and cohabiting with one's betrothed, as Isabelle and Hugh had been doing, and not by sexual intercourse. Gratian wrote that 'betrothed girls, whom others have abducted, should be returned to those whom they first betrothed, even if the abductors used force on them'.[40] Moreover, Gratian supported the concept that mutual consent was understood to make a marriage.[41] If Isabelle was living at the court of Hugh de Lusignan, then mutual consent should be assumed and their marriage could have been declared valid, even if she was under the legal age and the couple had not yet consummated the marriage. Additionally, a betrothal cannot be broken by the parents if they consented to the contract.[42]

However, Gratian was a jurist and most likely a clergyman. As a result, his arguments were far more black and white in theory than they would be in real-world practice. As we have seen, breaking a betrothal did not seem to be too great a difficulty, especially if the bride is not of age. Moreover, because a father's consent was at least desired in a marriage for medieval couples, if Count Aymer gave Isabelle to John after first betrothing her to Hugh, the legality of either betrothal or marriage can quickly become muddied.

Adding to the confusion is the medieval understanding of coercion, abduction, and rape as these relate to marriage. If Isabelle's parents had coerced her into marrying Hugh, the expectation in medieval society was that she ought to obey her parents as the proper behaviour for a child. The use of abduction and rape to force a marriage, while technically illegal, was exceedingly difficult to prove, especially since the Church's requirements to prove that a rape happened were so stringent. For example, one of the requirements was that rape cannot happen to a woman if it occurred within her house, or even up the road from her house. The idea is that abduction is part of what makes for a rape case, and being so close to one's own home does not constitute abduction.[43] Even if Isabelle had tried to claim this with regard to either Hugh or John, it is unlikely to have been successful in the ecclesiastical courts. While there appears to be no evidence that she wanted to claim rape or abduction, it is one legal option that either party could have tried if they wished to press the issue. Such claims seem to be mostly confined to the lower classes, though, not the aristocracy, so even if the thought of rape had occurred, it is unlikely Isabelle would have taken that approach. Claiming rape could have done irreparable harm to her reputation, so it was a fairly uncommon strategy. Besides, as mentioned above, she was following her father's apparent desires for her to marry John, as an obedient child should do.

The question of having legitimate heirs may also have been foremost in John's mind when he chose Isabelle. He had ten years of marriage to Isabella of Gloucester and no children had been produced from it. Whether Isabella's lack of children was due to her being barren, to the couple not living together very often, or to any number of other reasons was by this point irrelevant. John had bastards aplenty by this time of his life, but he needed heirs. Isabelle was young and healthy and so there was no real reason to suspect she would not be able to give him heirs. One possible sticking point in this argument, though, is that infertility can sometimes run in families due to conditions such as endometriosis or polycystic ovarian syndrome (PCOS), which of course were unknown in the thirteenth century. Isabelle's own mother, Alice de Courtenay, only had two children, or at least only two who survived to adulthood; any others she may have miscarried or delivered but who died in infancy are not recorded. Certainly, she could have had many children who did not survive to adulthood. That was not an uncommon tragedy for medieval parents but it was not usually documented by contemporary chroniclers. Theoretically, if Alice did not have many children, then it could have been a reason for concern as related to her daughter's fertility. That such topics did not seem to cross John's mind could imply either that Isabelle's mother had at one time produced a plentiful brood that did not survive into adulthood and therefore Isabelle's fertility was not a concern to him, or that he truly was smitten with Isabelle and took her despite this additional risk factor. We will likely never know for sure.

Marriage and Disappointment

As mentioned above, John held a coronation for Isabelle when they arrived in England, and he participated in a second coronation for himself alongside her. Some may choose to see this as a sign that he genuinely cared for her and married her based at least in part on affection, even if that is not the whole of it. There are few specific details actually recorded in chronicles which describe John's second coronation alongside Isabelle. One chronicle recorded only that the ceremony was 'extremely impressive' and that there was a sumptuous feast after the coronation, with few details beyond that.[44] A short entry in the Norman Rolls for 10 October 1200 noted also that the king appeared deeply appreciative of the singers at the ceremony. These rolls note that two royal clerks were paid 25s for singing *Christus vincit*, and that £74 19s 9d was spent on ceremonial robes made just for the coronation. This was a large sum of money at the time and implies that the ceremony would have plenty of 'visual splendor'.[45] There are few other records of the event, though. The general lack of description in the chronicles implies that, despite the expenses of the robes and services, it was an otherwise ordinary coronation ceremony.

Having Isabelle crowned as queen and doing so alongside a second coronation for himself (and in fact, a third time for himself, a second time for Isabelle, on Easter 1201 at Canterbury) may have implied that John had intended to have Isabelle co-rule with him. It also validated Isabelle's role as John's consort and legal wife by showing that their marriage had 'spiritual backing at religious sites associated with two of the Angevin dynasty's most favoured saints' cults, those of St Edward the Confessor at Westminster and St Thomas Becket at Canterbury'.[46] This crowning and anointing would also further strengthen Isabelle's status as John's wife in light of the fact that her earlier relationship with Hugh le Brun was legally quite murky. John's intention to allow Isabelle to co-rule is highlighted when considering that she was also anointed with holy oil at her coronation, an action usually taken for reigning monarchs, and there was precedent in the thirteenth century for queens to have vice-regal power. There was a long tradition of Norman queens being more than just the consorts of kings. A queen would have been called upon to act as vice-regent in the king's absence, on occasion, and oversee many aspects of his court even in his presence. By the time Isabelle was crowned, it had been nearly fifty years since a crowned queen of England had filled that co-ruler role. Richard's wife, Berengaria, certainly did not, nor did she ever even set foot in England during Richard's reign. However, Eleanor of Aquitaine was 'a living witness of the position which custom gave to an English queen. ...[Isabelle] was now expressly occupying Eleanor's place, hardly [leaving] room for doubt that the intention was to re-establish the queen in the position that was hers a half century earlier'.[47] But this did not actually happen. What did happen is exactly the opposite. By all accounts, other than providing heirs, Isabelle never filled an expected role as a reigning queen and was at best the consort of the king despite being crowned and anointed.

Considering how she had been brought up and by whom, Isabelle's own marriage may have fallen far below the expectations she might have developed in her childhood. Although the English royal records of John's reign indicate that he and Isabelle had a solid relationship, some arguments can be made that her marriage was less impressive than she may have wanted. Isabelle's parents set forth an example that ended up being far different than her union with John. Her mother, Alice of Courtenay, was a noblewoman descended from French kings. Alice's father was Peter of Courtenay, a younger son of Louis VI and brother of Louis VII; through her mother, Isabelle was not only a cousin of Philip Augustus, Louis VIII, and Louis IX from the French royal family, but also related to many of the royal families of Europe. She also had connections to most of the other major families through her mother's two marriages prior to her third to Aymer Taillefer. Isabelle's father was also from one of the most respected noble houses in Europe, and was a powerful count who came into his inheritance in roughly 1186.[48] In *The History of William Marshal*, there is a reference to a man with the surname Taillefer who sings a song before a battle. Beyond his surname, this person is unnamed, but it seems possible that he might have been Isabelle's father or perhaps an uncle, as it was not unusual for there to be references to other men of powerful families in the *History*. If true, then he was at least known as a high-profile man to Marshal's biographer. In fact, Isabelle's mother is also specifically mentioned in Marshal's biography and is said to have a face and body as perfect as Nature could fashion.[49] Beauty, it seems, ran in the family.

Isabelle's family had a long tradition of fierce independence, bordering on insolence, particularly where it concerned the dukes of Aquitaine, their rightful overlords. The Angoulême nobles in general refused to give fealty to dukes of Aquitaine as they were supposed to as their vassals; they would only swear their fealty directly to the French king. Isabelle's mother was an example of a strong medieval woman who exercised the power that was available to her. She appears to have been an active participant in the ruling and management of her lands, whether her own *suo jure* lands or the dower lands from her marriages. Alice de Courtenay issued charters and documents on her own and alongside her husbands. She had her finger on the pulse of events in her demesne and it appears that her input was valued and approved of by her husbands. Isabelle's parents seem to have had a mutually respectful relationship, with Alice issuing charters and other documents alongside Aymer and sometimes on her own. When Aymer died in 1202, Alice 'may have assumed the government of the city of Angoulême, whilst the county was expected to answer to John's seneschal for Poitou'.[50] In 1203, Alice was granted a monthly pension of 50 livres, which might have been in exchange for any dower rights or other claims she had over the county, to be paid out by John's Norman exchequer. After that, she retired to an estate she had acquired as part of her dower lands from her first marriage and lived there as late as July 1215, where she was still issuing charters. Alice set an example for her daughter of how an aristocratic woman could rule alongside her husband, but she was just one example among many the young Isabelle might have had. Moreover, Aymer and his forefathers had a well-earned reputation as rebels and independent lords, semi-autonomous within their lands. As noted above, these noblemen refused to give fealty to their rightful overlords, the dukes and duchesses of Aquitaine, and instead gave fealty directly to the French king. This stubborn independence led often to military and political conflict between the lords of Aquitaine and Angoulême. Indeed, John's elder brother, Richard I, astute military strategist that he was, had just barely managed to strike a delicate balance of power in the region by carefully playing the Taillefers against the de Lusignans in their territory dispute over the lands of La Marche. A strong-willed family, a history of rebellion, and a maternal example of competence and hands-on rule would, without a doubt, have left an impression upon the young Isabelle.

It is possible that Isabelle's parentage and family history caused her to create more conflict in her marriage than needed. If this is the case, it is understandable, given her examples growing up. In fact, it seems very likely that Isabelle was disappointed in her marriage to John and that it did not live up to the expectations she would have been raised to anticipate, and which were hinted would come her way during her coronation. When Isabelle was crowned at Westminster in October 1200, the ceremony implied that she would be vested with some sovereignty.

John had a second coronation for himself at the same time, and during the ceremony, Isabelle was not only crowned but anointed with holy oil. By doing so, the implication is that she would be viewed as an authoritative co-ruler with some form of sovereignty of her own, at least in theory. John was showing to all and sundry that he was sharing his own power with her as his queen. Agreeing to grant her such authority may even have been understood, if not expressly stated, when John made the marriage arrangement with Isabelle's father.

In practice, however, Isabelle was kept utterly dependent upon John and was given no true authority at all, not even over the lands she held in her own right. By keeping her on a short leash and forcing her dependence on him for her finances, Isabelle was denied the potential political influence that was available to many queens who came before her. A queen, and indeed many married women of the medieval aristocracy, would often issue charters alongside her husband, would be given lands to be held in dower for her, have her own income, and generally would take up a position of management over her household, and such was the example she had received throughout her childhood by way of her mother. The issue of Isabelle's dower lands was somewhat unusual because both Eleanor of Aquitaine and Berengaria of Navarre were still alive when John married Isabelle. They had their own dower lands as part of their marriage portions to Henry II and Richard I, respectively. John could not take their lands to give to Isabelle as part of her own dower, and so her dower was granted from other Angevin lands not typically associated with English queens. More specifically, Eleanor's dower, which was given to her in 1189 after the death of Henry II, took up all the lands that 'traditionally comprised the dowers of the Anglo-Norman queens'.[51] Under normal circumstances, Isabelle would have been endowed with revenues from John's lands on the day they married. In truth, it seems the revenues did not actually come to her until the death of Eleanor of Aquitaine, which occurred 1 April 1204.

Isabelle had gone back to Angoulême a few times after her marriage to John, but during those visits, she did not have any authority over the region. Nicholas Vincent states that, 'although she received the country's homage in 1206, and in 1214 may have been allowed various seigneurial privileges, she appears to have exercised no direct authority there until after the death of John'.[52] That John waited six years to bring Isabelle back to Angoulême to receive oaths of fealty gives a good indication that he never intended to share power with her. As her father's only child, she was the heiress *suo jure* of Angoulême, but she did not ever get to rule her lands in her own right during her marriage to John. She was dependent upon him for her livelihood and means of support, and this dependency perhaps underscored her lack of authority as queen. To be fair, though, there are many reasons why she might have been denied more authority, some with more merit than others. For one thing, it is possible Isabelle's youth and lack of practical experience prevented John from letting her co-rule or have much independence at all. She was a child and John treated her accordingly.

Even though she was raised by her parents to be a nobleman's wife, she probably would not have been allowed full control over her household anyway if she were truly as young as she seems to have been. If her parents had passed away before she was able to tend to her own estate, a regency of some kind would have been established to help her learn her new adult roles; since her parents were living at the time of her marriage, no regency was needed. However, older aristocratic women might have been selected to help rear her and teach her skills she would need in her position, similar to a regency though far less formal. Such arrangements may well have been why John left her in the care of Isabella of Gloucester in 1205. She could have been under the care of other noblewomen prior to that, and it went unremarked since it was not out of the ordinary as her living arrangements with her husband's first wife were. This position also seems like it would lend further weight to the argument that she was not actually of age to marry in 1200. However, even when she did reach a more mature age where she could have learned to co-rule with John, he did not allow her to do so, nor did she have any direct control over her dower lands or Angoulême itself once her father died and she came into her inheritance. Instead, John appointed a governor, Bartholomew de Le Puy to control Isabelle's lands and handle the administrative work, and he retained that position until John's death in 1216.

Also, Isabelle did not immediately receive her queen's gold. As discussed earlier, the queen's gold was a common source of income for Norman queens, stemming from a percentage of voluntary fines owed to the king from his vassals, but it appears that Isabelle did not receive hers for many years after her marriage to John, not even after Eleanor of Aquitaine died. While there could be several reasons for this, it seems that two are the most likely combination. First, Eleanor was still alive for the early years of John's reign and marriage to Isabelle. She was, of course, a force unto herself and she had been the official intercessor for both Richard's and John's reigns while she was able to carry out that role. Eleanor was accustomed to her authority and it seems unlikely that she would have surrendered it, nor that John would have asked her to, especially not to a young, untried girl. Second, John himself was relatively stingy with his money and largesse, making it more likely he would choose to enjoy the income from those lands himself. Rolls from the royal household indicate that he did in fact make use of any money Isabelle should have received. Moreover, records indicate that he still maintained Isabella of Gloucester's household, and that the amount he spent on her income was almost as much as what he spent on Isabelle's. Either he was incredibly generous with his former wife, an unlikely scenario, or he was tight-fisted and accommodated Isabelle with barely more income than he had to. John was also petty enough that it might very well have pleased him to take those incomes for himself which should have gone to Hugh de Lusignan, by way of Isabelle's domains in Angoulême, had Hugh married Isabelle as he had originally planned. This might also support the theory some historians have floated that John married Isabelle because he wanted to take something away from the de Lusignans and he did not care much what it really was, whether a betrothed or something else. That idea seems to have been largely ignored, but given his reported temperament, it bears a quick mention here. However, it seems far more likely that John simply wanted to make use of the funds available to him, much as his own father had done during his lifetime by using income from Isabella of Gloucester's lands.

Isabelle may also have been disappointed in John because he was cowardly. She implied that Hugh le Brun was a better knight than John in all ways when she claimed to have lost the best knight for him. But her disillusionment with John could have also stemmed in part from events leading up to her being trapped in the castle at Chinon by Poitevin rebels fighting for Philip Augustus. It was in January 1203 that Isabelle sent a request to John, asking him to rescue her since she was besieged at Chinon. This must have been terrifying to her, for at the very most she could have only been 15 years old and not at all familiar with battles. John set forth to save her with a group of mercenaries, but along the way, he learned that a nobleman who had but days before been loyal to him had switched over to Philip Augustus's side. John was concerned that he would be penned in on all sides by his enemies if he continued on the route to Chinon, so instead of rescuing his wife himself, he sent the mercenaries along without him and he hunkered down in Le Mans, waiting for his hired men to bring his wife safely to him. Later, in December 1203, John claimed he needed to go to England to get the advice of his barons and would sail from Calais, but fearing that his Continental barons would turn him over to Philip Augustus, John fled in the middle of the night. Many positive things may be said about John in terms of his penchant for administration, but in terms of bravery, it seems to be a different matter. It is difficult to imagine Richard, Henry II, or Philip Augustus waiting for paid soldiers to take care of matters if their wives were in danger. If Isabelle had been in any way influenced by tales of knights fighting for their loves, as depicted in many of the courtly love tales with which she might have been familiar, John's cowardice and failure to come to her rescue may have come as a shocking blow to the young girl and her beliefs about how kings should act.

Loss of the Continent, Loss of Reputation

In looking back over the year 1203, the year in which John began to lose his lands on the Continent, Warren notes that contemporary chroniclers could only see it as a year of shame and that 'many men were bewildered at John's apparent helplessness'.[53] Isabelle was typically blamed by these chroniclers for the loss of John's Continental lands. Her reputation suffered from, and in large part was created by, the near-contemporary male clerics who were inclined to distrust women and whose writing was biased by their knowledge about John's disastrous reign.[54] Roger of Wendover claimed that Isabelle was an ideal mate for John since he was one of the most unpleasant kings of England; Matthew Paris, Wendover's successor at St. Alban's, contributed further to sully Isabelle's reputation, using an unverified story that told how one of John's emissaries to the ruler of North Africa told how Isabelle hated her husband and called her an adulterous woman. Chroniclers seemed to relish placing blame at her young feet by labelling her a temptress and sometimes even toying with the term of witch, suggesting that John's helplessness was because Isabelle cast a spell upon him. Matthew Paris in particular was especially antagonistic towards her, describing her as 'more Jezebel than Isabel', though others were similarly ill-disposed towards the queen. There may be various reasons for them to have viewed her so. Chroniclers of the time certainly tended to regard Isabelle as the prime cause in and of herself for the loss of Angevin lands on the Continent. But other than using the misogynistic terminology that was common for the era and blaming her marriage to John for the loss of the Continent, the chronicles that survive actually list very few specific reasons for viewing her with such contempt.

One possible reason for blaming Isabelle is simply that John was disliked by most of the nobility, and so that sentiment could easily have been transferred onto Isabelle. As the saying goes, one is guilty by association. However, disliking the spouse of a hated ruler does not always happen – for example, Katherine of Aragon, Caroline of Brunswick, and Lady Diana Spenser were all popular spouses of unpopular royals – but in Isabelle's case, no one seems to have been willing to give her the benefit of the doubt. From the start of her marriage to John, she was blamed for the loss of lands the Angevin Empire suffered during John's reign. Roger of Wendover recorded that John spent his nights in 'riotous living' and stayed in bed with Isabelle until noon every day instead of taking care of his kingdom. He was so besotted with her that some people suggested that she had bewitched him. For evidence, they claimed that when messengers arrived with news that Philip Augustus was making war on his land, seizing his castles, and dragging off his castellans, John replied, 'Let be, let be, whatever he now takes I will one day recover.'[55] Wendover goes on to say that John's attitude remained similarly truculent and unconcerned because 'he was enjoying all the pleasures of life with his queen, in whose company he believed that he possessed everything that he wanted'. Given that this record is dated from 1204, after the initial loss of John's Continental lands, it seems likely that it is pure gossip from John's detractors since Isabelle was possibly not even cohabiting with him at the time.

Even John himself apparently blamed Isabelle for the loss of his lands. According to some accounts, John himself blamed Isabelle for the loss of his Continental lands. The author of the *Histoire des ducs de Normandie* documented an argument John and Isabelle apparently had when he was suffering loss after loss to Philip Augustus. The chronicler writes that John, having received news of yet another loss of his lands on the Continent, told Isabelle, 'Listen, my lady, I have lost everything for you,' to which she responded, 'Sire, I lost the best knight in the world for you'.[56] While we have no real way to determine the validity of this exchange, it seems in line with Isabelle's known temperament to have a sharp retort, based on some of the letters she wrote which survive to us. There were plenty of medieval women who had a biting wit and a ready retort, like Eleanor of Aquitaine, but in Eleanor's case, she tempered these with her political and diplomatic acumen. Isabelle never seems to have acted similarly and so, combined with a populace already disposed not to like her, her wit probably contributed to her poor reputation right from the start of her marriage. She did not often display the traits that were desired or expected of queens.

Isabelle's poor reputation may have been further degraded by her use of queenly intercession. Or rather, her lack thereof. It does not appear that Isabelle made much use of her intercessory role during her marriage to John. As previously discussed, one of the roles of queens prior to John's reign was to be an intercessor both for nobles desiring access to the king and for common citizens. While it does not seem that chroniclers made any actual note about this aspect of her queenship, did Isabelle's apparent lack of intercession impact how she was portrayed in historical documents? Could it have had an influence, one way or another, upon how John reigned? Certainly, it seems more than likely that it influenced how others saw them both. Isabelle may have participated in a display pardoning at her coronation, though we cannot know for certain since very few details about the ceremony are actually recorded. Traditionally, coronations were a time for newly crowned queens to show mercy. However, queens' roles were shifting during the reigns of Richard and particularly John, so it is not at all certain whether Isabelle would have performed any coronation pardons or not. It is also possible that the chronicles simply do not document any intercession she may have performed, though it does not seem likely there would be no record of it if she had interceded; she was so unpopular that her performing a respected queenly act would have probably surprised at least one of the chroniclers into making a note of the event.

Additionally, as we have seen, it appears that Eleanor of Aquitaine retained her role as royal intercessor during the reign of Richard and of the early years of John's reign before she died in April of 1204. More significantly, Eleanor presented a vision of feminine diplomacy and intercession. One instance of such was in late 1199 or early 1200, at the very start of John's reign, before he even married Isabelle. He needed the aid of Amery of Thouars to win against his nephew Arthur's supporters. John gave control of Chinon to Amery along with naming him seneschal of Anjou and Touraine, but as soon as his battle was won, John stripped Amery of those offices. Eleanor wrote to Amery and begged him to assure John of his loyalty, which was now in doubt because of his treatment at John's hand. Through her persuasion, Amery did so, and thus Eleanor averted a potential disaster for her son. A letter dated in 1200 from Eleanor addressed to John recounts her actions on his behalf. It highlights her diplomatic and intercessory skills. She wrote,

> Especially you should know that I and your faithful Guido de Dina asked and showed him so much that he was altogether in your service, since he himself had done you no harm nor held any of your land unjustly, as your other Poitevin barons do. And again we showed him that he should feel great shame and sin that he suffered your other barons to disinherit you unjustly ... and because we spoke right and reason to him, he freely and willingly conceded that he and his lands and castles were from now on at your command and will ... And since he conceded benevolently what we had asked, namely that he will be in your service well and faithfully against all men, I, who am your mother, and your faithful Guido de Dina, have undertaken that you will be towards him as a Lord ought to be towards his loyal man.[57]

While Eleanor's death occurred early in John's reign, it may have been just enough time for Isabelle to become accustomed to others filling that role instead of her. Given her apparent youth and assuming that teenagers across time periods are at least a little bit similar, it may not have occurred to her to do anything differently, especially since John kept her dependent on him for her livelihood.

It also seems unlikely that she had the personality for intercession, or that John would have tolerated it. Often described as arrogant or prideful, Isabelle was known to be overweening with her titles. While we have to take descriptions of her by her contemporaries with a healthy dose of skepticism, given their antagonistic feelings toward her, it is true that Isabelle was vain when it came to her titles and she remained so for her entire life. She was sensitive to slights and insults, real or imagined, and it does not seem too far a stretch to believe that she just would not have been inclined to exert herself on behalf of someone who she felt to be beneath her in social class. She also held grudges based on how others treated her, such as Blanche, the dowager queen of France. Though Blanche did indeed insult Isabelle, a person with a less volatile temper and more political skill would not have risen to the bait. Isabelle seems to have been unable to rise above and her subsequent crusade against Blanche contributed to the detriment of her social standing later in her second marriage.

John and Isabelle both were reputed to have extremely volatile temperaments, which most likely had an impact on their personal relationship, and in turn that probably influenced the ways in which John ruled. We do not know for certain because, as Church notes, the relationship they had is almost completely obscure. Just from the perspective of general domestic life, the influences of one's spouse can have an impact on behaviours outside the home setting. Basic personality traits naturally are a major influencer as well. In John's case, he was distrustful of his barons and the more monied and powerful they were, the less he trusted them, even if they were loyal to him. Some scholars have claimed that John had revolting personality traits, including a tendency towards pettiness and spitefulness, which were dangerous and had the potential to become tyrannical.[58] He was not often regarded with a lot of respect by many of his peers and contemporaries.

Chroniclers depict a general lack of respect for John from a young age, beginning primarily with his disastrous expedition to Ireland in 1185 when he was around 18 years old. John's father, Henry II, made his youngest son the future ruler of Ireland in 1177 when John was only a little boy. The Anglo-Norman lords in Ireland were promised their own semi-independent lordships over the Irish lands they inhabited, taken over from the native Irish. In turn, these nobles first had to conquer the native

Irish, who were, from Henry's perspective, irredeemably stubborn and resistant to Norman rule. When he was 18, John mounted his first actual expedition to Ireland. It was an unmitigated disaster, at least according to the expedition's official chronicler, Gerald of Wales. John had chosen some of the younger nobles to go along with him and, when they arrived, the young men laughed at and mocked the garb and beards of the native Irish chieftains. Some reportedly even tugged at the beards, a dire insult. Gerald of Wales recorded that John was 'a mere youth' and 'a stripling who listened only to youthful advice'.

This account, while painting a negative and probably at least somewhat accurate picture, fails to highlight some of the actions John had attempted to fulfil while he was in Ireland. In fact, he was not idle during his time in Ireland as some records indicate but had issued more than 20 land grants while he was there, which foreshadows his administrative skills. He was busy attempting to build up a future administration and following for himself for when he would truly be King of Ireland. The grants were, alas, mostly given to his younger companions who had sailed with him, a move which further alienated the Anglo-Irish elite. Many groups who had previously not been allies apparently decided to join forces to oppose John. He also began the construction of castles at important spots around the country so he could take advantage of the rivalries of the local Irish. These actions are either not listed by Gerald of Wales or they are given a biased slant against John, making him appear to be nothing more than a callow youth with bad instincts and worse advisors. John acquired other skills of a more dubious nature on his first Irish expedition. These included learning how to play off subordinates against one another to increase tensions to his own benefit, which would ultimately backfire and result in the barons' rebellion against him, and the native Irish military tradition of collecting the heads of dead enemies as trophies, which he later allegedly introduced in his campaign against the Welsh.[59] Whether truly deserved or not, Gerald of Wales helped to solidify the reputation John earned on the expedition, and Roger of Howden also seems to have believed it as well. Unfortunately, that reputation followed John out of Ireland and throughout the majority of his reign.

Richard himself had not helped John's reputation. As noted earlier, his comments about John during his captivity and after his release when Richard forgave him tarnished his already sullied stature. John had an uphill battle to fight if he wanted to restore his good name, which was not that great to begin with thanks partly to the Irish expedition. It did not help matters that he kept undermining his own reputation through his words and deeds, such as his actions with regard to Amery of Thouars. John then made matters even worse for himself by marrying Isabelle and then becoming defensive about his marriage to her, or at least giving the appearance of such. When Philip Augustus and his army were picking off John's lands on the Continent one by one, John's advisors told him that he needed to take a stand and stop the French king. John's flippant response that he would take back later what Philip took today seems to have genuinely shocked many in his circle. Records indicate that Isabelle was reviled by the population and that she must have had some sort of spell on John to make him forget his responsibilities on the Continent as he had. Within two years of his marriage to Isabelle, the majority of John's lands in Continental Europe were lost; within four years, all of them were lost, and he fled to England, never to return south to the vast territories his family had held for generations.

It is perhaps unfair of history to place the blame on Isabelle. Even if she did influence John's actions in a negative manner, the fact remains that he was the monarch, not her. The responsibility was with him. Moreover, if Isabelle really was as young as she may have been, she was just a child and probably lacked a true understanding of the impact her actions could have on global politics. While she may have been educated in her childhood about certain aspects of politics, Isabelle was possibly too young to understand some of the nuances of politics and diplomacy. Moreover, she failed to learn as she matured. To be fair, though, she did not have an example from which she could have learned when even her own adult husband seemed to lack this understanding at vital moments, and it resulted in catastrophe for his reign.

The Birth of Children and the King's Personal Life

Any parent knows the profound changes that come with the birth of a child, especially a first child. Most await the birth with excitement, trepidation, and a variety of other emotions. For a child to be the heir to a kingdom must come with its own unique set of emotions and issues. The birth of the future Henry III must have had a similar impact on his parents. He was the first legitimate child of his father and his role would be to ensure the continuation of the Plantagenet dynasty, greatly eroded though it was. His birth was another large step closer to a peaceful transfer of power upon John's death, something which England had hardly seen since the Anarchy of the 1130s -1150s. But in what ways could the birth of their children have impacted Isabelle and John as a couple, and specifically as a reigning monarch?

Isabelle gave birth to her first child, the future Henry III, on 1 October 1207, almost exactly seven years after her marriage to John. There can be a great deal of speculation about why it took so long for Isabelle to deliver her first child. There are no known records left which might have indicated if she had any miscarriages, though that is certainly a possibility. Most chroniclers did not bother with documenting miscarriages, or even the deaths of infants and children. However, if Isabelle were as young as 8 or 9 when they wed, she would have been around 15 years old at Henry's birth. This is still a very young age for childbirth with many associated risks that may not have been as dangerous for a slightly older woman giving birth for the first time. Many, though not all, husbands of the time held off on consummating their marriages if their wives were very young because of the greater risk associated with young girls giving birth. It seems that the more likely scenario is that Isabelle was probably not yet fertile in the early years of her marriage, as previously discussed.

There is a lack of evidence to indicate that John had fathered any illegitimate children during these early years of his marriage, either, suggesting that possibly he was both faithful and chaste, at least according to historian Marc Morris. Morris bases the lack of children before 1207 to the possibility that John was not sleeping with Isabelle, even though various chroniclers said he stayed in bed with her most of the day. Because of that, '[W]e have to entertain the alarming possibility that, during the early years of his marriage, John may have been both faithful and chaste.'[60] Why John's potential chastity and faithfulness would be considered alarming is somewhat odd. It would be more alarming if he were definitively sleeping with Isabelle and no children were forthcoming. A legitimate heir was needed, so even if he had fathered numerous children by mistresses, it is not likely any of them would be considered as his heir. Some historians have taken the lack of illegitimate children born during his second marriage to imply that John was devoted to Isabelle and had no mistresses at all during this time, but given his personality, this also seems unlikely. However, given John's documented lustfulness and the social acceptance of royal husbands keeping mistresses, it seems more likely that he either did not father any illegitimate children on his mistresses during these years, that he did not acknowledge any such children, they died or were miscarried, or they were simply not documented.

In fact, it was the accusation that he attempted to rape the daughter of the Earl of Essex that was used as one of the justifications for the barons to revolt, ultimately resulting in the creation of the Magna Carta. Moreover, in 1214, John allegedly abducted a noblewoman called Matilda FitzWalter and tried to force her to become his mistress. She refused, no doubt at least in part because she was already married, and John, so the story goes, sent her a poisoned gift which killed her. Some scholars believe that he locked her in the Tower to force her compliance. The chroniclers Matthew Paris, known to be very negatively biased against John, and Anonymous of Bethune, both record this situation between John and Matilda, though they seem more concerned that John, who was known to love food and wine, did not take an interest in one of the serving wenches instead. If he had, no one would have even given it a moment's consideration. It was the fact that Matilda was a noblewoman that caused the problem. Paris and Anonymous were primarily focused on the dishonour John did to Matilda's husband and father than on his attempted rape of the woman herself. Ironically, Matilda was married to Geoffrey FitzGeoffrey de Mandeville, who in 1216 became the second husband of Isabella of Gloucester and a Magna Carta baron.

To further the discussion of childlessness, we know that Isabelle spent at least one year, and possibly longer, in the care of Isabella of Gloucester, based on evidence from John's household accounts. From 1205 to at least 1206, according to household expense reports, Isabelle lived with Isabella of Gloucester at Winchester Castle, and that Isabella's household was still being subsidised by John. We have no way to know exactly why or how this arrangement came about, whether it was a sign of trust from John to his first wife, a way to cause her embarrassment, or some other motivation. Whatever the reason, it does not seem that John lived with Isabelle at the time, which is another explanation for why Isabelle did not deliver a baby before 1207. Regardless, there were no known royal children or bastards born during this time, which could, perhaps unrealistically, indicate that

John was chaste and that he and Isabelle chose not to live together until she was old enough to deliver a baby more safely. Again, though, it seems more believable that he had mistresses and any resultant children are simply lost to history.

Once Isabelle had delivered her child, a couple interesting things happened. One was that on 22 November 1207, John ordered the queen's gold for Isabelle to be managed separately at the exchequer once again. He even assigned a man as keeper of the queen's gold, indicating that it had not been going to her before Henry's birth. We do not know for certain how the gold was accounted for prior to this date, but marginal notes in one of the rolls suggests that it was paid at the Chancery earlier in John's reign.[61] Upon the delivery of the baby boy, John instated, or possibly reinstated, Isabelle's queen's gold. This could indicate it was a reward to her for delivering a son and heir. The allotment of queen's gold could have been a recognition on John's part of her importance as the mother of his heir, or possibly a reward for her fertility, but either way, the receipt of the gold generally indicated that it 'was a gift of a king contented with his wife'.[62] Isabelle's gold appears to have been the first time in her marriage that she had any source of her own income since John kept control of her lands. However, now that he had his legitimate heir, John might have issued orders for the queen's gold to be given to Isabelle so that he no longer had to bother himself with keeping up her income or comfortable standard of living.[63] There is no way to verify this, but if it is true, it is certainly an argument that the royal marriage was not a very affectionate one. Considering that it was also a part of Isabelle's public and political duty as a queen to give the king heirs, her allotment of queen's gold may simply have been in payment for her public services.

From an outsider's point of view, this may seem to have been a relatively happy time for the royal couple, though whether this was actually so is a matter of debate. Immediately prior to the birth of Henry, John was frequently in residence with Isabelle, according to the accounts of his household expenses, which could indicate that he was excited about the imminent birth of his first legitimate child. Marc Morris states that John interrupted an almost endless round of hunting in July and August to make four separate visits to Isabelle, and that he remained at Winchester starting from the later part of September so that he was present at the time of the birth. By many standards, John seems to have been a good father and loved his children; he was also quick to acknowledge his illegitimate children and arranged good positions or marriages for them in adulthood. It stands to reason that he would be even more attentive and caring towards his legitimate children and heir.

It is less certain that he was a good or loving husband, and arguments can and have been made that he was not. The birth of children alone does not imply marital bliss or harmony, only that each knew their duty to provide an heir and other children to use for making political alliances. John forged one such alliance with the Welsh when he wed his eldest and illegitimate daughter, Joanna, to the Welsh king Llywelyn Fawr in 1205. This was also the year when John sent Isabelle to live with Isabella of Gloucester. This move could indicate that, setting aside the question of her youth, political issues prevented him from trying to father an heir on Isabelle at that time and he may have sent her away for her safety. Some scholars have argued that John was devoted to Isabelle because of the existence of Clause 61 of the Magna Carta, sometimes called the security clause, that specifically forbids the barons from harming her or her children by John.[64] Such an inclusion should not automatically be taken to mean that John valued Isabelle so highly.

In fact, Matthew Paris recorded that John hated that particular clause. Paris's chronicle of John and his feelings about Clause 61 should certainly be taken with a grain of salt in light of the considerable animus Paris seemed to feel toward John. Also, there is still debate as to who created Clause 61, with some arguing in favour of Archbishop Stephen Langton being its genesis and others arguing that the various barons came up with it themselves. It seems like including that clause in the Magna Carta was an astute political clause which would help to protect the line of succession and prevent the potential for a violent transition of power. Regardless of who originated the clause, protecting the mother of the king's children could simply be a smart move considering that John's children were at that time all very young and still needed their mother; the royal children of different monarchs should also be protected for similar reasons of succession. It should be noted, however, that John did make arrangements for Isabelle to remain with one of his most trusted servants, Terric the Teuton, who kept her under armed protection in 1214–15 following the degenerating relationship between the king and the barons. Since by that time, Isabelle had given John at least four children, it may be that he genuinely was devoted to her and cared for her well-being, though keeping her safe could just as easily have been for the benefit of his children as for her own protection.

As with most of John's reign, there were many political and military events and conflicts prior to and during the time of his heir's birth. The continuing struggle to reclaim his lost lands on the Continent pressed heavy upon John. But could another source of stress have been the very lack of an heir? If some of his actions seemed unstable to the chroniclers, a possible explanation could be that John was worried that he still had no legitimate heir and his anxiety caused erratic behaviour in other areas of his life. This could be an argument in favour of Isabelle having been at least 12 years when they married and that John was getting impatient for a baby since Isabelle would be entering fertility after a couple years of marriage. John blamed her in at least one chronicle for the loss of his lands, as we have discussed, and Isabelle was quick to retort that she was not the only one who lost out on a good thing. Other chronicles and letters which survive document separate instances where John and Isabelle appear to be engaging in witty banter together; given their similarly volatile temperaments, though, it raises the question of whether they were bantering or arguing. The health of their relationship is important because it could easily have influenced the political events plaguing John's reign; some scholars do believe that John's personal life very much affected the way he ruled. Though it is doubtful most chroniclers of the time would have been too sparing of Isabelle's feelings, given that she was wildly disliked, it is still possible to misread a situation or put a more positive spin on it if the observer were witnessing something that made them uncomfortable. Being present during a royal domestic argument might be one such exceedingly uncomfortable situation. More importantly, perhaps, John was almost 41 when the future Henry III was born. Richard I died at 42, and their other brothers died much younger than that. John's mortality may have been starting to loom over him, for he knew full well from family experience that any number of injuries or illnesses could cause death. The proverbial 'heir and a spare' cannot have been far from his mind, and more so as his marriage progressed without children.

Once Henry was finally born, the birth of John and Isabelle's other children happened in relatively short order. Whether this was because

John had not frequently cohabited with Isabelle prior to 1207 due to her youth or for some other reason, beginning with Henry, the queen produced five children within the span of nine years. One incident worth some exploration which may have impacted John's reign occurred beginning in 1210. In 1210, John made a second, much more productive expedition to Ireland. This was shortly before the birth of his third child by Isabelle, a daughter named Joan, in July of 1210. Joan had been preceded by another son, Richard of Cornwall, in January 1209. There is a four-year gap between the birth of Joan and Isabelle's next child, Isabella. It was during that span of time, on the Irish expedition, that John committed one of the most shocking acts of his reign.

William de Braose, one of the Anglo-Norman lords of John's court, was once a loyal and favoured noble. He held extensive lands and titles in England, Normandy, Wales, Ireland, and the Welsh Marches. He fought for both Richard and John against Philip Augustus and appeared to be one of John's most loyal supporters. De Braose's ascension in the king's favour caused plenty of rancour and jealousy among the nobles. However, his sudden and dramatic fall from grace came as a shock to the other lords of the time. Historian Sydney Painter described John's actions as the biggest mistake he had made in his reign, for it revealed to his barons just how cruel he could be. De Braose himself died in exile in the summer of 1211, but worse was the manner in which his wife, Maud, and their eldest son, William, died. While de Braose fled in exile first to Ireland and then to Wales, Maud and her son were starved to death in the dungeons, possibly beneath Corfe Castle.

There is a lot to unpack with this scenario. The true reasons for de Braose's fall from favour and the horrific manner with which John dealt with the family are not entirely known. John himself claimed it was because of late fees and taxes de Braose owed him from his various estates. However, that is an unsatisfactory reason considering the violence John inflicted upon the family and is far too harsh simply for recovering owed monies. Unless John truly had an unstable mental state, it seems likely that there was a different reason for the way he treated de Braose. It is possible, and has been argued at times, that de Braose knew the true events surrounding the disappearance and assumed murder of John's nephew, Arthur. If de Braose were, for some reason, threatening to disclose his knowledge about Arthur's fate, that could have been a motivation for John to act against him. That does not, though, explain why de Braose would not just reveal what he knew when John sent him into exile.

John's actions could have been explained by a combination of circumstances, but we might consider whether it was related, at least in part, to rumours that Isabelle had taken a lover of her own. Matthew Paris recorded that Isabelle was a temptress, incestuous, and depraved, and that she was not faithful to her husband. As we know, Paris was solidly in the anti-John camp and did not hesitate to disparage him or Isabelle. It was Paris who reported that Isabelle was committing adultery and incest, presumably with her half-brother, Peter of Joigny, who had visited her in 1207 and 1215. John was reputed to have had one of Isabelle's lovers hanged and then suspended over her bed. Such tales seem very far-fetched, particularly given their source. But, as with many myths and tall tales, they may have contained a kernel of truth. If Isabelle had indeed taken a lover, it would have been valid grounds for John to divorce her. Since he did not do so, it seems more likely that the mere accusation was enough to ruin her already poor reputation. Women were, as we know, held to entirely different standards of sexuality than men were. A queen taking a lover would not have been tolerated at the time. Perhaps she enjoyed a flirtation with another man and John became jealous. Perhaps none of these things happened, but some other reason caused an estrangement between John and Isabelle. There need not be a specific reason like adultery to create a rift between married couples, particularly when both were of volatile personalities.

Louise Wilkinson states that a contemporary writer had reported on various, short term spats between John and Isabelle. Moreover, the chronicler Gervase of Canterbury had written that John imprisoned Isabelle at Corfe Castle in 1208 and at Devizes in 1209. Gervase died in 1210 and so his record of John's marriage does not cover any potential disputes between the king and queen in the later years of the reign, but there is precedent to show there had been a couple occasions where Isabelle was kept at a castle. Whether these were actual imprisonments for some reason or simply putting Isabelle in a safe place due to political events is unclear. However, an estrangement and eventual reconciliation that occurred later in their marriage could explain the four-year gap between the birth of Joan in 1210 and the birth of their fourth child, Isabella, in 1214.

During the years in question between 1210 and 1214, it does seem that John and Isabelle spent time in each other's company. They went together to La Rochelle in February 1213, because of a threat of invasion from Philip Augustus into the territories John and Isabelle still held. Considering that they were traveling together, any estrangement they may have had at this time seems to have come around to a reconciliation, at least enough so that they were traveling together. So, it is possible that there was no estrangement caused by adultery or anything else, but rather a string of miscarriages that caused the gap between Joan and Isabella's births. As we know, chronicles are very unlikely to record miscarriages. Sometimes, given medieval understanding of conception and how long it can take for foetal quickening, it could take several months before a woman realised she was pregnant at all. Irregular menses may not have been uncommon as well, depending on a woman's general health and diet. Even a birth followed by the death of an infant or of a young child frequently went unnoticed and unmourned, unimportant to most beyond the immediate family. It seems like miscarriages or a failure to conceive may be the best explanation for the gap between the two royal daughters as much as any potential estrangement between John and Isabelle.

These discussions are relevant to John's reign because they could cause deep anger and resentment, in the case of adultery, or grief and disappointment, in the case of miscarriages. Either of these scenarios could result in an irrational outburst from John if he were as prone to being swayed by his personal life as some have suggested. However, as so often happens, the people we are angry at are often not the ones at whom we strike out. John may have been angry and took out that anger on the de Braouses instead of on his queen. If he had lashed out at Isabelle, it would likely have gone better for him politically since husbands were permitted to discipline their wives. If he was influenced by his personal life and struck out at the de Braoses, though, the other barons would naturally have wondered when John would choose to strike out at them. It was one of the worst mistakes John made during his reign and led to the barons' rebellion which resulted in him being forced to sign the Magna Carta.

It may seem odd to think about a king's private life having a drastic impact upon the way he rules. Perhaps many of us think monarchs should be able to separate their public life from their private. History has shown us, though, that the opposite is at least as often true and that a ruler's private life can have a tremendous influence on their political actions. From King John and Henry VIII to Bill Clinton and Donald Trump, the personal desires and priorities of leaders often overshadow their decision-making processes with regard to politics. Perhaps there are times where this causes something good to happen in the political realm; just as often, though, the effects can be devastating both to the ruler and to the people. That John may have allowed his personal life to influence his reign directly led to the loss of his Continental lands and the signing of the Magna Carta. The impact of that document upon modern governments and politics, though, cannot be overstated. Without John's difficulties, we may have been living in a world without any document like the Magna Carta at all. Whether that is good or not may depend on who one asks.

Chapter 5

Life After John

John's reign is remembered mainly by a few specific events, most notably the forced signing of the Magna Carta. However, many of the events that happened during the years from 1189 to 1216 also had a huge impact upon the women to whom he was married, and conversely they must have influenced John as both a man and a king. Both of John's wives led interesting, sometimes turbulent, lives after their marriage to him ended. However, despite what some may be inclined to think, their lives did not end with their marriage to John, whether it ended because of annulment or widowhood. Isabella of Gloucester had a rough time gaining any meaningful sort of independence even years after their annulment, which is the opposite of what we might expect once she was out of the control of a marriage. Indeed, her life after John seems to have been more interesting than life with him. Isabelle of Angoulême seems to have learned bad lessons concerning how to rule during her marriage to John and she continued to make similar mistakes after his death and during her second marriage. This section will focus more on the ways in which John had a continuing influence on each of his wives.

Isabella of Gloucester

John had his marriage to Isabella of Gloucester annulled in late 1199 or early 1200, just as he came to the throne upon Richard's death. Whether the annulment happened before or after John's coronation is irrelevant; John did not have Isabella crowned with him, signalling from the start of his reign that he had no intention of having her as his queen. Based on the experiences of many other women of the time, one could be forgiven for assuming Isabella would quickly remarry. She was, after all, still one of the greatest heiresses of her day. However, such was not to be the case. Rather than arranging another marriage for her, or allowing her to find one herself, John kept Isabella nearly a prisoner for the next fourteen or fifteen years. Officially, she was given into his wardship, as was the common practice when a great estate was left without a male heir or other suitable guardian. However, wardship was most commonly used for young boys who had not reached their majority yet, or for younger unmarried women, not fully adult women who had been married for many years. The reality of Isabella's situation was that she was still every bit as much in John's control after the annulment as she was when she was married to him. By keeping control of Isabella as he did, John was able to continue to gather the revenue and income from her Gloucester lands for his own use.

Isabella's household was still subsidised by John even after he divorced her and married Isabelle. It is not possible to determine what exactly this arrangement might have meant. Most likely it was just a way for John to keep control of her Gloucester lands and make use of the revenue generated from them rather than having to give them to any other man Isabella may have married later. By retaining control of Isabella's household expenses as his ward, John could make free use of the money from her lands, despite being the sole heir *suo jure* of the Gloucester estates. He also kept her under his wardship, so as to maintain her household expenses. By keeping Isabella as his ward, John was almost imprisoning her, although some chronicles have described it as an 'honourable confinement'.

The rights of wardship worked in John's favour, though, and he used it to secure funds for his treasury. Isabella could, in theory, have protested being kept in wardship, possibly appealing to ecclesiastical authorities for assistance to help her regain the control over her own lands, to help her remarry, or to avoid a new marriage that was not desirable to her. Wardship was originally created so that a lord could protect a minor heir or widow from relatives who would attempt to take their lands, whether through force or killing the heir or other unscrupulous means. Part of the justification for wardship was that minor heirs or women, whether married or not, were unable to give military service to their lord. Since they could not, the thought was that a lord should be able to take the income from lands during wardship for military use. In general, a lord also was supposed to approve any marriages for widows or others under their wardship. This did not always happen, of course, a notable exception being John's own mother Eleanor marrying Henry Plantagenet without the approval of the king of France.

There is no record that indicates Isabella had attempted to remarry or to protest her treatment at John's hands after their marriage was annulled, though, so either any such records did not survive or they never existed in the first place. Given what we know of Isabella, it seems most likely that she simply accepted her fate. However one defines it, Isabella was still under John's control, unable to manage her own lands or income, unable to remarry without his permission, essentially a captive in all the important ways.

In one of the more bizarre events of Isabella's life after John, she was also put in charge of John's new wife, Isabelle of Angoulême, for a couple years in 1205 and 1206 at Marlborough Castle. The reasons behind this arrangement are not at all clear. Certainly, it was not uncommon for very young nobles or queens to be left in the care of other noblewomen, so in that regard there was nothing out of the ordinary. However, it probably would have been an awkward, even uncomfortable situation for Isabella to have been required to care for the new child-bride of her ex-husband. Possibly this arrangement was set up as a way for John to save some money. He gave almost as much to Isabella's household as to Isabelle's; prior to Isabelle being boarded with her, Isabella received around £50 a year for her household, but after Isabelle came to stay with her, that amount increased to around £80. The additional £30 may have been adequate to cover most expenses in a combined household, though it was not a large amount. Taking a brief look at these household expenses may help to shed some light on the reasons for this living arrangement.

On the one hand, some have argued that John was fairly miserly when it came to supporting the women's households. That may well be the case, considering that the total amount for both seems to have been that £80 total, a fairly small sum even by medieval currency. Eighty pounds in 1220 is roughly equivalent to £126,577 today.[1] Granted, it sounds like a decent sum, and inflation would mean that such an amount would go a lot further in the thirteenth century than it would today, but it is still hard to imagine living on that amount when compared against the costs of some items listed below, which are nearly half of this annual amount on which Isabella's household was maintained. On the other hand, John is sometimes viewed as being surprisingly generous. It is true that John was often generous with his own retainers and household knights; Warren states that John may not have been given to extravagance, although he did like many of the finer comforts in life, unlike his famously austere father who was widely known for his plain, unadorned clothes and simple taste in food. The truth seems to be that John was extravagant. He usually had the best food, wine, and clothing, not just for himself but for his wife and retainers. He even insisted that anyone entering service in his household required new clothes, which was paid for out of the king's money. John wanted his servants to be well dressed. He even sent gifts of new tunics and dresses to the wives of his crossbowmen.

Isabelle herself had a large dress allowance and often even received presents of cloth and wine from John. One of John's purchasing agents documented that John had sent for 110 yards of linen, several ermine furs, towels, brass bowls, 9 ½ yards of scarlet fabric, fur gowns, and robes to be delivered to Isabelle for part of her wardrobe. Moreover, the accounts of John's household show the purchase of many varieties of spices like cinnamon and cloves, indicating that he had a preference for flavourful and rich foods. The first purchase order for sugar ever to appear in the accounts of any English king appeared in John's books for 1206.[2] John clearly was not stingy with his own household expenses. He liked his people to look good, and for there to be good food and wine for himself as well as when he held large feasts for the poor, which he always had prepared for Christmas and Easter. The cost of his Christmas feast in 1211, for example, was £32 12s 11d according to the Pipe Rolls for that year. Another roll documents a single robe costing £23, which was a huge sum.[3]

It may be the case, though, that he was generous with himself and his own household, including those in it, because he wanted the appearance of a generous and free-giving liege lord. Having a household filled with servants and knights who were all well kitted out would reflect well on him, but it need not have transferred to generosity in other areas of his life. However, although it seems he was very generous in some ways, it appears that John did not spend a lot of money on the households of either Isabella or Isabelle, so it may be that combining their households saved him some extra funds he felt it unnecessary to spend. Court records indicate that John paid around £80 a year to maintain Isabella's household, plus frequent gifts of cloth and wine. The contributions John made to Isabella's household, which included paying for ladies in waiting and household knights, was nearly equal to what he paid out for his queen's household.

After Isabelle delivered the future Henry III in October of 1207, John's contributions to Isabella of Gloucester's household 'were gradually scaled down, from more than £80 a year to just over £50'.[4] It is possible that he reduced the household income for both of them because, now that Isabelle had given him a son, he felt he had done his part in keeping her comfortable and now was not obligated to do so. If John was maintaining both Isabella's and Isabelle's households, giving Isabelle the queen's gold may have offset the cost he was incurring to maintain her expenses in other ways. Isabella had never received the queen's gold since she was never crowned queen, but Isabelle was, and she was due her own income. In any case, John reduced the expenses given to Isabella of Gloucester's household and was pretty miserly about what he gave to her, but he still continued to maintain her expenses and gave her gifts over the next fourteen or so years. Considering that John retained control of the Gloucester lands after their annulment, Isabella would have been destitute had he not given her money for her household, even if it was a relatively small amount.

It is remotely possible that John put Isabelle under Isabella's care as a sign of trust in his former wife. Especially since John was often traveling or battling in the earlier years of his reign, it made the most sense for him to leave his young queen with a trusted older woman. John trusted almost no one, which was partly what got him in so much trouble with regard to his noblemen. He rarely trusted even someone as famous for his honour as William Marshal. However, while John's marriage to Isabella of Gloucester does not seem to have been a happy one, it must have been at least amicable after the fact, enough so that he felt secure in leaving Isabelle in her care for more than a year. This could be a somewhat unfortunate indication of the sort of personality Isabella had, for she was never documented as complaining or appealing any of her various situations, from wardship to marriage and back to wardship again. She gives us no reason to believe she would have argued about housing her ex-husband's new wife. Perhaps she was a passive and submissive woman, which would certainly have made her a darling of the chroniclers if they had noticed her at all, as they seemed to like women to be quiet. Or perhaps she was politically astute enough to know that appealing or arguing against her situations would get her nowhere and could possibly backfire on her, and so chose to hold her tongue.

It is also possible that John left Isabelle with his first wife because he was known to be petty and mean-spirited, at least if we believe the admittedly biased chroniclers. Some of his actions do seem to support the notion that John was a petty individual. W.L. Warren notes that, 'Unlike Henry and Richard, [John] could never quite bring himself to be generous in victory. Success invariably bred in him an overbearing confidence, and he could not resist the temptation to kick a man when he was down'.[5] Granted, Warren was referring to John's military or political victories, not marital, but the argument can be used for his private life as well. If he wanted to do something humiliating to Isabella, leaving his young new wife with her would have been a good way to do it, though why exactly he would want to treat her so is not documented.

We do not even know what John and Isabella thought of one another when they were married; the historical record is as sparse for their impressions of each other as it is for Isabella's childhood and life before her betrothal to John. Henry II had kept the pair unwed for the better part of a decade so he could use John's marriage as leverage if need be in political machinations against his scheming sons, and Richard then insisted upon the marriage taking place as soon as he came to the throne; considering this, it does not seem likely John and Isabella were all that taken with each other or that she was sorry to see the end of her marriage. That still does not explain what reason he might have had to wish to embarrass her by keeping his new wife under her care except if he had connected her somehow in his mind with some of the more devastating defeats he endured while he was married to her.

However, some chroniclers such as Adam of Eynsham, the biographer of Bishop Hugh of Lincoln, do not deny that 'when ragged beggars and feeble old women accosted [John] on the road, the prince spared time to talk with them and acknowledge their greetings – behaviour by no means common among the domineering nobles of the era'.[6] This account of John is at odds with the general consensus among contemporary chroniclers that he was an immoral, irreligious tyrant. The various chronicles actually agree in one respect – completely inadvertently, of course – and come together to show that John was a complex human being in reality, capable of acting in several different ways simultaneously, and that not everything about him was awful.

Isabella's age, which we discussed previously, may come into play in her life after John. Assuming the year of her birth was somewhere around 1173, she was around 26 years old when John divorced her. She would have still been well within childbearing years. After her marriage to John ended, Isabella waited approximately fifteen years to be allowed to remarry. Robert Patterson states that 'John's remarriage did not essentially alter the status of the Countess of Gloucester or her earldom; the king kept both in custody. Isabel was not to be free for someone else to marry because John had new plans for the earldom'.[7] At the time of their annulment, John was working on various military campaigns to try to save his Continental lands, all of which required funds. Clearly, he was not successful in those endeavours and all his lands on the Continent were lost by 1206.

After their marriage ended, John had given Isabella's lands to her nephew, Amaury, the son of her eldest sister, Mabel, making Amaury the Earl of Gloucester. Years later, in 1213, John had confirmed a will which Isabella had made regarding her estate, which was no doubt written after Amaury's death. At the time, John was trying to raise funds for two separate events: paying for his part of an attack with Otto of Brunswick against Philip Augustus to reclaim Normandy, and he also had plans to reimburse the clergy for their losses during the interdict that had been placed upon his lands. When Amaury died in 1213 without issue, John decided that he would take quick advantage of the opportunity. If he had given the succession of the Gloucester estates to Isabella or her ancestral family at that time, John would not have been able to gain many funds for his military or ecclesiastical debts. Instead, he effectively sold Isabella to Geoffrey de Mandeville, the Earl of Essex, for the astronomical sum of 20,000 marks. That was the biggest fee any heiress in medieval England had ever gotten.[8] The betrothal was announced on 28 January 1214 and the marriage likely took place within a couple weeks of that date. More than a decade after he left her, John was still able to use Isabella for his own purposes.

To return briefly to the idea that perhaps John and Isabella never consummated their marriage, it could have been a possible explanation for the exorbitant fee John charged to Geoffrey de Mandeville if Isabella were still a virgin. Geoffrey may have paid a high price for the dubious honour not only of marrying the king's former wife, but also for her maidenhead. However, even with the vast Gloucester lands, if she was too old to give her new husband an heir, he wouldn't get to keep the earldom of Gloucester if she died before him; rules of inheritance entailed the Gloucester lands to Isabella's nephew, the son of her youngest sister, since she did not have any children of her own who would inherit the lands in her right. As noted earlier, John had given the Gloucester earldom to Isabella's nephew, Amaury, investing him with the title Earl of Gloucester. The Gloucester lands had only reverted back to Isabella when Amaury died in 1213 without any children of his own, at which point she was able to use her comital title again and make use of the lands' revenues herself. This was really the first time she was ever able to act as a true Duchess of Gloucester, since she had been in wardship or married to a man who controlled her lands ever since she was a child. Isabella was once again a wealthy heiress in need of a husband.

Although the exact date of the wedding is not known, she was married to Geoffrey FitzGeoffrey de Mandeville, the second Earl of Essex, in 1214. At the time of her remarriage, she was around 41 years old and her new husband, at around 23 years of age, was almost twenty years her junior. At her presumed age, Isabella was pushing the limits of conception and childbirth, though conceiving and delivering a child in one's forties was not impossible. Though fertility declines beginning around the time a woman is 30 years old, conception can still occur into the forties; however, by the mid-forties, 'fertility has declined so much that getting pregnant naturally is unlikely for most women'.[9] That age is not set in stone, of course, as women have varying degrees of fertility, but it is a good general guideline. Exceptions exist. John's own mother was in her mid-forties at John's birth in 1166, although he would prove to be her final child and possibly the last time she would have conceived anyway.

Eleanor's rebellion with her sons against Henry began in 1177, eleven years after John's birth. Potentially, she and Henry had plenty of time to have another baby or two before they became completely estranged, unless she had passed her window of fertility by then. Given the typical age range for women's fertility, this seems to have been the case. It is possible that Isabella, too, had passed her fertile years by the time she was finally remarried. At any rate, she was probably past the age of safe childbearing by the time she married de Mandeville.

If the earlier year of 1160 for Isabella's birth is accurate, then she would have been closer to her mid-fifties at the time of her marriage to the Earl of Essex, which was almost certainly well past any potential childbearing years. Furthermore, since the Earl of Essex was much younger than she was when they married (he was around 25 at his death in February 1216), Isabella's year of birth may be even more relevant if Geoffrey felt she was simply too old for him and he was uninterested in bedding her. No matter how wealthy she was as an heiress, it would be difficult to envision a young man in his early twenties taking a woman to bed who was almost old enough to be his grandmother and who had no chance of giving him an heir. Even if Isabella were around 41 when she married for the second time, that would have been nearly twice as old as her new husband. Even that slightly smaller age difference would probably have been hard to overcome by many standards, though of course it did not have to be an insurmountable issue. If Isabella were in her early forties, there was still a possibility for children, and thus for de Mandeville's children to inherit the rich Gloucester titles and estates. Such was not to be, though Isabella's alleged barrenness does not automatically need to be the reason.

Geoffrey's first wife, Matilda FitzWalter, also died without children. This may be a simple coincidence. There are many reasons why Matilda might have died young and childless, from an illness or injury to death in childbirth or from a miscarriage; no confirmed cause of death was recorded. There is no record of his first wife's age or exactly when they were married, though it would have been before 1214 since Matilda made it into the historical record in a rather horrifying way in that year.

John had a troubled history with Geoffrey de Mandeville, which should come as no surprise considering that he had troubled histories with most of his barons. It likely began at least as early as 1212 when Geoffrey's father in law, Robert FitzWalter, participated in the Barons' Revolt against John. At that time, John seized FitzWalter's lands and laid waste to two of his castles and forests when FitzWalter fled into exile. Moreover, FitzWalter gave his full-throated support to his then son in law, Geoffrey de Mandeville, when John accused him of killing a servant and threatened to have him hanged. According to the *Histoire des ducs de Normandie*, FitzWalter told John that 'you will see two hundred lanced knights in your land before you hang him!'.[10] FitzWalter did, indeed, bring 200 knights with him when Geoffrey appeared at trial.

John's difficulties with FitzWalter and de Mandeville did not end there, though. Far more troubling is the tale recounted by Matthew Paris and the anonymous chronicler of Bethune. These chroniclers both claim that Matilda FitzWalter was the woman John tried to force into being his mistress somewhere between 1212 and 1214. Matilda, according to the chroniclers, had caught John's fancy. He began a flirtation with her, but all of his advances were rebuffed. Offended by her lack of interest, John allegedly imprisoned Matilda in the Tower, telling her that he would release her if she would just look on him a little more favourably. Imprisoning one's potential love interest may not be the best approach to win a woman's affections.

Unsurprisingly, Matilda still refused and, according to Matthew Paris and Anonymous of Bethune, John sent her either a poisoned egg or a poisoned bracelet. Given John's penchant for starving his prisoners, a famished prisoner eating a poisoned egg seems the most believable part out of the whole outrageous tale. It is easy to imagine, given John's past dealings with the Lady de Braose, that he would have followed a similar plan with Matilda FitzWalter until she was hungry enough to eat anything she was offered. The chronicles must be viewed with scepticism, of course. Whether the death of Matilda is made up as anti-John propaganda or whether it is based in fact, it would not be difficult to understand why de Mandeville would have been inclined to insurrection if this were how his wife was treated at John's hands.

A far more plausible, though certainly less titillating, explanation for Geoffrey's rebellion against John was pure politics; John had banished Geoffrey's father-in-law, Robert FitzWalter, in 1212 for his role in the barons' rebellion. John destroyed the FitzWalter castles and seized control of his lands. Robert made a statement that his rebellion was because John had tried to seduce Matilda, though the financial and political tensions seem a more likely catalyst for his rebellion. Geoffrey would have been more inclined to side with his father-in-law and against the king who had unjustly exiled him and destroyed his lands. Regardless of Matilda's cause of death, this was the atmosphere Isabella of Gloucester entered when she married Geoffrey and his rebellious family. Isabella's marriage to Geoffrey was certainly driven by pure politics. John needed the cash for his various campaigns and debts, so selling the rights to marry Isabella for 20,000 marks was one way to do that. Or rather, coercing Geoffrey de Mandeville to buy the rights to marry Isabella is probably closer to the truth. Some scholars seem to think that de Mandeville made an offer for Isabella's hand of his own volition. Geoffrey de Mandeville 'was prepared to contract for her.'[11] However, considering Isabella's age, the fact that she was probably past childbearing, and the 20,000 mark fee John demanded, it seems unlikely that the earl was eager to wed Isabella. It could well have been a way for John to force punishment upon the FitzWalter and de Mandeville families since the sum he required was staggering. The income from the Gloucester estates was at the time about 800 marks a year, so John was requiring a fee twenty-five times the amount the Gloucester lands would even bring in. This makes Isabella's marriage to de Mandeville appear to be the result of retaliation from John for Geoffrey's role in the barons' rebellion, for she was certainly too old to give Geoffrey an heir and he was effectively bankrupted from having to pay to marry her. Their marriage had to have been arranged and insisted upon by John, and all things considered, it seems unlikely that Geoffrey was an eager bridegroom for Isabella. De Mandeville being a target of John's political retribution also makes sense when we consider that, by being forced to marry a woman too old for childbearing, John was effectively truncating the de Mandeville family line of inheritance. Geoffrey and Isabella both had ample cause for outrage at John.

All the same, it seems that Geoffrey and Isabella actually had a relatively contented marriage, for they regularly issued charters together and Isabella had her own seal. This is the first time there is evidence that she was treated as a noblewoman and wife who was respected, for it does not appear that she had a seal during her marriage to John, and no records exist past 1191/1192 for Isabella and John issuing charters together. The end result, whether stemming from Geoffrey's anger over his first wife's treatment, having extreme financial burdens imposed on them by John, or pure politics, is that Isabella and her new husband became high profile rebels against the king. Geoffrey ended up being one of the twenty-five barons who witnessed the signing of the Magna Carta, along with Robert FitzWalter. It is interesting to think about the influence Isabella may have had on her new husband with regard to joining the rebellion against John. After a decade of marriage plus another fifteen years of being under his wardship, she likely had some unique insight into the man behind the Crown.

Isabella was married to Essex for two years and did not have any children during that time. While Essex was a young man at the time of his death, it seems that no questions have been raised about his own fertility despite his own childlessness. No records exist which show he fathered any illegitimate children, though a lack of documentation does not necessarily mean anything, and his legal wives did not bear him any children. It is always possible that de Mandeville was unable to father children. While we will likely never know whether the second Earl of Essex was infertile or not, it seems irresponsible not to at least consider the possibility, given that neither of his wives apparently conceived during their marriages to him.

Isabella and Geoffrey were married only about two years before his death on 23 February 1216, brought about by injuries sustained in a tournament, just a few months before John's death from dysentery. After both King John and Geoffrey de Mandeville died, Isabella enjoyed her first true taste of freedom. Widows in the Middle Ages were sometimes seen as a wholly different species, often living independently and without being under the authority of any men. Many widows managed their own businesses or estates, and some chose to enter convents, either as a lay person or to take the veil and live as a nun. The remarriage of royal widows as opposed to noble or aristocratic widows was sometimes a little different. Isabella was never crowned, never ennobled, and was not born to royalty. She did not provide John with a royal heir. Her remarriage was therefore one closer to that of a noble widow than royal, despite having been married to a royal.

Typically, for a woman to remarry still required the input and approval from her family. Widows were 'part of a web of familial relationships. The family would regard her remarriage in light of its impact on the position of the family as a whole and thus would feel entitled to involve itself'.[12] A widow often had more say in her remarriage than a woman whose marriage was annulled, but such does not seem to have been the case for Isabella. Since John kept her under his wardship, he acted in the place of any male relatives she had who would have made the arrangements for her future marriage. However, since both John and de Mandeville died within a few months of each other, Isabella appears to have made her own decision in her choice of third husband.

In September of 1217, she married Hubert de Burgh, the 1st Earl of Kent, Chief Justiciar of England, and one-time handler of Arthur of Brittany, John's nephew who had a rival claim to the English throne. As a noble widow, Isabella would have made most of the arrangements of her third marriage on her own, as was expected for both the time and social class, and it seems like she did very well for herself.[13] She managed her lands in Gloucester successfully on her own when the lands came back to her, and she made a very advantageous marriage to Hubert de Burgh, presumably without much input from family or friends, who were few and far between. Sadly, Isabella did not have time to enjoy her third marriage. She wed Hubert in September and died in October, less than two months later.

Isabelle of Angoulême

The primary reason for taking the chronicles of Matthew Paris with a healthy dose of salt is that he was writing some 40 years after John's death. Paris took over as the scribe of St Albans monastery after the death of Roger of Wendover in 1236. In addition to writing well after the death of John, Paris made no attempt to hide his bias against John. In fact, at one point, he wrote about John's death by saying, 'Foul as it is, Hell itself is made fouler by the presence of John,' a truly harsh condemnation. It is a sentiment with which Isabelle of Angoulême may have entirely agreed, though, depending on one's interpretation of her marriage to John and their life together.

Upon the death of John, Isabelle made what may be her only attempt at queenly intercession when she tried to act on behalf of her nine-year-old son, now Henry III. She quickly had him crowned on 28 October 1216 at Gloucester Cathedral, aligning her actions with those of the loyal barons who decided that crowning the young boy would help to reinforce his claim to the throne. Isabelle used her own gold coronet instead of the royal crown, which had been lost in the Wash in October 1216, just before John died, along with most of the rest of his royal treasury and jewels. Upon his deathbed, John had appointed a council of loyal barons to oversee the reclamation of the English throne, which had been claimed by Louis, the son of Philip Augustus, with the aid of rebel barons. Henry III's hasty coronation was made amidst huge political upheaval and contributed in part to his having a second coronation three years later at Westminster Abbey on 17 May 1220. By that time, Isabelle had long since returned to France to take control of her lands in Angoulême, leaving all but one of her children behind in England.

It is difficult, perhaps, for modern audiences to understand why Isabelle would have chosen to abandon four of the five children she had with John. Such was the case, though, and when Isabelle left England for good, she apparently never looked back. Some scholars suggest that abandoning her children was an indication that Isabelle in fact hated John and was quick to divest herself of anything that could remind her of him. Others argue that her actions were simply political and she chose to leave her children because one was now a king under the regency of William Marshal rather than Isabelle herself, and the others were already or would soon be betrothed to the political benefit of their brother the king. The only child Isabelle ever saw much of after she left England was her eldest daughter, Joan, who was betrothed to Hugh X de Lusignan, the son of Isabelle's first fiancé, Hugh le Brun. Young Joan was already living at the court of Hugh X, in accordance with social customs. As is so often the case, the truth is likely somewhere in the middle.

There is plenty of evidence to suggest that John and Isabelle did not have a loving marriage, some of which has been addressed in previous sections. Adding to this idea now is the fact that, after Isabelle gave birth to Henry, John appears to have never mentioned her in any of his correspondence again. He did not even mention her later in his will or in any charters made to the religious institutions to request prayers for her soul, which was a customary and even expected action which would have shown some concern for his queen's welfare. Similarly, Isabelle mentioned John three times in awards to religious houses in exchange for prayers for his soul and then she, too, never mentioned him again in any of her surviving correspondence. Even these three awards struck an indifferent tone, for two of them simply confirmed awards that had already been made by John or Geoffrey fitz Peter, the man who had been in custody of her lands in England. The third was related to a grant of a fair at a monastery in Exeter. All three awards were in England and related specifically to that country, not to any Continental lands, and once Isabelle permanently left the country, none of her charters after that ever referred to John again. In neither John nor Isabelle's charters is there evidence of 'convivial, pious solicitude', asking for prayers or masses to be said for the security of the other's soul.[14] Of course, this does not necessarily mean that John and Isabelle had a miserable marriage or that they did not care for each other. But it does seem odd that neither ever mentioned the other in documents where we might expect to find them, making it fairly easy to assume that theirs truly was a political union and nothing more.

The politics of the time also left no room at all for Isabelle to have any input into raising Henry or his guardianship. She was not listed in John's will in any way, let alone appointed to be one of young Henry's guardians or regents; that role went specifically to William Marshal, the Earl of Pembroke and the peerless Greatest Knight, and Hubert de Burgh, the Earl of Kent and chief justiciar of England. The council, and Marshal and de Burgh in particular, quickly made it clear that they would tolerate no interference by Isabelle in their regency of England during Henry's minority. This could in part have been because, as a woman, Isabelle would have no knowledge of military tactics nor could she have gone to battle on behalf of her son. These military actions were required immediately upon the death of John and coronation of Henry III, since at the time of John's death, Louis the Lion, son of Philip Augustus, was waging an invasion of England and had taken control of London. Despite being around 70 years old, William Marshal was still a brilliant military strategist and strong fighter, and he led the forces against Louis to rout the French from English soil. Isabelle would not have been any help in that military matter, having no practical experience with fighting and having been prevented from participating in council meetings and planning during her marriage to John, when she might have learned about military and diplomatic tactics. Having no authority left to her at all in England, Isabelle returned to Angoulême just a few short months after Henry was crowned.

Given her station in life and her probable expectations, it is very likely that Isabelle would have been disappointed at best at being locked out of her son's life and not allowed to be a co-regent to him. She was not allowed even to be simply the queen mother, a role where she might have been able to give some input into Henry's reign and upbringing. Perhaps she was reflecting upon her own coronation at which she had been anointed with holy oil, the implication being that John intended to let her share power. However, rather than being permitted to continue in a minor role to the young king, Isabelle did not appear to be even an afterthought to the men in charge. Even the biographer of William Marshal did not mention any potential role for her; when Marshal's biographer wrote of the death of King John and the coronation of Henry, he did not indicate that Marshal himself considered her, either, despite being the very image of chivalry toward women. If anyone might have made a token protest on Isabelle's behalf, it probably would have been Marshal. Even though he did not seem to like Isabelle much more than any of his peers did, he probably would have spoken up for her if his honour demanded it. Rather than offering a small bit of consolation to John's widow, Marshal said, instead, that the king's final words were, 'And because I trust in [Marshal's] loyalty above all others, I pray you, let him be my son's protector, his guide and guardian in all matters: without his help and his help alone, he'll never govern these lands of mine'.[15] Later, when Marshal met Henry at Gloucester, the boy king did not ask about his mother, either. He merely welcomed Marshal and said that he entrusts himself fully into his care and asked that Marshal take care of him as a loyal friend. Thus overlooked by both her son and the men now in charge of him and who were, for all intents and purposes, the de facto rulers of England, Isabelle instead turned her attention to her ancestral lands, which she held in her own right.

She arrived back in France in the summer of 1217 and appears to have been busy with the administration and rule of her lands, including possibly seeking assistance from the Church in dealing with Henry's council. She had a few correspondences with Pope Honorius III between 1217 and 1222, some of these exchanges indicating that Isabelle had nearly as tumultuous a relationship with the Church as John once did.

In 1220, Isabelle stirred up scandal once again by remarrying. The new marriage is not in and of itself scandalous since she was highborn, wealthy, and still in her childbearing years. In fact, although laws and customs varied slightly from country to country, most of them were basically the same across Christian Europe and as a result, widows and widowers tended to remarry quickly and repeatedly. Rather, her second marriage highlights how unscrupulous and calculating she may have been, for the man she married was Hugh X de Lusignan, the Count of Le Marche. Not only was he already betrothed to Isabelle's own daughter, Joan, but he was the son of her first fiancé, Hugh le Brun. That she chose to marry him herself, causing her own daughter to be jilted, was viewed by many as deeply unethical. By marrying as she did, Isabelle effectively lived up to the reputation various biased chroniclers had created for her – a scheming, immoral, power-hungry temptress who had no qualms about making questionable decisions if she thought she would get more benefit from it than damage. This may be an unfair assessment of Isabelle, but there is no denying that marrying the fiancé of one's own child truly does smack of underhanded political scheming at best. It is probably this act as much as anything else that has helped to cement Isabelle's tainted reputation throughout history.

Abduction of wealthy heiresses was not legal, but it did occasionally occur, as we have discussed. Sometimes those abductions occurred with the eager cooperation of the woman since it may have been just about the only way for her to pick her own husband. There is, of course, no evidence that Hugh X abducted Isabelle for her second marriage as she essentially was for her marriage to John. However, she was not granted permission to marry Hugh X de Lusignan from the English regency council as was required for dowager queens. It is not clear exactly when Isabelle and Hugh X may have come to an agreement nor whether or not she had been advised regarding the marriage by any of her other family members or peers. Based on her letter to Henry, it seems as though she had attempted to consult with his council on the marriage and received no help from them, so if this is true, she did try to adhere to protocol. Whether the council responded or not, or if they gave her advice she did not wish to hear, is unknown. It does seem that Hugh also discussed the marriage with some close confidants because they recommended that he find another bride not as young as Joan who could give him heirs right away, though whether he referred specifically to Isabelle or whether he was speaking of a hypothetical match to a French lady is also not known.[16] It seems that Isabelle quickly came to understand that her actions were considered to be devious and attempted to smooth over the political disturbance her marriage to Hugh X had caused. Indeed, she would have had to be completely obtuse not to understand that her actions infuriated many of her peers, not the least of whom was her son the king and his council. When word reached Henry that Isabelle had married Hugh X, the council retaliated by confiscating her dower lands in England and ceasing payment of some 3,500 marks a year that King John had established for her pension.

Based on a letter that has survived, after she remarried, Isabelle tried to intercede on her own behalf to her son Henry to only limited success. When her dower lands and pension were seized, she wrote to Henry to ask him to release them as they rightfully belonged to her, John having endowed them to her. Theoretically, she was within her rights to demand her dower lands and pensions, since the Magna Carta forbade kings from arranging the remarriages of noble widows and until the end of the thirteenth century, a widow could pay a fine to be allowed to marry as she wished. Since Henry was still a minor at the time and his council was mostly in charge of England, they could have simply fined Isabelle for remarrying without their permission or approval, though it would be an incredibly steep fine if they tried to use her pension and dower lands for such. She wrote that she only married Hugh because his friends were urging him to set young Joan aside and instead take a bride from the French nobility who was old enough to give him heirs right away. Since Joan was still a young child, only 9 or 10 at the time, it would be several years before she would be able to safely carry and deliver a child. Isabelle's letter to Henry reads:

> Hugh of Lusignan remained alone and without heir in the region of Poitou, and his friends did not permit our daughter to be married to him, because she is so young; but they counseled him to take a wife from whom he might quickly have heirs, and it was suggested that he take a wife in France. If he had done so, all your land in Poitou and Gascony and ours would have been lost.[17]

Hugh X, born in 1183, was still a few years older than Isabelle herself, and nearly thirty years older than Joan. While many aristocratic girls married men as old as their parents or older, such unions would have to wait to produce children, as with Hugh and Joan had they wed.

Moreover, if Hugh had been left to follow his friends' advice and take an older woman of French birth, Henry would have been left with a very difficult battle to retain his greatly reduced land holdings on the Continent, as well as his mother's own lands of Angoulême. What likely would have happened is that Hugh could have easily allied with Philip

Augustus or his son, Louis the Lion, and staged a successful military campaign to take over any lands that had once been a part of the Angevin territories.

This seems to have been Isabelle's thought as well, or at least she presented it to Henry as such: 'But we, seeing the great danger that might emerge from such a marriage – and your counsellors would give us no counsel in this – took said H[ugh], Count of La Marche, as our lord.' By marrying Hugh herself, Isabelle was giving him both a French wife and a woman who was already known to be fertile, to give him heirs quickly, and who would now be unlikely to rebel against her son or his Continental interests. She even went so far as to suggest that she married Hugh for Henry's good more than for her own, writing, 'God knows that we did this more for your advantage than for ours'. She makes it sound as though she married Hugh reluctantly, but that reluctance seems feigned. If she had spent any amount of time in Hugh le Brun's court while she was betrothed to him, she probably would have gotten to know the younger Hugh as well. Marrying a man she knew from her childhood might have seemed a desirable choice to a woman who had been used as a pawn by her parents and John when she was a child.

In fairness, despite the ethical dilemma the marriage posed, Isabelle probably was not wrong with regard to the benefits of her new marriage; in practical terms, Isabelle's marriage to Hugh actually makes a lot more sense than if Joan were to have wed him instead. She may have been able to convince Henry and his council of the practicality of her new marriage had she persisted in her efforts with Henry's council members. However, such circumspect and diplomatic actions did not seem to be in Isabelle's personality.

As mentioned earlier, and somewhat related to her style of conversing, Isabelle is not recorded as having carried out any acts of queenly intercession during her marriage to John. She made attempts on behalf of Henry upon his accession and a couple times for herself after she returned to her homelands. Possibly she tried to intercede for herself or others more than that, but if she did then those letters and related documentation have not survived for us to review today. However, based on the letters we do have, Isabelle really does not seem to have been any good at intercession, despite almost certainly having seen many examples of it being carried out by various people throughout her life. In one of her earliest letters to Henry, dated around 1218 or 1219, she seems to gripe at, and browbeat, Henry more than she appeases him. The letter adheres generally to the standard format, but there is without a doubt a harassing tone to it, as though Isabelle were attempting to guilt Henry into giving her what she seeks.

The letter has a very different feel to it than the letters we have seen from her first mother in law, Eleanor, for example, who knew how to cajole, flatter, and smooth ruffled feathers while still getting her way. In this 1218/1219 letter, Isabelle tells her son that she needs his help to defend her lands, though whether from rebellious tenants, opportunistic neighbours, or avaricious French monarchs is not entirely clear. She does write that she needs Henry to give her the dower funds which should have been hers by right of John, noting that even if she had no money at all, Henry should want to help her since her interests and his coincide: 'Whence it is necessary that you give such fruitful counsel without delay for your land and ours in this region that neither you nor we lose our land for lack of your counsel and help. ... you should still help us by right with your goods, so we might defend our land, since your advantage and honour is involved.'[18] By comparison to Eleanor's letter to John telling him of her actions regarding Amery of Thoarc, Isabelle's letter reads as demanding and shrill.[19] Granted, she was concerned about her lands and how to defend them, but several of Eleanor's letters were written while she was under various stresses and yet they retained a diplomatic and persuasive tone as appropriate. Isabelle's lack of intercessory skills helped to cement her role as a failed queen.

When Isabelle remarried, her new husband held her hereditary lands *jure uxoris*, by right of his wife. He issued charters either alone or with Isabelle and managed most of the defence of their lands, but because Hugh X appears to have been fairly weak willed, often changing allegiance between his stepson, Henry III, and the French king, Louis IX, son of Philip Augustus, the power he had through his marriage to Isabelle was important. Their relationship with the royal house of France was always tempestuous, partly because the lords of the Angoumois were naturally rebellious and partly because the Plantagenet and Capetian houses had a long history of antagonism. Some of that sentiment must have made an impression on Isabelle in the sixteen years of her marriage to John. However, Isabelle herself caused as much damage to the relationship between her own house and the French royals as John ever did.

By disposition a proud woman, Isabelle seems to have had a difficult time adapting to her new station in life. Having had her hopes dashed of holding the regency for Henry, no longer a queen and not even with the authority reserved for the queen mother, Isabelle seems to have become bitter about being merely a countess. She was often conscious of her rank during her first marriage, and to the end of her life she insisted on signing her correspondence as 'queen of England, lady of Ireland, duchess of Normandy, Aquitaine, countess of Anjou and of Angoulême', despite the fact that she was no longer any of those titles beyond Countess of Angoulême and La Marche. Her pride made her fractious at times, easily offended, and matters came to a head in 1241.

As with apparently everything involving the French royal house and those connected with the English court, the relationship between Blanche, the queen of France, and Isabelle was complex. Blanche was King John's niece, the daughter of his sister Eleanor of England. Beginning in 1216, Blanche, not surprisingly, strongly supported the French invasion of England during the First Barons' War because her son Louis claimed rights to the English throne through his relationship with John. That war led to John's death, for he died of dysentery while on campaign against the barons and the invading French. Whether Isabelle cared for John as a husband or not, his death led to her drastic change in social status and fortune. It would be an easy assumption to make that Isabelle blamed Blanche for the change in her status, especially if Isabelle were as volatile and superficial as she appears.

In the mid-1220s and early 1230s, Blanche was regent to her son, Louis, for he was not yet of age when he came to the throne. Unlike John did for Isabelle, Blanche's husband, Louis VIII, had explicitly instructed in his deathbed testament that she would be France's regent. Blanche acted quickly to have Louis knighted and crowned, and then, with the help of Theobald of Champagne and the papal legate, she took charge of military forces and organised several strategic campaigns to put down rebellions by nobles who had refused to recognise Louis's coronation. Blanche was almost single-handedly responsible for preserving the throne for her son, and because of the gratitude he felt for her, she remained highly influential over her son for the rest of her life.

These reasons alone would have been likely to make Isabelle jealous of Blanche, for she probably felt that she should have been allowed to be the regent for her own son in England and she wanted to continue to have influence on him. Adding insult to injury, acting in her role as regent, Blanche twice turned down Henry's offers of marriage to daughters of French nobility; her plan was to prevent Henry from gaining any more land on the Continent through marriage. Undoubtedly this must have felt like a snub to Isabelle, who would want her son to marry a woman who would bring him additional lands.

Later, in 1230, Henry III staged an invasion of France to try to reclaim the Continental lands his father had lost. Isabelle had promised to give him support, but when it came to it, she backed out and Henry did not receive the support he had been counting on to make his invasion successful. Blanche had managed to get Isabelle not to support her son's invasion, possibly through politically strong-arming her, but more likely by offering Isabelle and Hugh some kind of financial pension in exchange for their support. Between Blanche being regent to her young son, denying the betrothals of Henry, and convincing Isabelle not to lend support to her own son, the two women must have had a miasma of dislike and disdain surrounding them when they met in later years. Although Isabelle reconciled with her son, she continued to use the antagonism between the English and French rulers against them.[20]

In 1241, Isabelle and Hugh were summoned to the French court to give their oath of fealty to Alphonse, the brother of Louis IX and newly invested Count of Poitou, as their liege lord. However, when they came before Louis and Alphonse, the French queen mother openly snubbed Isabelle. Already quick to take offence and conscious of her social status, Isabelle was reluctant to cede authority to anyone who she considered to be her social equal; she likely also felt that Alphonse was beneath her status since he was a count and she had been a queen. Infuriated, she and Hugh left Paris and at that point, Isabelle began to actively plot against Louis. Along with their son in law Raymond of Toulouse, they attempted to form an English-supported confederation of rebellious nobles from the southern regions. These nobles, already in revolt when Louis IX acceded to the throne, were unhappy with Blanche's administration of the government and needed little additional reason for insurrection. The major nobles involved in the confederation were Peter Mauclerc, the Duke of Brittany; Theobald, Count of Champagne; and Isabelle's husband, Hugh, Count of La Marche.

The confederation ultimately failed and, by 1244, Hugh had made his peace with and swore allegiance to Louis IX, ending any more potential rebellions from Isabelle herself. Nevertheless, she was not finished with revenge upon the Capets. Later in 1244, two cooks at the French court were arrested and charged with attempting to poison the king. They both confessed and claimed that Isabelle had paid them to kill him. Her arrest was ordered but before she could be taken into custody, she claimed sanctuary at Fontevraud Abbey, where she stayed until her death in 1246.

During her second marriage and even before, when she ruled over Angoulême on her own, Isabelle displayed a general lack of leadership ability. History has not been kind to her, and her actions after John died do not help to improve her reputation. However, it is perhaps unfair to saddle her with a reputation as a terrible or incompetent ruler. While it may be true from a purely objective standpoint, Isabelle's missteps and bad decisions during her tenure as countess of Angoulême may have been partly because she never genuinely learned how to rule when she was married to John. She was a child who seems to have had a good example from her parents on what a successful marriage looked like. But while she was at home with her parents, it is unlikely she would have been given administrative tasks as part of her education at such a young age. Then, once she was married to John, he kept her on a short lead and she had no authority at all during her royal marriage. So, despite the fact that she should have at least observed many examples of feudal lordship, she never seemed to apply them herself. It is sometimes easy to forget, because she was a queen and lived nearly 1,000 years ago, that Isabelle was still a child when John married her. Regardless of her upbringing, social status, and the attendant expectations attached to each, she was still too young to have a genuine understanding of national and global politics, and during her marriage to John, she would have had little to no opportunity to cultivate any diplomatic experience. Age aside, there are many reasons for Isabelle never to have gotten a full grasp of the finer points of ruling.

Isabelle is often discussed in relation to her status as her parents' only child. For all the differences in society and how children were raised, there is nothing to suggest that medieval parents did not love their children every bit as much as modern parents do and it is possible that Count Aymer and Alice of Courtenay could have spoiled their daughter. Certainly, there were spoiled children even in the Middle Ages; the argument can be made that John was one such child, given that he was his father's apparent favourite son. Isabelle might well have been cherished and pampered, and that could be even more likely if she were not just the sole child, but the sole surviving child. If her parents had had other children who died, it would be no surprise if such an event strongly impacted them. Keeping that sole heiress safe, happy, and healthy as much as any parent has the ability to do so would have naturally created a bubble around Isabelle. What penetrated that bubble may not have been the skills or education she would have needed to be an effective queen or ruler. Indeed, there are some authors of historical fiction who have taken this approach to Isabelle's governing abilities.

Beyond the possibility that she was simply spoiled and did not learn what she needed to know, Isabelle also spent many of her formative years when she would have learned about queenly duties with John himself. As we know, John was not considered to be a good ruler himself, although he was an excellent administrator, and Isabelle would never have learned any other way of ruling once she was in John's control. He was her only example from the time she was 12, being generous in assuming she was actually of age when they married. John, for all his deftness with administration and what appears to be a genuine desire to tend to the lower classes, was a Plantagenet and was raised in an ambitious and quarrelsome family, full of back-stabbing and jockeying for power. He learned statesmanship through violence and secret alliances made behind closed doors. While his style absolutely impacted his reign, it also would have made an impression on Isabelle, who could see for herself up close how he ruled. Perhaps monarchs of the Middle Ages had to rule with a more authoritarian style over whole countries, but nobles ruling over their various territories and smaller holdings probably needed a different approach.

Gerald of Wales also seems to have considered this possibility as he discussed the difficulties Angevin rulers had with Ranulph Glanville, who ran the administration of both England and Normandy for a time. Ranulph believed that the Angevins had greater resources than the Capetians but they were too spread out, accounting for their increasingly weakened position. He was probably right to an extent. However, Gerald noted that when the Plantagenets took over England, 'they learned how to rule as monarchs' and that their authoritarianism did not sit well with the Normans' independent nature.[21] This more imperious style of ruling is what Isabelle observed for the sixteen years of her marriage to John. It is logical to believe that she would have been influenced by it and taken it with her when she returned to her native home of Angoulême. If the Plantagenet royal form of leadership chafed the Norman nobles when John came to the throne, it would probably have been even less welcome more than a dozen years later in the form of Isabelle.

Under Richard's reign, the Normans were generally cooperative, assuming that Richard would be successful in his endeavours. He was a strong leader and was able to deflect the waning loyalty of nobles, a strength that was only damaged when he was held in captivity and unable to assert his authority. It was at this time that Norman loyalty started to flag because, as William of Newburgh wrote, the nobility were like sheep without a shepherd to keep them on track. Then, when Richard died, he was replaced by John, to the eventual wrath of the Norman lords. John 'could be tough, he could be ruthless, he could plan a bold manoeuvre, but he never displayed the courage that rouses and inspires'.[22] Richard had bravery in droves, being the only medieval English king to be remembered by his epithet, 'Lionheart'. John, however, does not enjoy such distinction, neither today, nor during his lifetime. In fact, there has been no English king after who has been named John, probably in response to his horrible reputation and a disastrous reign defined by paranoia and a fear of betrayal. Treachery and deceitfulness were part and parcel of John's own childhood, so it makes sense that he might have absorbed those lessons and imparted them, even unknowingly, to Isabelle. By the time she returned to her hereditary lands, ruling by way of distrust must have been second nature given her experience as queen of England.

Marriage to John had a lasting impact on both of the women who called him husband. From preventing remarriage and using their income as his own, to imbuing them with his own version of rule, both of his wives continued to be shaped by their time with him even years later.

Chapter 6

Changing Roles

As with so many figures from history, there is a great deal we do not know and will probably never know, and that is as true for John and his wives as anyone. The written record can be spotty, especially depending on what the topic is under discussion, documents lost or destroyed, and views of the people themselves shift over time. Actions a person takes in life can have lasting influence over a great deal of areas from politics to social expectations to art. In their own time, John and Isabelle of Angoulême were viewed with scorn, derision, and even hatred. Isabella of Gloucester, on the other hand, seems hardly to have been noticed at all. And yet, the reputations of all three of these people have been regarded in various ways when viewed through the lenses of historical time period, politics and current events, and social movement.

As royal wives, and especially queens, women were able to effect changes in society simply by existing in certain social positions. As discussed in the section on the role of queens, such women were able to influence people in ways big and small, from fashion to international politics, peasants to monarchs. Some of the changes brought about by John's wives may have gone unnoticed or are lost to history. Other changes may be obvious or have had an impact on the ways in which women of their status were treated later.

Isabella of Gloucester

Isabella of Gloucester may have changed the roles for the women who came after her in a few ways, though her impact may be more subtle than other women who came after her. Matthew Paris, who never hesitated to malign John or Isabelle of Angoulême, does not mention Isabella in his works, which may be noteworthy. Even though she has been largely overlooked by history, it is possible that Isabella was seen by chroniclers as a proper example of feminine virtue. Her absence from the historical record overall may be an indication that the chroniclers actually approved of her. At the least, they took little notice of her, which they certainly would have done had she behaved in a way that was perceived as inconsistent with her social status. Acting in a manner that was aligned with one's station in life was simply expected and not necessarily something worth noting; had she been the queen, it is most likely that the chronicles would be more forthcoming about how she was viewed by her contemporaries. Perhaps Isabella was, from our modern perspective, quiet and maybe even meek. She did not outwardly protest on either occasion to being held in wardship despite those wardships lasting for many years each. She also did not seem to object to the annulment of her royal marriage and made no appeal to the pope to assist her that we know about. Granted, she may have kept silent because she was happy about the annulment, seeing it as a possible path to freedom. We should not assume that Isabella wanted to stay married, at least not to John. She should be forgiven if she assumed she would be free to live for a time as a wealthy heiress on her own before remarrying; that was the usual practice for women of her status after the end of a marriage.

Absent any documentation about her private thoughts one way or the other, we have no way of knowing for sure what Isabella might have felt about these matters; she may have been thrilled not to have been married to John. The fact that she never said anything can be interpreted as her being an obedient woman, exactly the kind chroniclers seemed to like best. If she had been anything other than obedient, the clerics writing the chronicles would most likely not have passed up the opportunity to denigrate her. Ironically, her very absence in most records says as much about her and how her contemporaries viewed her as anything that might have been written. We can guess that Isabella did her best to be a good wife to John, whether he was with her often or not, and that she was conscious of her social status and acted in a manner appropriate to her station.

If Isabella made any changes for women who came after her, they might have simply been along the lines of providing an example of a patient and virtuous lady. She seems to have handled the various injustices done to her with at least an outward appearance of serenity. Certainly, some of the treatment Isabella received during first marriage gives a preview to how John would later treat his second wife and possibly, on a much less horrifying scale, even his dealing with the de Braose family.

Isabelle of Angoulême

Isabelle of Angoulême might have changed the ways in which queens were viewed far more than Isabella of Gloucester did, though whether she changed roles in a positive way or not is open to debate. Isabelle may have been a factor in why thirteenth-century women in England saw a bit of a rise in the misogyny that appears in writings of the time, or it may be unrelated to her or anything she actually did; however, because medieval society was still based largely on biblical texts, particularly those of Paul and his views on women as subservient to men, and of how the male chroniclers viewed Isabelle specifically, she comes to the generations that have followed with a tarnished reputation.

Chroniclers created a deliberate image of her for their contemporaries which may bear little resemblance to the reality of the woman herself. Matthew Paris, as we have discussed, was especially antagonistic toward her and his writings did nothing to mitigate the negative image she presented for all women. Isabelle's reputation may have suffered greater damage from Paris's writing than it might have if both had lived elsewhere other than England. Prior to the thirteenth century, many ecclesiastical laws varied from region to region and some places were less misogynistic than others according to local tradition. Secular laws, though still influenced by ecclesiastical law, were sometimes quite open to recognizing the agency of queens. In thirteenth-century Castile and Leon, for example, laws written by Alfonso X showed a strong ideal of parity between the king and queen, which gave a significant amount of power to the queen's role.

The Middle Ages were not always as misogynistic as we sometimes think and allowed women to have a say in a variety of issues. For example, in some ways, Eleanor of Provence, the wife of Henry III, appeared to have had fewer freedoms than the queens who came before her. We have touched previously on the fact that she had her queen's gold suspended for a time, and she was not normally allowed direct input into the operations of the government. However, Eleanor of Provence was also able to influence her husband indirectly since he reportedly doted on her; as a result, she was able to convince Henry to appoint many of her family members to prominent positions over English barons, resulting in bitterness and resentment among the various English noble families. There is no evidence that Isabelle had similarly been able to influence

John or his politics in any way during her marriage to him. Probably the biggest difference between Isabelle and Eleanor, though, is that Henry III eventually entrusted the regency of England to his wife in 1253 when he left England to quell some rebellious nobles in Gascony. During that time, Eleanor ruled in her husband's stead, and recent scholarship has shown that she actually called England's very first parliament into session, on Henry's behalf. This is a drastically different experience from Isabelle's, who was not permitted even to oversee her own queen's gold or hereditary lands, despite her vassals swearing an oath of allegiance to her as the countess of Angoulême *suo jure*. Isabelle was never placed in charge of England or Angoulême, nor was she permitted to become regent to her son when John died. While he lived, John kept Isabelle under his total control, and after his death, his barons were not inclined to change her standing in government.

Isabelle might have had an early influence on Henry III as his mother, with regard to his devotion to his patron saint, Edward the Confessor. If we assume that Isabelle fulfilled one of her queenly duties by teaching her children to be religiously devout as part of their childhood education, then it is likely that she introduced to them the importance of St Edward the Confessor as one of England's native saints. This approach to the Confessor would have incorporated Henry's religious education while helping to prepare him to take the throne – a practice which might make even more sense if Isabelle were actually conscientious about her son's role as England's future king. And, certainly, based on her letters that survive, it seems she was, indeed, concerned of her son's education as the future heir to the throne. If Isabelle adhered to the ideals of Marian devotion and used this form of acceptable authority to her advantage to educate her son, her teachings would probably have appealed to Henry, who by many accounts was devout even as a child. It would also fulfil a part of Isabelle's role as a queen and mother, despite having a reputation as being bad at both.

Medieval motherhood gave a woman as queen an identity and voice which could not be ignored or silenced. If Isabelle used her natural authority over Henry as his mother, she would have carried out the most essential role of a queen and at the same time, helped prepare her son for kingship. Whether chroniclers chose to recognise that element of her or not, the fact remains that Isabelle likely did inhabit this space in her role as queen, mother, and woman.

Social Expectations

Beauty and fashion standards are areas that are undeniably influenced by a queen. The queen set the standard for beauty or how a woman is supposed to act. Conversely, though, established social expectations also influenced the queen. This was especially true if she was foreign-born. It seems, too, that if a queen was popular with the citizens, she held more influence over society than she did if she were disliked. For example, in the sixteenth century, Catherine of Aragon was foreign but beloved; Anne Boleyn was English but despised. Isabella was never crowned queen, so she had little opportunity to influence anything in a wider sphere. If she had any sway on social mores or expectations, it would have been in a smaller way, probably confined to her own household and immediate family. We do not know what she looked like or whether she was considered to be beautiful or not, though probably she was at least attractive enough or there could well have been some kind of comment about it in a document somewhere. It is also possible that wealth equals beauty and any physical shortcomings she had were overlooked by the richness of the inheritance that made her one of the most eligible women of her generation. Being the heir to vast lands and fortune probably made up for a great many sins.

Isabelle, on the other hand, was considered to be a rare beauty even in her own lifetime, described as having long blonde hair and blue eyes. As we know, later historians called her the Helen of the Middle Ages, and clearly she must have had some sort of charm about her to tempt John. Regardless of the politics involved in stealing her away from Hugh de Lusignan, it is difficult to believe John would have taken her as a wife had she been entirely unattractive. It stands to reason that Isabelle could have influenced areas such as fashion, for many women of the nobility would want to emulate the queen. We have seen this imitation in many time periods, although later eras had stricter sumptuary laws which prevented some people from wearing certain kinds or colours of clothes; during John's time, though, neither fashion nor sumptuary laws were set in stone.

However, we can conclude that Isabelle was not a well-liked queen even beyond the misogyny of the chroniclers and their thoughts about her, though her lack of popularity may well have been made worse by some of their writings. Her ability to influence even something like fashion might have been stymied because of her deep unpopularity. The nobility viewed her with suspicion, which in turn added fuel to the fire for John, who was suspicious of most of his barons anyway. Her failure to grow into the role of queen could not have helped her cause at all, nor did her lack of opportunity to mitigate any political tensions on her husband's behalf. Because of how Isabelle was viewed by the general population, it helped cement an anti-French sentiment and later resentment among the nobility during the reign of Henry III. Isabelle did not behave in ways that were expected for queens, such as performing intercessions or coronation pardons. When she returned to Angoulême after John died, she did nothing to help shift that negative image in English minds. Instead, she failed to provide her son the help she had promised to win back his father's, uncle's, and grandfather's Continental lands and restore the Angevin empire.

Standards of beauty may seem a trivial thing to focus on, but they are often reflective of various aspects of society. In the Middle Ages, a lot of religious thought was embedded even into things like the concept of beauty. To medieval society, what was inside was supposed to be reflected on the outside. If a person was virtuous and good, then they should also be beautiful or handsome. Conversely, if a person was wicked, then their body should reflect that. This notion is tied to the Great Chain of Being, a philosophical construct that described the hierarchy of all things, with God at the top of the hierarchy, down through the ranks of angels, humans, animals, plants, and minerals at the very bottom. There were various subdivisions as well within each group. For humans, kings were at the top – their place within the hierarchy was assured in part because of the connection between the Great Chain and the divine right of kings – then nobility, gentry, merchants, and peasants. Women were considered to be below, or less noble, than men, but generally speaking, what a person's virtues were like were believed to be reflected through their physical appearance and personality.

It was therefore disconcerting when someone's personality and behaviour were at odds with their physical appearance. Often, an unattractive person was simply ignored unless they were of a social class where that was not an option. Sometimes they were persecuted, reviled, and shunned. It seems that the more unsettling scenario was if a person was physically beautiful and yet acted in a manner that was thought to be inconsistent with their appearance. While there are examples throughout history of handsome men who were reviled for their actions, it was, of course, the women who took the brunt of it. When a woman was considered a beautiful but a terrible person, such as Isabelle of Angoulême, she was generally said to have a demon ancestress or was herself some kind of witch. We saw this when the chroniclers described her as 'more Jezebel than Isabel' and claimed that she had bewitched John. Clearly, a beautiful woman who was wicked must be descended from demons and witches because no other explanation was acceptable to explain her lack of feminine traits. Of course, Isabelle was not a witch, nor was she the ancestor of demons, but her poor reputation throughout the years is a function of this line of thought.

Double Standards

Discussing women who were called Jezebels, witches, or descendants of demons highlights a sizable double standard that existed in medieval society. As we all know, there were different expectations of behaviour for men and women in the Middle Ages, and honestly for every other time period as well. Men in medieval society, especially of the ruling classes, not only were forgiven for having many mistresses, but were practically required to have them. They had to prove their manhood and virility and the best way to do that, in addition to fathering many children, was to have a series of extramarital affairs. Nearly every medieval king did so, including Henry I, Henry II, John, Edward IV – and those were just a very few of the English kings who kept mistresses. It was simply expected that men of a certain rank would have mistresses and illegitimate children; it seems to have made them more manly and a virile king was to be desired. Virility equalled strength and the ability to defend the country. The motivation for kings having affairs was not difficult to understand. As we have discussed previously, the vast majority of marriages for the nobility and royalty were political arrangements in which love was not relevant. Marriage was for politics and dynasty; mistresses were for fun. For women, on the other hand, especially those of noble or royal birth, having a lover outside of marriage was absolutely not tolerated. They, too, had political marriages that were generally loveless, but the difference is that, because of the rules of inheritance and primogeniture, only legitimate children were allowed to inherit titles, lands, and revenues.

Illegitimate children generally did not inherit anything, though there were plenty of children conceived on the wrong side of the sheets who were granted important roles in adulthood; Geoffrey, the archbishop of York, was one such illegitimate child of Henry II who later had incredible power and influence over the political climate of the time. Similarly, Joanna, the illegitimate daughter of John, was married to the Welsh king Llywelyn Iorwerth for political reasons. Other noble or royal illegitimate children have occasionally been legitimised in one way or another and managed to inherit estates and titles or important roles. This was the case with Robert, the 1st Earl of Gloucester, who was given Mabel FitzHamon as his wife. He was made the Earl of Gloucester by his father, Henry I, after the sinking of the White Ship in November 1120, which killed Henry I's only legitimate son. The difference, of course, is that only men were really permitted to acknowledge their illegitimate children or grant them titles or prominent placements in government. Women could not do so if they had a child out of wedlock. If a man acknowledged a child as his own, it was permitted because there was no other way to prove paternity, which is naturally why a woman was not allowed to take a lover other than her husband. No one wanted a bastard to inherit lands or titles that did not belong to him.

Legitimacy was especially important for the throne. A queen had to be impeccable in her behaviour so that there would be no question of the legitimacy of her children. That is why allegations of adultery were so serious; the personal betrayal was perhaps painful but not important compared to the possibility that an heir to the throne may be illegitimate. One only needs to do a quick review of Tudor history to know what a nightmare it was for an heir to be, or thought to be, illegitimate. Isabelle was thus accused of adultery as a way to show that she was unfit to be a queen, though only the chroniclers seemed to make this claim, saying that she had affairs with servants and low-class men, and committing incest with her half-brother. Chroniclers tended to accuse women of adultery first partly because they could hardly accuse the king himself without great risk. It was less risky to accuse the queen.

Accusations of adultery or witchcraft must be viewed with scepticism. Considering how infrequently Isabelle was left on her own, let alone left to manage herself, adultery is not very likely to have happened. However, records indicate that she had been accused of incest, sorcery, and adultery and that the man she was supposedly sleeping with was strangled and hung over her bed. Naturally, we tend to take these kinds of tales with a grain of salt, but they do give at least some indication of the kinds of rumours that were circulating during Isabelle's own lifetime. Matthew Paris proves once more that he loathed both John and Isabelle when he wrote that Robert of London was sent by John to the court of the Muslim emir in Morocco, where Robert told the emir that John was married to a woman who hated him and that she was incestuous, adulterous, and performed sorcery. Interestingly, there is an Irish chronicler who also wrote, in the early 1230s, that Isabelle had an illegitimate child called Piers the Fair with her half-brother Peter de Joigny. Piers supposedly materialised in the county of Cavan, claimed he was the son of the English queen, and was killed in battle fighting in the army of Walter de Lacy. The name Piers could have been significant considering that Piers or Peter was the name of Isabelle's half-brother as well as her grandfather. However, nothing more is known about this tale and it is little more than 'the malicious rumours that the ruled put out about their rulers. Like devotees of the modern tabloid newspapers, there was nothing that so titillated an observer of the Plantagenet court as sexual misdemeanor'.[1] Nevertheless, rumours and accusations of adultery, along with witchcraft and incest, were effective weapons in the arsenal for a king who may wish to annul his marriage and marry anew, and plenty of kings made abundant use of it. Even Eleanor of Aquitaine was not immune from rumours, having been accused of an incestuous relationship with her uncle, Raymond, when she went on crusade with her first husband. This accusation could have been a reason why her marriage to Louis was annulled with relative ease, thus emphasising the power rumour had to change a person's fortune.

Contemporary Views

Looking at the various ways in which Isabella of Gloucester and Isabelle of Angoulême were viewed by their contemporaries can be enlightening. We have already covered many of the views the chroniclers had of each woman, at least as much as they bothered to record anything about them, but those clerics, as we know, were very biased against John and that bias spilled over onto Isabelle in particular. We can guess that Eleanor of Aquitaine at least had no major issues with either of John's wives. She could hardly have objected to his marrying Isabella since doing so gave to John the honour of Gloucester and made him one of the wealthiest lords of England. She does not appear to have objected to John annulling his marriage to Isabella of Gloucester either, so perhaps Eleanor felt that Isabella was in some way not an adequate wife for her son. Neither is she documented as being bothered by or upset about his marrying Isabelle of Angoulême. If she did not approve of him marrying Isabelle, we can assume Eleanor would absolutely have made an objection of some sort, as was the case when she prevented John from leaving his first wife to marry Philip Augustus's sister around 1192. We do not know what other women may have thought about John's wives and it is frankly a little sad that not one friend or family member wrote anything personal about either of them, nor did the women themselves leave any surviving evidence. It makes one wonder if they had any friends at all they could confide in and lean on, or if they were just surrounded by women John had chosen for them with no real bonds of friendship.

While the chroniclers of the time were all men, it is generally unknown what most men outside the Church thought about either of John's wives. Isabella of Gloucester had a single mention in *The History of William Marshal*, and she was unnamed, only referenced as John's wife. Marshal's biographer wrote that the king 'separated from his wife, a divorce which, it's said, proved to do him no favours'.[2] Isabelle of Angoulême has slightly more mentions in *William Marshal* and, to the biographer's credit, he seems to have tried to be neutral in his descriptions of her. He does not blame the girl herself for the loss of John's lands, but rather said, 'I can't explain it in detail, but [John stealing Isabelle from the de Lusignans] was the initial cause of the disastrous war that was to cost the king his land.'[3] Marshal's biographer seems not to have had any issues with Isabelle, at least not that he wrote about openly. It is not likely he would have been too harsh toward either John or Isabelle; William Marshal's son commissioned the biography during the reign of Henry III and, as the head of a major noble house, it would not be prudent to denigrate his monarch's parents.

The biographer did, though, make several references throughout the text about the traits a proper woman should have, including 'wit, generosity, beauty, grace, charm'.[4] The implication is that she did not have all these qualities. Of course, the author was commissioned by Marshal's son and as such, the text was effusive in its praise of that family specifically, not Isabelle. Nevertheless, it seems that the text is slanted in a way that indicates the author felt Isabel de Clare was virtuous in ways no other woman, even a queen could be. Isabelle clearly had beauty, as she was considered a gorgeous woman even in her own lifetime, but we cannot be certain regarding the other traits. Surviving documents indicate she was also witty, though her particular brand of wit may not have been appreciated much in a woman at the time.

Isabelle and John were given to bouts of verbal jousting, though whether this was a cover for arguing or genuinely felt dislike or not is undetermined. In a passage from *Les Histoire des Ducs de Normandie* the author relays one of these verbal jousts. John had sent his mercenaries to rescue Isabelle from being besieged in one of their castles and, upon her return to him, tells her not to worry because he knows a place where she will be safe for ten years. She replies that she thinks he wants to be 'a king checkmated by a square'.[5] This was, apparently, a typical conversational style for Isabelle and it did not make her many friends. Given her apparent abrasiveness as well as the way she was excoriated in the chronicles, there is no reason to think the writers would suddenly reverse course and begin describing her in complimentary terms.

Another way we can get a sense of what Isabelle's contemporaries thought of her is actually by looking at her effigy, which is in Fontevraud Abbey in France. She appears to be depicted as recently dead, wearing a blue robe with a white chemise and red girdle, lying supine and with her hands crossed over her chest, a pose implying the preparation of her body. While this is a common enough pose for effigies, it is notable here because Isabelle's effigy is beside the effigies of Eleanor of Aquitaine and Richard the Lionheart, neither of which implies that the people they depict are dead. Eleanor's effigy shows her alive and reading, and Richard's hands appear to be in motion as if he is orating. Both Eleanor and Richard's effigies depict them in active postures, a contrast to Isabelle's effigy. Eleanor, regardless of what one thought of her, was a vibrant and involved queen and regent, seen as a hands-on administrator. Showing her in death as reading could imply that she was better educated than Isabelle as well as more interested and involved in the events of her day. Richard, of course, was a very active warrior-king. Isabelle, on the other hand, was neither a warrior, nor a hands-on queen. It is perhaps because of her perceived inactivity that her effigy is reflective of the sentiment toward her.

Another curious difference is that Isabelle's effigy is made of wood which has been painted over many times, while those of Eleanor's and Richard's are made from limestone, a more durable material. It is possible that a big enough piece of limestone could not be found, or a stonemason to carve it. It may also simply be that it was intended as a template to show Henry III, who had requested a monument for his mother, and then was left unfinished. That does not seem likely, though, since the limestone used for the other effigies is easier to carve than wood is. In some sense, her wooden effigy could be reflective of Isabelle's reputation and general unpopularity. That it was created with a material that had a higher chance of being lost, burnt, or destroyed over the years than the others, is suggestive of the notion that she may have been a woman that her society wanted to forget.

Chapter 7

Representation in Literature

Viewing historic figures by how they are represented in different time periods can be a very interesting and enlightening exercise. We have seen how the majority of the contemporary or near contemporary chroniclers thought about both John and Isabelle. But what about non-clergy authors? There were still men and women writing tales, songs, plays, poems, and eventually over time, novels. How they chose to portray historical figures can tell us a great deal, not only about how changing times impacted how figures are viewed, but also some of the politics and social issues of the time in which they were writing.

Fiction writing, regardless of the era in which it was created, provides insight to the world surrounding it. It is in this realm, where history meets literature, that different avenues of interpretation take form. The very lack of documentation about certain figures, or the lack of any of their personal writing, may be the bane of professional historians. However, that unknown space, the private conversations in bedrooms or council meetings or birthing chambers, is where authors can explore different possibilities and motives, where many of the figures from history actually come alive. We do not always – or even often – have first-hand accounts of important battles, or of conversations, council sessions, or agreements between groups. We almost never, really, have any record of a person's private thoughts, recorded in a journal or in a letter to a friend. Instead, it falls to the authors, playwrights, composers, poets, and sometimes, yes, chroniclers, to fill in the gaps and create a whole, living person out of the most meagre of substances. Sometimes they miss the mark and contradict what we do know about a figure, but just as often they add a new depth to the person, a different take on a familiar event, or a unique motivation for an action that no one considered before. Authors take what is written in historical record and read between the lines, finding a person who may be entirely different than what we originally thought. By looking at the same elements of history in different literary works, we can begin to see some of the rich diversity that can make history tangible.

Because of the plethora of poems, plays, and novels written throughout the ages about King John and the events of his life, we will focus only on literature from some modern historical fiction authors. However, most eras had their own share of literature about this controversial king as well. The chronicles of Matthew Paris give us the first traditional view of John when Paris describes John's envoy and the Muslim emir of North Africa. This scene describes John as 'a tyrant not a king, a destroyer instead of a governor, crushing his own people and favouring aliens, a lion to his subject but a lamb to foreigners and rebels. ... He himself was envious of many of his barons and kinsfolk, and seduced their more attractive daughters and sisters.'[1] Although this is the sort of person we typically think of when considering John, this interpretation does not always remain constant. Tudor playwrights, for example, focused more on John's defiance of the Church, which aligned with the feuds Henry VIII and Elizabeth I each had with it. Authors of the Romantic Era were more concerned with reviving medievalism and finding beauty in the concepts of feudalism and chivalry. Victorian authors focused largely on morality and fell back to Matthew Paris's point of view, painting John as a wicked and morally bankrupt monarch. It was also during the Victorian era that historian Agnes Strickland first described Isabelle as the Helen of the Middle Ages, showing some overlap with Romanticism. The parallels between Helen and Isabelle make sense when considering that each woman was seen as the cause of great wars and strife.

Modern historical fiction, which for the purposes of this section we will define as literature written after 1940, is still a varied genre that comes with a huge range of interpretations. Authors of the modern period have also taken the gaps in the historical record and run with them, creating some very interesting and diverse approaches to various figures. As in the actual historical record, a lot of modern historical fiction seems to gloss over Isabella of Gloucester, but those that do include her often interpret her in as many different ways as she had names; indeed, in just the handful of modern books discussed below, Isabella of Gloucester is called Isabel, Isabella, Hadwisa, and Avisa. I retain the spelling of Isabella throughout, and Isabelle for John's second wife. There are not a lot of modern works of literature where Isabella plays a prominent role, and she is often used as a prop of some sort, made into whatever device is most useful to the author for advancing their plot. Some of the interpretations of all the main players involved, from Eleanor of Aquitaine to Richard, John, his wives, and even Matilda FitzWalter, are wildly different. Each new iteration of the characters provides new insight into the actual people behind the story; even the most fanciful interpretations are based in some way on real documents.

This section will discuss common elements of John and his wives through their portrayal in modern historical fiction novels. Each author has his or her unique explanation of events. While they all base their novels upon chronicled record, the different nuances between them all are fascinating, proving that history has a life of its own and there is often no one way to interpret the same event or historical figure.

What did they look like?

As with many figures from history, we often lack an accurate or detailed description of what a person looked like. Isabella of Gloucester is completely faceless in the historical record. We do not know if she was tall or short, light or dark, plain or beautiful. The descriptions of Isabelle of Angoulême are a little more detailed, telling us that she was blonde haired and blue eyed and considered a great beauty, but these are still generic descriptions. We do not know her height or build or anything else that gives a clearer picture of her. Historical fiction authors are happy to step in here and fill in those gaps.

In *The Devil and King John*, written by Philip Lindsay in 1951, Isabella of Gloucester is called Hadwisa, which is a variation of her mother's name; confusion in the records indicate that even her contemporaries may have been unclear as to what her name actually was. In this novel, Lindsay depicts her as a 'brown-headed girl, pale, and with huge grey eyes. She came shyly, and looked upon the ground while she curtsied', giving her a physical description that is entirely lacking in the historical record.[2] Though initially Isabella is depicted as shy, she shows some fire and political awareness when, later, she and John discuss the need for her to bear him a son. She ruminates that, once they are wed, she is determined to keep John as hers when he says he will live with her as brother and sister if she desires that, seeing a potential annulment as making her into a 'whore' and that 'her children would inherit England, she'd not be just one of his wenches, nor have her children coupled with the brood that called him father'.[3] Lindsay gives Isabella more of a feisty spirit than we can glean from what the chroniclers wrote of her, where she is essentially faceless and passive through her sheer lack of visibility.

Whereas Isabella of Gloucester was depicted as somewhat shy with brown hair and sharp intelligence, Isabelle of Angoulême is shown to be a spoiled, shallow, unintelligent girl. Lindsay implies that John fell in love with her and used that as his motivation for marrying her rather than for political reasons. 'And then at Lusignan,' writes Lindsay, 'John, for the first time, saw Isabel ... And to John she was so beautiful that, when she curtsied before him, for the moment, he could not even bow to her. He could but gape ... and John knew that statecraft, that all must be forgotten ... so long as he possess this girl'.[4] Lindsay immediately described John as a lecher for his attraction to Isabelle, who he described as just over the threshold of girlhood and barely old enough to wed. Lindsay goes on to describe John's thoughts toward the girl, describing how he dreamed of her naked in bed with her 'half-child's body sunk in cloth ... He would be to her half-lover, half-father'.[5] Lindsay portrays Isabelle as an object, a thing to be owned, and plays on the notion that, by any modern standard, John would be considered a paedophile. Isabelle's own father also seems to view her as an object, for when John approaches Count Aymer about marrying her, Aymer thinks that he cannot see what there was about Isabelle to so attract the king and that she looked too much like her mother for him to consider attractive.

Jean Plaidy's novel, *The Prince of Darkness*, written in 1978, does not mention what Isabella of Gloucester looks like, but portrays Isabelle as having dark hair and eyes that were so blue, they were nearly violet. This is a different description from the historical chronicles, which agree that she had blue eyes but blonde hair. She is almost immediately depicted, too, as being completely vain and self-absorbed, with Isabelle thinking to herself that it was clear to her that she was unusually beautiful and how 'she was always a little shocked if people failed to react to her beauty which they only did on rare occasions'.[6]

Sharon Kay Penman's novel *Here Be Dragons*, written in 1985, introduces her readers to Isabelle initially through the eyes of William Longespée, the Earl of Salisbury, John's bastard half-brother. Though they had heard of Isabelle's beauty, neither Longespée nor John were quite prepared for the reality. Longespée's own wife was of an age with Isabelle, and so he was expecting to see a young girl similar to his wife's looks. Instead, Penman describes Longespée's reaction: 'Will found himself staring, too, at the girl coming toward them. His mouth dropped open; the shock was all the greater because he'd instinctively cast Isabelle in [his wife] Ela's image'.[7] Isabelle was instead described as a vision of beauty, dressed in a turquoise gown, with an oval face. This initial description does not actually give insight to what she looks like, but many other references throughout the novel discuss her blonde hair and eyes that are so blue they were nearly purple.

Elizabeth Chadwick's novel *The Scarlet Lion*, written in 2006, does not describe Isabella of Gloucester's physical appearance, only that John is tired of her. Isabelle of Angoulême, however, is described in detail. She was 'as light and leggy as a young cat. She was just beginning to develop a figure: breasts the size of green apples were outlined by her close-fitting silk gown but her waist and hips were still flat and boyish'.[8] Chadwick goes on to describe Isabelle's golden hair and wide-set blue eyes. Initially, while Isabelle is seen as an undeniably lovely girl, she lacks the intense sexuality of some other descriptions, and the kind innocence of others.

Childlessness

As discussed earlier, there were many reasons why a woman might not have children in the Middle Ages. The lack of children from John's marriage to Isabella of Gloucester as well as the length of time before conception for Isabelle of Angoulême are areas where modern authors have had many different interpretations.

Philip Lindsay's novel assumes Isabella is barren but with a hint that it is through John's negligence as a husband that she has no children. Lindsay writes, '[Isabella] was rarely with him. ... there was no pretence of love between them, and as [Isabella] showed no signs of quickening, John soon despaired of having a child and placed the blame on her, for he had proof uncountable that he could be a father.'[9] Placing the blame on the woman seems an automatic reaction to a lack of children, even though it is clearly not always the case. When John goes to her to tell her he is having their marriage annulled, he tells her he does not want to since he was fond of her, '"but I am king now, and you have given me no child." [She responds], "Perhaps because you did not desire one.'"[10] Isabella's implication is that John does not want a child with her and so found ways to prevent that, whether through abstinence or other means, despite her years of faithful marriage to him.

Lindsay's John insists on delaying Isabelle's motherhood after their marriage. She thinks to herself that she would like a baby because it would be like a living doll, and often asks John to give her a child, though Lindsay does not specify the manner in which John prevents Isabelle from conceiving. John, however, tells her she must wait and that 'he must never forget she was very young, she would understand in time; and, he swore, he would not let her bear a child for many years. On that one point he remained stubborn, on that alone Isabel could not have her way.'[11] In part, John seems concerned for Isabelle's safety, for as we have discussed, pregnancy and childbirth were dangerous enough in medieval Europe, and more so if the mother was still a very young girl. Lindsay's John seems to be concerned with her health and safety first, rather than with producing an heir and a lasting dynasty. Although Isabelle herself initially begs him for children, when she does finally get pregnant, she resents the child and is a most reluctant mother. She hates being pregnant, hates how her body is changing, and hates the foetus growing in her. Lindsay says that Isabelle 'hated the child before it was born, and shuddered whenever she felt it move under her hand when accidentally she touched herself in bed. [She resented] this humiliation that made her the envelope of a ravenous parasite.'[12] She wishes the child would die before its birth and in portraying her emotions thus, Lindsay seems to be setting up the rationale for Isabelle's future abandonment of all but one of her children by John.

Jean Plaidy takes a slightly different approach to Isabella's childlessness. In her novel, it is a deliberate act on John's part that his first wife never gets pregnant, with John considering his options for a new marriage right from the start. He thinks to himself that Isabella is a mild woman who he is tired of 'and he was going to get rid of her. ... Her lands were safe in his keeping and he made no secret of the fact that that was all his marriage was about.'[13] Plaidy highlights here the importance of dynasty and wealth as well as the fact that most noble marriages had nothing to do with love.

The novel expands on Isabella's childlessness: 'She had no children, he had decided to avoid that complication so that when the moment came to cast her off there would be no question of the issue of the so-called marriage.'[14] This rendition of John comes across with a distinctly sinister tone. That dark aspect of John is further displayed in his pleasure at causing pain or fear. When reflecting on the early days of his marriage to Isabella, John remembers how 'he had struck terror into his poor shrinking bride and had thus obtained the only pleasure he ever had from her'.[15] The enjoyment John gets from terrorizing his first wife is shown again when he considers how best to rid himself of her. He considers poisoning her, showing the worst traits that have followed his reputation through the centuries. Once he decides on getting an annulment based on consanguinity, John considers the idea of raping her just to see her terror but decides against it in case she ends up pregnant. After all, 'One of his excuses for ridding himself of her was going to be that she was barren and it was a king's duty to get sons.'[16]

Plaidy similarly writes of the initial delay in children based on Isabelle's extreme youth. John tells Isabelle that he did not give his first wife much chance to have children, but that it will be different with them. He goes on to say, 'But I'd not have you bear children too soon. You are too young for it. I'd not have that perfect little body spoilt.'[17] When Isabelle does become pregnant, she thinks to herself that, though John had not wanted her to ruin her body with pregnancy while she was still so young, 'it may well have been that her extreme youth had prevented her from doing so'.[18]

The sometimes tenuous connection between menstruation and fertility aligns in the novel with the medical discussion on conception laid out by Mary Lewis, Fiona Shapland, and Rebecca Watts. Plaidy's Isabelle takes control of her own fertility, though, by deciding to have a gap in between the births of her third and fourth children. Plaidy writes, 'Having borne three children in the space of three years Isabella felt that she could give herself a rest from childbirth.'[19] This Isabelle, though, wants a break from pregnancy because she considers taking a lover. She knows the dangers of giving an illegitimate child to a king, especially to King John, but finds the excitement worth the risk. Of course, he eventually finds out and Plaidy here uses the chronicled accounts of John hanging the body of her lover over her bed as a plot device.

Sharon Kay Penman's take on the delay in pregnancy factors in a fear that Isabelle may be barren, as Isabella was thought to be. Upon the birth of their first child, John wonders whether Isabelle had ever despaired of conceiving or if she worried that he would put her aside in favour of another woman who would give him children right away. Penman writes that John was, 'gripped by an irrational belief that … God had played a macabre and sardonic jest upon him, giving him as wife and Queen the most beautiful woman he'd ever seen, the most desirable bedmate he'd ever had – only then to make her barren'.[20] No actual cause for Isabelle's childlessness is given in Penman's novel, only that it takes several years for her to conceive. Again, this fits with the possibility that Isabelle was too young to conceive and that her body simply was not yet ready to carry a child.

Elizabeth Chadwick's novel brings a particularly disturbing element to the lack of pregnancies in the first few years of John and Isabelle's marriage. Though it is not explicitly stated, it is implied that John did not wish to risk Isabelle's death in childbirth because of her youth. However, Chadwick's John takes other liberties which disturb William Marshal, who apparently knows of them. The passage reads, 'John had apparently sworn that he would not get her with child until her body was capable of birthing an infant, but such an oath did not prevent him from indulging in debauched and lecherous practices that would not lead to pregnancy'.[21] It is clear that Chadwick's John is molesting and possibly sodomizing his young wife which would, of course, avoid pregnancy, but which is seen as horrific by William Marshal and others. Marshal's wife discusses John and Isabelle with Ida of Norfolk, who says that when Isabelle has given John a son or two that he would leave her alone. Isabelle Marshal realises that Ida is right, and that there will be power and authority for the young queen once she is old enough to realise it, though the thought of having to bed with John is awful enough to negate any kind of compensation. Later, William Marshal witnesses further evidence of John's moral depravity when John shows Isabelle a new jewelled ring. She 'made an admiring sound and slanted John a look compounded of desire for the rings and apprehension at what she would have to do before he would add one to her jewel casket'.[22] Chadwick's interpretation plays upon the worst aspects of John's personality in a way that explains Isabelle's childlessness in both a believable and heart-breaking manner.

Marital bliss?

There is a lot of ground that can be covered when discussing whether or not John and either of his wives cared for one another. A traditional view of John might direct one to believe he cared only for what he could get out of a marriage, what lands and wealth, or what alliances. More romantic interpretations would suggest that John fell in love with his second wife and married her despite the inevitable political fallout that would result. Modern authors have taken both of these interpretations and more in their portrayal of marital bliss with John.

In *The Devil and King John*, it is not clear whether Lindsay's Isabella of Gloucester cares about John himself. However, she does seem to care about her own reputation, as evidenced by her anger when John suggests they live as siblings. She also seems interested in keeping John to herself, and not put her potential children on a level with his many illegitimate children. Isabelle of Angoulême, on the other hand, does not love John, viewing him as an old man and foolish. Lindsay writes that John's second wife 'had no love for John, and little tenderness. He was a big fool who must be petted and teased'.[23] She also continues to love Hugh de Lusignan and fantasises about him while making love to John. Lindsay does not speculate on Isabella of Gloucester's feelings very much beyond implying that she may be more interested in her status and reputation, but Isabella is also depicted as far more pragmatic than her young replacement. This Isabella knows marriage is for dynasty, not love. In Lindsay's novel, John decides on a controlling role in Isabelle's life before they are even married.

As in real life, Lindsay's novel paints a picture of control that is absolute; however, his rendition of John appears to be controlling for Isabelle's own good. He writes, 'He would make certain Isabel did not have such wicked creatures [ladies in waiting and courtiers] in his court when they were married. He would retain her soul's purity.'[24] The John of real life almost certainly did not consider his actions to be for the good of his wife, whether Isabella of Gloucester or Isabelle of Angoulême, but rather based these kinds of decisions on what gave him the most money and power. Lindsay's John carries on with his desire to control Isabelle out of a need to make her love him and feel as obsessive about him as he does her. However, Isabelle herself is shown to be terrified of marrying John and most definitely not in love with him. Upon his return to Angoulême to be wed, John kisses her in greeting and she welcomes him to her home, as is her duty, but she is sobbing. Her fears are written off by her parents as the normal fears of a virgin about to be married to a man she does not know, which appeases John. He reminds himself to be gentle with her because her body and mind are fragile and pliable. Initially, Isabelle is a scared girl who has not yet learned how to be manipulative, though she discovers it quickly enough. Whether she learns manipulation out of self-preservation or greed can be debated, but Lindsay writes it as a combination of both. She learns that John likes to give her things and soon figures out how to make him happy while getting what she wants as well. Lindsay writes, 'She had but to weep, and he was at her feet; she had but to smile, and he danced like a bear. … And life ahead of her seemed a lovely garden in which she would be able to do everything she wanted.'[25] She turns into a spoiled brat by just about any standard, verbally and physically abusing her ladies in waiting if they accidentally pull her hair or do not water her wine exactly as she likes. She is a person wholly absorbed in the superficial and shallow and does not seem to be interested at all in governing, in trying to influence John, or in having any active role as a queen at all. Neither John nor Isabelle seem to truly love one another, though John's obsession with her may seem so to some.

Plaidy does not shy away from bringing to light the many negative traits John reputedly had. It is clear in this novel that Isabella hates and fears John, and that he only gets pleasure from terrorising her. Plaidy picks up on a possible reason Isabella never appealed the annulment of her marriage to John to the pope which was that she wanted to get away from him. When John tells her he is divorcing her, Isabella is careful not to let him see the hope in her eyes in case he changes his mind simply to torment her. She promises John she will not complain to the pope and, in an act of intercession on her own behalf, convinces John that she is satisfied with his decision so that he will be free to father an heir. She tells him, '"you should marry again and perhaps this time you will get heirs." She was thinking: I pity your bride. But relief must necessarily be stronger than her pity.'[26] In this act, she proves herself to have strong potential as a queen since she is able to get away from her hated husband while still making him think it is his idea.

Plaidy's Isabelle of Angoulême initially likes John, and possibly confuses some complex emotions for love. This is made clear when John is thinking to himself about the attractions of power: 'John knew that power was one of the most potent ingredients of sexual attraction with some females. Many an otherwise virtuous woman had surrendered to him because he was the King's son, King's brother and later the King. Rank could be a powerful aphrodisiac.'[27] This seems to be the case for

Isabelle's attraction to John as well, though she does not consider it in quite those terms. She is looking forward to all the jewels and beautiful clothes she may get as a queen, which she feels would be finer than what she would get as the wife of a count. She is portrayed as a superficial person mainly interested in baubles; as long as she get what she wants, Isabelle is content. To her credit, though, Plaidy's Isabelle does truly care for Hugh de Lusignan and thinks him to be honourable even if he is not what she wants and does not marry him.

Penman's Isabella does not care much for John, and their marriage is depicted as neglectful at best. John tells his illegitimate half-brother, William Longespée, that he feels free to seek a new wife that will bring him more lands or a better title, and that 'we neglected to get a papal dispensation for our marriage[.] Nor need your heart bleed for [Isabella], the abandoned wife. We may not agree on much, but we do share a deep and very mutual dislike.'[28] John, in this novel, deliberately appears to not follow up on the papal dispensation required to legitimise his marriage to Isabella. He knows he will want to discard her eventually and quietly plans to make that easier for himself at the right time. Isabelle, though, does love John according to Penman's interpretation. In conversation with William Longespée, Isabelle implores him to help John regarding his lands on the Continent. She confides that she does not actually think John will be unduly troubled by the loss of those lands because he believes an island kingdom is better and easier to protect; however, but he feels duty-bound to try to preserve his brother Richard's empire. She is worried for her husband and wants to help ease his burden but knows she cannot, and so asks Longespée if he knows how to help instead. Penman writes, 'He'd wondered if Isabelle loved his brother, was pleased now to conclude that she did.'[29] Readers could come to the conclusion that Isabelle is concerned for the loss of the Angevin empire and its accompanying riches, but in the context Penman delivers, Isabelle's fear is simply for her husband's happiness.

Chadwick's portrayal of John and Isabella of Gloucester's marriage is utterly business-like. After John's coronation, William Marshal is talking with his wife and she comments that she had not seen John's wife at the coronation feast. Asking him if John did not intend to crown Isabella alongside him, Marshal explains, '"He married [Isabella] for her lands; they've never shared a bed." … Since Isabella and John had only paid lip service to their marriage, [Marshal's wife] could not see her being distraught over an annulment, but she might regret being denied the opportunity to be Queen.'[30] Chadwick moves swiftly away from Isabella of Gloucester to Isabelle of Angoulême. In her interpretation, John considers marrying Isabelle as a purely political move, even though he acknowledges that she is a beautiful girl. He tells William Longespée, 'I cannot afford to let Angoulême and Lusignan unite. Aymer's salivating at the chance to have his daughter crowned Queen of England.'[31] Chadwick's portrayal of the marriage is probably the most realistic of the novels discussed here, showing that dynasty and politics were the primary focus. Anything else was irrelevant.

Witches

Several chroniclers, as we know, mention that John was bewitched by Isabelle of Angoulême. It was the only conclusion they could come to that explained how the king could lie abed with his wife while his empire fell apart around him. Of course, this depiction is unlikely, but John's bad reputation stuck to his young wife as well. The result is a variety of interesting and sometimes strange perspectives in historical fiction.

In *The Devil and King John*, Isabella is depicted as an actual witch who practices the old religion rather than Christianity. Lindsay comments in his author's note that he does not actually believe Isabella practiced witchcraft in any way. Lindsay states that 'only in [Isabella] … have I let my imagination wander far, as we know very little of her beyond her plenitude of names … the studies of Margaret Murray on early Western religion are to me conclusive … the old religion remained strong in Europe for centuries until it degenerated into witchcraft'.[32] Lindsay's use of witchcraft here is an interesting, if highly unlikely, reversal.

In several chronicles, Isabelle of Angoulême is accused of being a witch, of having bewitched John and causing him to lose the Angevin empire. However, in Lindsay's view, Isabella is an actual witch, and nobody suspects it. In part, she is written this way to draw parallels to the old religion that was supplanted in Britain by Christianity. It is a nod to the ancient roots of the land, to the Druids and other pagan religions that flourished before the conversion to Christianity. Or rather, the old religion in this book is depicted as it was imagined to have been in the 1950s, which was when neopaganism began to rise in popularity. Neopaganism and the reality of these pre-Christian religions probably bear very little resemblance to one another, but it is one area where authors are able to fill the gaps in the historical record with topics and ideas that are entertaining and often reflective more of the current events surrounding them than any true historical representation.

In *The Devil and King John*, the nobles do not say Isabelle of Angoulême is a witch or that she put a spell on John. Rather, they place the blame appropriately on John himself, saying that John 'was like a man bewitched' and that 'his friends watched in horror to see the way he fawned on his child-wife … He must wake up, whispered his friends, or his realm would go.'[33] Lindsay goes on to say that John cannot tear himself away from the poison of kissing Isabelle, but even that is turned into a passive, unconscious action on Isabelle's part, not an intentional act. She is merely doing what she is supposed to as his wife. When John reflects on his wife's love for him, he believes that women are far more skilled in lying than any man and that deceit is bred into all women so that they are unable to prevent themselves from it. Lindsay's John is made a mockery of because of his apparent devotion to Isabelle, causing Philip Augustus to lose any respect he had for John and to think of him as weak. Lindsay writes, 'Philip watched amused, delighted at such weakness in one whom he had feared as son of Henry.'[34] While Philip does not seem to believe John was bewitched, he fully believes that John allowed a woman to supplant his kingly instincts, and Philip takes full advantage of that.

Writing Isabella of Gloucester as a witch also links John to witchcraft and his alleged ancestress, Melusine, who, according to legend, married a Plantagenet lord but turned into a demon and flew out the window when her husband saw her bathing and saw that her lower body was a serpent's tail. Other modern authors take up this Angevin legend, from Philippa Gregory to Sharon Kay Penman, using the legend to move plot points forward. In Lindsay's novel, the fact that Isabella is supposed to be a witch and no one but John knows it reads very much like a censure on McCarthyism, a modern-day witch hunt occurring at the time the novel was penned. Although the author, Philip Lindsay, was an Australian who emigrated to Britain, the McCarthy era of American politics influenced a great many things outside the US borders. Though McCarthyism specifically was a product of American politics, a similar anti-communist 'red scare' occurred in other countries, including the United Kingdom with its Cambridge Five spy scandal. Other literary works of the time were written as censures against McCarthyism, most famously *The Crucible* by Arthur Miller.

Additionally, linking John to 'the Old Religion' also connects him to the history of Britain more closely, making him a true British king rather than a king of foreign descent. Lindsay states that, since John was reared by a Devonshire nurse, John was more English than his brothers. 'He had learned with child's pertinacity of secret rites of the old religion and they had become almost sacred in his memory as if he had sucked them with the milk from that English breast.'[35] Later, John reflects on the differences between himself and Richard, who, John thinks, 'did not love this country as he loved it ... Richard would ... but drain gold from England and spend it on foreign slaughter'.[36] Lindsay writes John as a truly English king who loves his country, unlike his brother or any of his other ancestors. The emphasis of Englishness and nationality aligns with both the anti-foreigner sentiments that many English nobles felt toward specifically the French as well as with the McCarthy-era politics in which the novel was written.

Jean Plaidy writes that Isabelle of Angoulême's hold over John is unconscious, not deliberate witchcraft. John tells Aymer, 'She's a little enchantress. I tell you this; she has cast a spell over me.'[37] This line alone gives credence to Plaidy's depiction of John as an unrepentant lecher, playing up his negative traits and setting the expectation that he, and he alone, is responsible for the loss of his lands on the Continent. Any enchantment Isabelle may have over him is purely John's own deviant desires. Count Aymer wonders if John has gone mad, or if his plotting against Hugh de Lusignan for Isabelle's hand is a prelude to madness.[38] Other barons seem to think the same thing at various points. John, though, blames Isabelle for the loss of his lands, saying that she is a witch, keeping him chained to her bed, bewitching him.[39] Plaidy, though, turns this exchange into a joke between lovers and no other characters in the novel seem to think that Isabelle has bewitched the king.

Neither Penman nor Chadwick describe either of John's wives as witches in the novels discussed here. This in itself lends weight to the notion that Isabelle of Angoulême was in no way trying to actively harm John, and her actions were not the cause of the loss of his lands. Both novels are based in a more nuanced, realistic view of events.

Sexuality

The sexuality of both of John's wives is often debated. Whether John and Isabella consummated their marriage, what made him want to set her aside, and whether Isabelle was truly promiscuous are topics which add spice to any novel. Authors of historical fiction naturally have plenty to say about these topics.

Lindsay's novel depicts Isabelle as a natural whore, saying that she instinctively knows all the tricks and practices of love, that John's passion only ignites hers further, and that she is completely uninhibited.[40] The assumption here is that women are naturally tarts, falling back on the virgin/whore dichotomy that is still so often prevalent in society. Isabelle often cajoles John into a good mood or into giving her something she wants by using her body, 'nuzzling him with her wet mouth' or wheedling him 'in baby-fashion'.[41] John is susceptible to this tactic, but it is not clear if this is Lindsay's interpretation of medieval mores or if it is a reflection of a 1950s male fantasy.

Plaidy's Isabelle is depicted as a precociously sexual girl, inordinately interested in sex from a young age. This Isabelle hides and watches the kitchen maids and male servants having sex in the garden and is initially 'greatly astonished by their activities and although she had seen them repeated many times she always liked to watch. This excited her more than anything she knew.'[42] Upon her first betrothal, she tries to convince Hugh de Lusignan to marry her sooner so that she may experience sex for herself. However, this version of Hugh is noble and he, while besotted with his young fiancée, insists on waiting until she is older before he will marry her. Plaidy writes that Isabelle is determined to make Hugh understand that she is young but still ready to be married, and that 'she might be innocent but she was not ignorant. She might be a virgin but she was anxious to cast off that not very exciting state'.[43] It is possible that second-wave feminism played a part in Plaidy's interpretation of Isabelle, for the novel was written in the late 1970s and the social climate permitted a freer approach to sex than previous decades. John is written as a revolting figure who is deeply drawn to rape and young girls. It is his observation, when her first sees Isabelle, that 'girls such as she was needed to be married young', the implication being that if she was not married and bedded soon, she would probably take a lover on her own and thus ruin herself and her family.[44]

Sharon Kay Penman's Isabelle is, like most other depictions, a vision of beauty. She is not, however, overly sexual or sexualised; instead, she is gifted with a natural grace and beauty which does not seem to have gone to her head. When readers are first introduced to Penman's Isabelle, it is from the perspective of William Longespée. Longespée thinks Isabelle will be shy and awkward as his own very young wife was, but instead she is gorgeous and self-assured. Penman writes, 'Will had occasionally seen young girls who'd matured too early, overly ripe and knowing beyond their years. Isabelle d'Angoulême was not one of these, had not forfeited the touching and poignant appeal of innocence. And yet she held the eye of every man in the hall.'[45] There is nothing prurient about how Longespée looks at Isabelle, even though John is as lascivious as he is usually portrayed. After John and Isabelle are betrothed, he steals a moment with her and, emboldened by her apparent approval of his quick kiss, he 'kissed her again, this time as a man would kiss a woman, and found that the entrancing flirt who'd invited such intimacies was but an illusion …, found himself holding a fearful little girl'.[46]

Penman's Isabelle is accomplished in the ways of courtly love, the illusion of flirtation, of give and take, but is utterly inexperienced at and fearful of actual physical love. She has yet to learn the power she can wield over men through sexuality, and in the context Penman creates, it is an appropriate way for her to behave. She does not display any untoward promiscuity as other authors have portrayed, though John remains a lecher. Longespée's attempts to convince John to wait to consummate the marriage fall on deaf ears, even though he reminds John that Count Aymer is trusting him to care for his young daughter. Isabelle has in Longespée a champion she does not realise she may need.

Chadwick's Isabelle initially is a terrified, molested girl. While John and others look at her lustfully, she herself does nothing to encourage them. Her introduction to sex was through degradation at John's hands. It is difficult to imagine this version of Isabelle willingly provoking sexual advances from John or anyone else.

Queenship, ruling, and regency

Isabelle's role within government is always open to debate, and as we know, it is possible that she never made any real effort to act in a queenly manner. John's control over her also probably made any such attempts difficult at best. Some novels portray her as ambitious but stymied, others as utterly uninterested in the various roles of a queen.

In Lindsay's novel, she generally shows an utter lack of interest or intelligence to participate in ruling until Henry is born. Then, she finally realises that his birth helps to secure the throne; moreover, once she recovers from the birth, she begins thinking of her son in terms of the king of England. She often 'wished that John would die, so that she could rule as regent. Otto of Germany, or his cousin, Blanche of Castille, would never get the throne now. It would be her son's, and therefore, hers.'[47] This is the only time in Lindsay's novel that Isabelle demonstrates any real interest in being her son's regent or in ruling at all.

In Plaidy's novel, Isabelle is described as having worked hard in the schoolroom and having a natural aptitude for learning. The novel reads, 'She wanted to be first in everything … she wanted also to be the cleverest. True, she had to work a little harder to achieve that, but she was purposeful and made a point of getting what she wanted.'[48] Her mother, Alice of Courtenay, seems to reinforce her belief that she is better than everyone else, having come from the lineage of French kings. This education and upbringing make Plaidy's Isabelle expect to be treated as an equal, or at least to be given a wife and queen's authority in certain decisions. Little mention is made, though, of her thoughts on being her son's regent after John's death.

Penman's novel, *Here Be Dragons*, shows that Isabelle is distraught to think that after John's death she is of no value despite having been his queen for sixteen years and the mother of the new king. During a conversation between Isabelle and John's illegitimate daughter Joanna, Penman writes, 'I might as well be a deaf-mute for all the heed they pay me. Without John, I count for naught.'[49] Penman's Isabelle is not depicted as shallow or vapid as she is in other novels, but instead is generally kind and confident. Her feelings of uncertainty are out of character for her as written in this novel, and the differences reveal a possible social shift in how women perceived themselves during the time the novel was written. Isabelle continues her discussion with Joanna, saying, 'It never occurred to me – or to anyone else, obviously – that I should act as regent. But I ought to have some say in my son's upbringing, and I have none at all. Nor will I, as long as Chester and Pembroke have the government.'[50] She goes on to tell Joanna that Marshal and the other men governing her son think she is frivolous, vain, and a bad influence on Henry, even though she is not written so in this novel. This version of Isabelle is shown as defeated, deciding that, as painful as it is for her, she will return to her own home and take up the ruling of Angoulême. She reasons that the four children she would be leaving behind in England would be well cared for. The implication is that she will be a good leader over her lands which she holds in her own right.

Chadwick's novel does not discuss Isabelle's thoughts or desires in much detail regarding queenship or regency of her young son. Occasionally, John allows her to help him make a decision, but usually that is so that he can toy with whomever is before him. For example, when John tries to decide whether to allow William Marshal to take his wife and family to visit her kin in Ireland he says, "'Let the Queen decide. … Do I give the Earl of Pembroke leave to go to Ireland, or do I leash him here at court where I can see him?" [Isabelle] shrugged indifferently. "Does it matter whether he goes or stays?" "That's what I'm trying to decide.'"[51] Isabelle ultimately says that Marshal's wife is nice to her, but if she is as difficult as John claims she is, then perhaps it is best for her to be in Ireland. Chadwick shows John appearing to let her make the choice, when it is certain he already made up his mind. He allows Isabelle to contribute in order to belittle Marshal. Later, after John's death, Isabelle is forced to surrender her valuable wardrobe to help pay for Henry's coronation, which she does only after being warned that she can give up her wardrobe or give up her son's chances of being king. Even then she does not display much interest in the matters of ruling, focusing only on her own desires.

Matilda FitzWalter

The treatment of Matilda FitzWalter, the daughter of William FitzWalter and one of the leading barons of John's England, is a story ripe for the picking, particularly for modern authors. While we may never know if it has any basis in fact, the chronicles of the day being rife with bias against John, it sheds light on his reputation throughout the ages as well as giving potential insight into the relationships between John and his wives and the politics behind the barons' rebellion. It is for these reasons I have included a discussion here about Matilda's depiction in literature.

Some authors take it as gospel truth that John did bring about the young woman's death, while others take a more measured approach. Regardless, it is a tale worthy of note because of the wide range of interpretations in modern literature.

In Lindsay's novel, Robert FitzWalter is depicted as a liar, and a stupid one at that, for his lies regarding his daughter Matilda and John are easily disproved. FitzWalter tells Stephen Langton, the archbishop of Canterbury, that John tried to seduce his daughter, Matilda, then married to Geoffrey de Mandeville, but she refuses John's advances. The chronicles of both Matthew Paris and the anonymous chronicler of Bethune indicate that Matilda was murdered, either from eating a poisoned egg or by wearing a poisoned bracelet. However, in Lindsay's interpretation, Matilda dies of unnamed causes after her father has fled to exile in France, an action he took after John allegedly killed Matilda in most other accounts. The entire sordid event is relatively short in this novel, and is used mainly as a catalyst to rationalise the barons' rebellion against John. Although Lindsay's novel does not linger on the event, its use emphasises the ramifications it held for John's political and personal life.

In *The Prince of Darkness*, John's treatment of Matilda is also used as a primary reason for the rebellion, but goes into much more detail than Lindsay's book. In Plaidy's account, John encounters Matilda FitzWalter when he comes to the baron's Castle Bayard. John is suspicious of Isabelle and angry at the thought that she might have a lover, and he sees Matilda as a way for him to distract himself from these thoughts. Deviating from most accounts of the situation, Plaidy makes Matilda an unwed virgin rather than the young wife of Geoffrey de Mandeville. John is once again taken by her youth and makes it clear that he expects FitzWalter to send the girl to his bed. The baron and his wife plan an escape, but John finds out about it and abducts the girl on the road, keeping her in one of his castles.

Although he enjoys raping young girls, John's plan is to convince Matilda to come to him of her own free will so that he can flaunt his conquest in the face of her parents. He visits her often, trying to persuade her that his attention is an honour and that he is doing her a favour for her future married happiness. Eventually, he tires of trying to persuade her and gives the castle's cook 'a hint which was immediately taken'.[52] The cook gives Matilda a poisoned egg, keeping faith with most of the other accounts, and Matilda dies. Plaidy's version of events is memorable in that it highlights the depths of this John's depravity and cruelty. As with many other authors, John's treatment of Matilda, and of other barons' wives and daughters, is used to justify their rebellion against him. John, of course, considers himself the victim, thinking to himself that just because Matilda 'had been a little fool and had held out against her King's advances, her father was now helping to stir up trouble'.[53] Plaidy's John reads very much as a malignant narcissist and the story of Matilda FitzWalter shows his very worst traits in full, which also has the effect of highlighting some actual reasons why the barons rose in rebellion against him.

Penman and Chadwick do not discuss the episode of Matilda FitzWalter in either of their novels discussed in this chapter. Likely this absence is because neither book focuses on John himself, but rather are from the perspective of Joanna, John's illegitimate daughter, and William Marshal, respectively. Neither of these figures were vital to the events surrounding the death of Matilda FitzWalter, though William Marshal's continued loyalty to John even through the signing of the Magna Carta could indicate that John's planned seduction of Matilda was fictitious even in John's own lifetime.

John and the barons

As with many topics related to John, a whole tome can be written just about the specific relationships between John and his barons. Why they revolted, how John reacted, events leading up to Runnymede, all are incredibly complex and outside the scope of almost all but the most specialised history texts. That does not stop authors from taking their own approach, though, and readers are rewarded with a variety of scenarios.

Lindsay's novel is, oddly, the one that seems the most relevant to current times, considering that it is the oldest of those discussed here. Some passages related to John portray him as being almost Trump-like, which is, of course, unintentional as the novel was written well before that unfortunate rise to power, as are the other novels discussed here. Seeing the resemblance between the two men is, of course, a function of reading *The Devil and King John* in the climate of 2016–2020 Trumpian politics and is in itself an example of ways in which literature, whether being created or being read, reflect the social issues of the time. However, Lindsay's King John often blames others for his own actions, gaslights those around him, has an explosive temper bordering on insanity, and so on. He takes no responsibility for his betrayal of Richard, conspiring with Philip Augustus while the Lionheart is held captive. Lindsay writes, 'Yet he could not blame himself. It was others' suspicions that had driven him to this corner.'[54] Further on, John debates the value of oaths with his nephew Arthur, specifically the breaking of oaths, saying, '"And has Philip, do you think, never broken an oath? ... Who knows his cunning better than I, when he strove to turn me against my brother, and did turn that brother, and my other brothers, against our father? All France's fault."'[55] John attempts to gaslight Arthur here, placing all the blame onto Philip Augustus for the various betrayals of him and his family when they were entirely John's choosing. Later, John has an epiphany but still vows vengeance on those he sees as traitors. Lindsay writes, 'The Marshal was right ... Himself had wrought his own destruction ... Traitors everywhere, ay, but he had made traitors, he had jeered at men, have turned them from him ... But he would make them suffer yet. He would come back. He'd take revenge on all.'[56]

Pettiness is another facet of John in many modern literary interpretations. Lindsay implies that John repudiated Isabella in part because she was given to him by Richard, who insisted upon their marriage proceeding after years of betrothal under Henry II's reign. Lindsay writes, 'and now John, Richard made count of Mortain, as their father had intended, and decided that he marry his betrothed, [Isabella] ... Yet all these favours but sharpened John's anger. They were given with such casual generosity, like largesse to a beggar.'[57] Here, John feels belittled and condescended, which is, in the novel, transferred onto Isabella, despite the fact that he likes her and remembers her as one of his childhood playmates. His pettiness and resentment overshadow his potential for happiness with Isabella, and directly impact his relations with his barons.

Plaidy does not spare John in his relationship with his barons. Throughout *The Prince of Darkness*, she sprinkles tidbits and comments made to, by, and about John, underscoring the growing resentment the nobles feel toward him. Matters rapidly become worse for John after he kills his nephew Arthur in a fit of rage. John and a mute manservant dispose of Arthur's body, but the Breton nobles start asking where the young man was. Plaidy writes, '"Where is Arthur?" the Bretons were asking the question and the King of France joined his voice to theirs. They wanted to know why King John's nephew had suddenly disappeared.'[58] His disappearance contributes to the nobles' wavering loyalty to John, especially once Philip Augustus began to inflame their discontent. William Marshal notes that those seneschals who remain loyal to John are often captured by Philip and 'tied to their horses' tails and dragged to prison'.[59]

John bleeds his people dry to raise funds for his wars against Philip, which also takes its toll. He found any cause, no matter how trivial, to fine people to enlarge the treasury, which naturally contributes to anger on all sides. Later, John's treatment of Maude de Braose and her son further shocks and enrages the nobles. Plaidy's John, however, sees their horrific deaths by starvation as a just punishment for their accusations that he killed Arthur; in this novel, it is true, but John does not wish anyone to accuse him of murder or anything else. John sends a guard to the dungeons to see what had happened to Maud and her son. 'They were both dead. The son had died first and in her agony the mother had gnawed at his flesh in the very extremities of starvation. John laughed aloud when he heard. So died proud Matilda! That would be a lesson to any who thought they could accuse him of his nephew's murder.'[60]

His actions toward Matilda FitzWalter further fueled the rebellious tendencies of the barons, and Plaidy writes that FitzWalter uses his considerable influence to take revenge, saying that his hatred becomes his inspiration. John is aware of the growing resentment but is indifferent to it, believing that they must live with it because he is the king. Plaidy crafts him as a brutal and ruthless ruler, which is true to an extent. However, his treatment of the barons, making them give over their wives and daughters for him to bed, and ignoring the indignities he inflicted upon them, lead directly to their rebellion.

Penman's novel homes in more closely on John's relationship specifically with Llywelyn Fawr, to whom John gave his illegitimate daughter Joanna in marriage. Here, John uses Joanna as a way to make an alliance with the rebellious Welsh king, hoping that he will be able to bring Llywelyn to heel. Over the course of the novel, John insults and humiliates Llywelyn, forcing from him some brutal concessions. John takes several sons from Welsh lords as hostages, including Llywelyn's eldest son Gruffydd. The events leading up to the Magna Carta are almost entirely from the Welsh king's point of view, which makes sense given that the 58th clause of the charter specifically orders John to 'give up at once the son of Llywelyn and all the hostages from Wales and the charters that were handed over to [John] as security for peace'.[61] John ordered several Welsh hostages to be hanged despite giving his word that he would not harm them. Even though there was no love lost between the Norman barons and the Welsh, even John's men advise him not to harm the hostages as it went against every rule of medieval warfare. William Longespée in particular is horrified. Penman writes, 'Will had been listening in appalled silence. He'd known this war would be a brutal one, but the cold-blooded killing of helpless hostages, many of them youngsters, far exceeded his worst expectations.'[62] The Welsh lords were not a part of the signing of the Magna Carta, but their treatment at John's hands makes it clear why there was a clause included that explicitly referred to the Welsh hostages.

Elizabeth Chadwick, in *The Scarlet Lion*, depicts John as deeply untrusting towards his barons even from the beginning of his reign. Upon the death of Richard, William Marshal defends John's claim to the throne, as he did in real life, and goes to swear his fealty. John tells him '"Get up. ... Save your oath for England and my coronation. More privileges will follow providing you know where your loyalties lie." William lurched to his feet. ... He wondered how many times he would have to repeat his loyalty to John before John was convinced.'[63] William Marshal was known even in his own lifetime as the noblest of knights and the most loyal. For John to question even Marshal's loyalty did not bode well for how he treated other, less honourable, barons.

A Final Word

While we may lack concrete evidence for many events in the lives of Isabella of Gloucester and Isabelle of Angoulême, making the best effort to understand their life and times can be a rewarding, if sometimes frustrating, experience. We live in an age where we can have instant communication, ease of writing and documenting, and immediate access to the sum total of human knowledge. It can therefore be difficult for us to understand how a woman who was married for ten years to a future king and another woman who was married to a king for sixteen years and the mother of one of England's longest-reigning monarchs can remain almost entirely unknown. That important historical figures can and do still fall through the cracks just shows us that history is never really over.

Students of medieval history live in the hope that one day, a long-lost manuscript will be discovered which sheds light on a previously unknown figure. How amazing it would be to unearth a document detailing the life of Isabella of Gloucester, or the personal diary of Isabelle of Angoulême! It could happen – after all, *The Book of Margery Kempe* was hidden from the 1400s until its discovery in a manor house library in the 1930s. Until then, the best we can do is continue to learn and study what we have in the hopes of better understanding our past, and to see where tomorrow might take us.

Acknowledgments

So much more goes into the writing of a book than just research. When I took this task on, I had never written anything so long in my life. The process was daunting, to say the least, and there was more than one time I wondered if I was up to the task. The fact that I completed this book is because of the support I received from so many people.

First, thank you to my family, especially to my parents, Jacque and Joe Hodges, and Steve and Mary McQuinn. You all never stopped believing I could do this even when I questioned it myself.

Thank you, too, to my best friend, Lynn Coleman. Your ability to make me laugh even when I was frazzled, and to offer suggestions for ways to power through, were always exactly what I needed at exactly the right time.

To Amy Olsen, Becky Anderson, and Ashley Purviance, thank you for being excited for me and being my cheer squad. I am lucky to have you all in my tribe.

To Blaine "Captain" Garfolo, your mentorship, guidance, and friendship over the years have helped me become a better scholar and better person. I am deeply grateful to you.

To my awesome beta readers, Cathy Smith and Anna Wheatley, your help during the writing process was invaluable. When I was simply too close to this to see what I needed to change, you helped guide me back on track. Thank you!

To my editors at Pen & Sword, Danna Messer and Claire Hopkins, thank you for giving me this opportunity and trusting me enough to tackle the topic of John's wives. It was the most difficult and most rewarding challenge I have ever had. Thank you so much for everything!

And most importantly, to my daughter, Shannon. This writing process was as hard for you as it was for me. Thank you so much for being patient with me on the many weekends when I didn't have time to play with you as much as I would have liked. Your sweet nature and exuberance get me through every day and I am so grateful you are my child. I love you.

Notes

Chapter 1: Introduction

1. Monica Brzezinski Potkay and Regula Meyer Evitt, *Minding the Body: Women and Literature in the Middle Ages, 800–1500* (London: Twayne's Women and Literature Series, 1997), 1.
2. Potkay and Evitt, *Minding the Body*, 1.
3. H.G. Richardson, 'The Marriage and Coronation of Isabelle of Angoulême', *The English Historical Review*, 61/ 241 (Sept. 1946), 289-290.

Chapter 2: Childhood and Education

1. Matthew S. Kuefler, '"A Wyred Existence": Attitudes Towards Children in Anglo-Saxon England', *Journal of Social History*, 24/4 (Summer, 1991), 823.
2. Willem Frijhoff, 'Historian's Discovery of Childhood', *Paedagogica Historica*, 48/1 (February 2012), 11.
3. Kuefler, '"A Wyred Existence"', 824.
4. Kuefler, '"A Wyred Existence"', 824.
5. Frijhoff, 'Historian's Discovery of Childhood', 11.
6. Frijhoff, 'Historian's Discovery of Childhood', 12.
7. Frijhoff, 'Historian's Discovery of Childhood', 12.
8. Frijhoff, 'Historian's Discovery of Childhood', 19.
9. Cited in Frijhoff, 'Historian's Discovery of Childhood', 19.
10. Mary Lewis, Fiona Shapland, and Rebecca Watts, 'On the Threshold of Adulthood: A New Approach for the Use of Maturation Indicators to Assess Puberty in Adolescents from Medieval England', *American Journal of Human Biology*, 28 (2016), 48.
11. Lewis, Shapland and Watts, 'On the Threshold of Adulthood', 48.
12. Everett U. Crosby, 'Children of the Middle Ages', Review of *Medieval Children* by Nicholas Orme, *The Virginia Quarterly Review*, 78/4 (Autumn 2002), 770.
13. Frijhoff, 'Historian's Discovery of Childhood', 23.
14. Cited in Nicholas Orme, *Medieval Children* (Yale University Press, 2001), 4.
15. Quoted in Crosby, 'Children of the Middle Ages', 766.
16. Orme, *Medieval Children*, 9-10.
17. Edward E. Gordon, *Centuries of Tutoring: A Perspective on Childhood Education* (PhD Dissertation, Loyola University, 1988), 52.
18. Christine Clark, 'Women's Rights in Early England', *BYU Law Review*, 207/1 (March 1995), 216.
19. *Oxford English Dictionary.* "Neoplatonism, n." *OED Online*, Oxford University Press, March 2021, www.oed.com/view/Entry/126068.

20. Willemien Otten, 'Christianity's Content: (Neo)Platonism in the Middle Ages, Its Theoretical and Theological Appeal', *Numen* 63 (2016), 245.
21. Otten, 'Christianity's Content', 248.
22. Brian D. FitzGerald, 'Medieval Theories of Education: Hugh of St. Victor and John of Salisbury', *Oxford Review of Education*, 36/5 (October 2010), 576.
23. FitzGerald, 'Medieval Theories of Education', 576.
24. FitzGerald, 'Medieval Theories of Education', 580.
25. FitzGerald, 'Medieval Theories of Education', 580.
26. FitzGerald, 'Medieval Theories of Education', 582.
27. Salisbury I.21, 61. John of Salisbury, *The Metalogicon of John of Salisbury: A Twelfth-century Defense of the Verbal and Logical Arts of the Trivium*, translated by D. McGarry (University of California, 1962).
28. FitzGerald, 'Medieval Theories of Education', 583.
29. FitzGerald, 'Medieval Theories of Education', 583.
30. Richard Green, 'Introduction', in Boethius's *The Consolation of Philosophy*, translated by Richard Green (Martino Publishing, 2011), ix.
31. Green, 'Introduction', xi.
32. Green, 'Introduction', xv.
33. Green, 'Introduction', xix.
34. Nicholas Vincent, 'The Great Lost Library of England's Medieval Kings?: Royal Use and Ownership of Books, 1066–1272', in *1000 Years of Royal Books and Manuscripts*, edited by Kathleen Doyle and Scot McKendrick (British Library, 2013), 83.
35. Vincent, 'The Great Lost Library', 85.
36. Sam Riches and Miriam Gill, 'Saints in Medieval Society', *Pilgrims and Pilgrimage*, paragraph 4; www.york.ac.uk/projects/pilgrimage/content/med_saint.html.
37. Katherine J. Lewis, 'Model Girls? Virgin-Martyrs and the Training of Young Women in Late Medieval England', in *Young Medieval Women*, edited by Katherine J. Lewis, Menuge Noël James, and Kim M. Phillips (St. Martins Press, 1999), 27.
38. Katherine Harvey, 'Episcopal Virginity in Medieval England', *Journal of the History of Sexuality*, 26/2 (May, 2017), 274.
39. Harvey, 'Episcopal Virginity', 273.
40. André Vauchez, *Sainthood in the Later Middle Ages* (Cambridge University Press, 1997), 287.
41. Jessica Brewer, 'Etheldreda: Queen, Abbess, Saint', *The Medieval Magazine*, 3/4 (March 2017), 34.
42. Glyn S. Burgess and Keith Busby (eds), 'Introduction', *The Lais of Marie de France* (Penguin Books, 2003), 18.
43. Quoted in Burgess and Busby, 'Introduction', 11.
44. Dolliann Margaret Hurtig, '"I Do, I Do": Medieval Models of Marriage and Choice of Partners in Marie de France's 'Le Fraisne', *The Romanic Review*, 92/4 (2001),363.
45. E. Jane Burns, 'Courtly Love: Who Needs It? Recent Feminist Work in the Medieval French Tradition', *Signs: Journal of Women in Culture and Society*, 27/1 (2001), 26.

46. Burns, 'Courtly Love', 47.
47. Burgess and Busby, 'Introduction', 20.
48. William W. Kibler, 'Introduction', in Chrétien de Troyes, *Arthurian Romances* (Penguin Books, 1991), 2.
49. Burns, 'Courtly Love', 27.
50. Pamela Raabe, 'Chrétien's Lancelot and the Sublimity of Adultery', *University of Toronto Quarterly* 57/2 (1988), 259.
51. Raabe, 'Chrétien's Lancelot and the Sublimity of Adultery', 263.
52. Kibler, 'Introduction', 14.
53. Rabbe, 'Chrétien's Lancelot and the Sublimity of Adultery', 260.
54. David Lyle Jeffrey, 'Courtly Love and Christian Marriage: Chrétien De Troyes, Chaucer, and Henry VIII', *Christianity & Literature*, 59/3 (2010), 516.
55. Rebekah M. Fowler, 'Caritas Begins at Home: Virtue and Domesticity in Chrétien's *Yvain*', *Arthuriana*, 27/1 (2017), 43.
56. Fowler, 'Caritas Begins at Home', 69.
57. Gerhard Herm, *The Celts*, (St. Martin's Press, 1975), 275.
58. Geoffrey of Monmouth, 'Introduction', in *The History of the Kings of Britain*, translated by Lewis Thorpe (Penguin, 1966), 19.
59. Thorpe, 'Introduction', *The History of the Kings of Britain*, 9.
60. Thorpe, 'Introduction', *The History of the Kings of Britain*, 11.
61. Geoffrey of Monmouth, Geoffrey, 'Dedication', *The History of the Kings of Britain*, 51.
62. Thorpe, 'Introduction', *The History of the Kings of Britain*, 15.
63. Thorpe, 'Introduction', *The History of the Kings of Britain*, 18.
64. Thorpe, 'Introduction', *The History of the Kings of Britain*, 28.
65. Greg Molchan, 'Anna and the King(s): Marriage Alliances, Ethnicity, and Succession in the *Historia Regum Britanniae*', *Arthuriana*, 24/1 (2014), 28.
66. Geoffrey of Monmouth, *The History of the Kings of Britain*, 209.

Chapter 3: The Role of Women and Queens

1. János M. Bak, 'Roles and Functions of Queens in Árpádian and Angevin Hungary (1000-1386 A.D.)', in *Medieval Queenship*, edited by John Carmi Parsons (Sutton, 1998), 13.
2. Pauline Stafford, 'The Portrayal of Royal Women in England, Mid-Tenth to Mid-Twelfth Centuries', in Carmi Parsons, *Medieval Queenship*, 143.
3. Jeffrey Richards, *Sex, Dissidence and Damnation: Minority Groups in the Middle Ages* (Barnes and Noble Books, 1990), 23.
4. St. Jerome, *Against Jovianus* (Aeterna Press, 2016), 1545 (Kindle).
5. Gabriel Radle, 'Bishops Blessing the Bridal Bedchamber in the Early Middle Ages: Reconsidering the Western Evidence', *Medium Ævum*, 86/2 (2018), 219.
6. Quoted in Radle, 'Bishops Blessing', 226.
7. Hurtig, '"I Do, I Do"', 373.
8. Margorie Chibnall, 'The Empress Matilda and Her Sons', in *Medieval Mothering*, edited by John Carmi Parsons (Garland Publishing, 1996), 281.
9. Hurtig, '"I Do, I Do"', 364-365.

10. *The History of William Marshal*, translated by Nigel Bryant (Boydell, 2016), 114.
11. *History of William Marshal*, 169.
12. Miriam Shadis, 'Berenguela of Castile's Political Motherhood: The Management of Sexuality, Marriage, and Succession', in Carmi Parsons, *Medieval Mothering*, 339.
13. Quoted in Hurtig, '"I Do, I Do"', 369.
14. *The History of William Marshal*, 213, 218.
15. *The History of William Marshal*, 224.
16. The debate on the happiness or success of either of John's marriages will be discussed in more detail in chapter four.
17. William F. MacLehose,'Nurturing Danger: High Medieval Medicine and the Problem(s) of the Child', in Carmi Parsons, *Medieval Mothering*, 15.
18. Shadis, 'Berenguela of Castile's Political Motherhood', 335.
19. Shadis, 'Berenguela of Castile's Political Motherhood', 367.
20. Monica Green (ed. and trans.), *The Trotula* (University of Pennsylvania Press, 2001), 85.
21. MacLehose, 'Nurturing Danger', 7.
22. MacLehose, 'Nurturing Danger', 5.
23. Green, *The Trotula*, 66.
24. Green, *The Trotula*, 76.
25. Green, *The Trotula*, 76.
26. Zeynep Özcan Dağ and Berna Dilbaz. 'Impact of Obesity on Infertility in Women', *Journal of the Turkish-German Gynecological Association*, 16/2 (2015), paragraph 1. Green, *The Trotula*, 89.
27. Green, *The Trotula*, 89.
28. Green, *The Trotula*, 77, 78.
29. Kristen Geaman, 'Anne of Bohemia and Her Struggle to Conceive', *Social History of Medicine*, 29/2 (May 2016), 226.
30. Orme, *Medieval Children*, 15.
31. Green, *The Trotula*, 77.
32. Green, *The Trotula*, 77, 82.
33. 'Reproductive Health', para. 8, https://www.cdc.gov/reproductivehealth/maternal-mortality/pregnancy-mortality-surveillance-system.htm; 'Maternal Mortality in 2000-2017', https://www.who.int/gho/maternal_health/countries/gbr.pdf?ua=1.
34. Orme, *Medieval Children*, 21.
35. Margaret Cormack, 'Introduction: Approaches to Childbirth in the Middle Ages', *Journal of the History of Sexuality*, 21/2 (2012), 207.
36. Cormack, 'Introduction', 17.
37. Orme, *Medieval Children*, 25.
38. Orme, *Medieval Children*, 17-18.
39. F.J. Erbguth, 'Historical Notes on Botulism, Clostridium botulinum, and the Idea of the Therapeutic Use of the Toxin', *NCBI.NLM.NIH.gov*, 19 March 2004, https://www.ncbi.nlm.nih.gov/pubmed/15027048.
40. Orme, *Medieval Children*, 33.

41. Jacqueline Murray, 'Thinking about Gender: The Diversity of Medieval Perspectives', in *Power of the Weak: Studies on Medieval Women*, edited by Jennifer Carpenter and Sally-Beth MacLean (University of Illinois Press, 1995), 1-2.

42. Murray, 'Thinking about Gender', 6.

43. Quoted in 'Abelard's Answer to Héloïse', *Peter Abelard (1079–1142) and Heloise D'Argenteuil (1090?/1100?–1164): Abelard's Answer to Heloise*, edited by C.D. Warner, et al. (The Library of the World's Best Literature, 1993), 32.

44. Christopher Baswell, 'Heloise', in *The Cambridge Companion to Medieval Women's Writing*, edited by Carolyn Dinshaw and David Wallace (Cambridge University Press, 2003), 163.

45. Mechthild von Magdeburg, *The Flowing Light of the Godhead*, edited by Frank Tobin (Paulist Press, 1998), 79.

46. Caroline Walker Bynum, *Jesus as Mother: Studies in the Spirituality of the High Middle Ages* (University of California Press, 1982), 242.

47. John Carmi Parsons, 'The Queen's Intercession in Thirteenth-Century England', in Carpenter and MacLean, *Power of the Weak*, 147.

48. Dylan Elliott, 'Marriage', in *The Cambridge Companion to Medieval Women's Writing*, edited by Carolyn Dinshaw and David Wallace (Cambridge University Press, 2003), 45.

49. Kristen Geaman, 'Beyond Good Queen Anne: Anne of Bohemia, Patronage and Politics', in *Medieval Elite Women and the Exercise of Power, 1100–1400*, edited by Heather J. Tanner (Palgrave Macmillan, 2019), 78.

50. Carmi Parsons, 'The Queen's Intercession', 149.

51. Carmi Parsons, 'The Queen's Intercession', 149-150.

52. Elizabeth Norton, *She-Wolves: The Notorious Queens of Medieval England* (The History Press, 2010).

53. Kristen Geaman 'Queen's Gold and Intercession: The Case of Eleanor of Aquitaine', *Medieval Feminist Forum*, 46/2 (2010), 11.

54. Geaman, 'Queen's Gold', 19.

55. Geaman, 'Queen's Gold' 19.

56. Stafford, 'Portrayal of Royal Women', 148.

57. Lois Huneycutt, 'Intercession and the High-Medieval Queen: The Esther Topos', in Carpenter and MacLean, *Power of the Weak*, 126.

58. Carmi Parsons, 'The Queen's Intercession', 150.

59. Stafford, 'Portrayal of Royal Women', 148.

60. Gillian Adler, 'Female Intercession and the Shaping of Male Heroism in the *Roman d'Enéas* and *Le Chevalier Au Lion*', *Medieval Feminist Forum*, 49/2 (2014), 76.

61. William Chester Jordan, 'Isabelle D'Angoulême, By the Grace of God, Queen', *Revue Belge De Philologie Et D'histoire*, 69/4 (1991), 826.

62. Carmi Parsons, 'The Queen's Intercession', 153.

63. Carmi Parsons, 'The Queen's Intercession', 104.

64. Carmi Parsons, 'The Queen's Intercession', 155.

65. Rachel F. Stapleton, 'Motherly Devotion and Fatherly Obligation: Eleanor of Aquitaine's Letters to Pope Celestine III', *Medieval Feminist Forum*, 48/1 (2012), 101.
66. Stapleton, 'Motherly Devotion', 103.
67. Alison Cotes, '"All of Them Saints of God ..."', *Social Alternatives*, 7/3 (1988), 11.
68. Berfu Duranta, 'Throne of Wisdom Sculptures', *Khan Academy*, para. 6.
69. Ps. 44:10; III Reg. 2:19; Carmi Parsons,'The Queen's Intercession', 156.
70. Douay Rheims.
71. Catherine Keene, 'Read Her like a Book: Female Patronage as *Imitatio Mariae*', *Magistra*, 24/1 (Summer 2018), 29.
72. Is. 8:1.
73. Keene, 'Read Her like a Book', 37.
74. Keene, 'Read Her like a Book', 38.
75. Carmi Parsons, 'The Queen's Intercession', 159.
76. Huneycutt,'Intercession', 127.
77. Esth. chapter 1-7.
78. Huneycutt, 'Intercession', 131.
79. Huneycutt, 'Intercession', 138.
80. Fiona Harris Stoertz, 'Young Women in France and England, 1050–1300', *Journal of Women's History*, 12/4 (Winter, 2001), 25.
81. John Carmi Parsons, 'Introduction: Family, Sex, and Power: The Rhythms of Medieval Queenship' in Carmi Parsons, *Medieval Queenship*, 3.
82. Carmi Parsons, 'Family, Sex, and Power', 4.
83. James A. Brundage, *Law, Sex, and Christian Society in Medieval Europe* (University of Chicago Press, 1987), 468-469.
84. Rebecca Slitt, 'The Boundaries of Women's Power: Gender and the Discourse of Political Friendship in Twelfth-Century England', *Gender & History*, 24/1 (2012), 1.
85. Julian P. Haseldine, 'Friendship Networks in Medieval Europe: New Models of a Political Relationship', *AMITY: The Journal of Friendship Studies* 1 (2013), 70.
86. Quoted in Alexandra Verini, 'Medieval Models of Female Friendship in Christine de Pizan's *The Book of the City of Ladies* and Margery Kempe's *The Book of Margery Kempe*', *Feminist Studies*, 2016, 42/2, 365.
87. Slitt, 'Boundaries of Women's Power', 1.
88. Slitt, 'Boundaries of Women's Power', 4.
89. Quoted in Slitt, 'Boundaries of Women's Power', 5.
90. Slitt, 'Boundaries of Women's Power', 5.
91. 'A Letter from Isabel of Angoulême (1220)', *Epistolae* (2014).

Chapter 4: John Plantagenet and Married Life

1. Vincent, 'John's Jezebel', 166.
2. Turner, *King John*, 166.
3. Fiona Shapland, Mary Lewis, and Rebecca Watts, 'Lives and Deaths of Young Medieval Women', *Medieval Archaeology*, 59 (2015), 282.

4. Lewis, Shapland and Watts, 'On the Threshold of Adulthood, 53.
5. Lewis, Shapland and Watts, 'On the Threshold of Adulthood', 54.
6. Alan Lloyd, *The Maligned Monarch* (Doubleday, 1972), 99.
7. Sharon Bennett Connolly, *Ladies of Magna Carta: Women of Influence in Thirteenth Century England* (Pen and Sword History, 2020), Kindle location, 2868-2871.
8. Lloyd, *The Maligned Monarch*, 99.
9. Warren, *King John*, 66.
10. Quoted in David d'Avray, *Papacy, Monarchy and Marriage 860–1600* (Cambridge University Press, 2015), 74.
11. Quoted in d'Avray, *Papacy, Monarchy and Marriage*, 74.
12. Samuel H. Dresner, 'Barren Rachel', *Judaism* 40/4 (Fall 1991), 443.
13. Warren, *King John*, 43.
14. Robert B. Patterson, editor, 'Editorial Introduction', in *Earldom of Gloucester Charters* (Clarendon Press, 1973), 6.
15. Vincent, 'John's Jezebel', 193.
16. Morris, *King John*, 74.
17. Patterson, *Earldom of Gloucester Charters*, 150, footnote to charter 163.
18. Kim Phillips, 'Maidenhood as the Perfect Age of Woman's Life', in *Young Medieval Women*, edited by Katherine J. Lewis, Noel James Mengue, and Kim M. Phillips (St. Martin's Press, 1999), 1.
19. H.G. Richardson, 'The Marriage and Coronation of Isabelle of Angoulême', *The English Historical Review*, 61/241 (Sept 1946), 294.
20. *The History of William Marshal*, 136.
21. Warren, *King John*, 76.
22. Warren, *King John*, 94.
23. Warren, *King John*, 46.
24. Vincent, 'John's Jezebel', 173.
25. Vincent, 'John's Jezebel', 167.
26. Lloyd, *The Maligned Monarch*, 102.
27. Richardson, 'Marriage and Coronation', 300.
28. Richardson, 'Marriage and Coronation', 300.
29. Richardson, 'Marriage and Coronation', 298.
30. Richardson, 'Marriage and Coronation', 299.
31. Jordan, 'Isabelle D'Angoulême', 824-825.
32. *The History of William Marshal*, 152-153.
33. Richardson, 'Marriage and Coronation', 303.
34. Richardson, 'Marriage and Coronation', 302.
35. Quoted in Richardson, 'Marriage and Coronation', 299.
36. Vincent, 'John's Jezebel', 174.
37. Richardson, 'Marriage and Coronation', 306.
38. Vincent, 'John's Jezebel', 175.
39. Vincent, 'John's Jezebel', 69.
40. Gratian, *The Decretum*, translated by John T. Noonan (Catholic University of America, 1967), ch. 47.
41. Gratian, *Decretum*, case 29, question 1.

42. Gratian, *Decretum*, case 32, question 3, c 1.
43. Sara M. Butler, "'I will never consent to be wedded with you!'": Coerced Marriage in the Courts of Medieval England', *Canadian Journal of History* (2004), 256.
44. Howden, as quoted in Jordan, 'Isabelle D'Angoulême', 826.
45. Louise J. Wilkinson, 'Maternal Abandonment and Surrogate Caregivers: Isabella of Angoulême and her Children by King John', in *Virtuous or Villainess? The Image of the Royal Mother from the Early Medieval to the Early Modern Era*, edited by Carey Fleiner and Elena Woodacre (Palgrave Macmillan, 2016), 104.
46. Wilkinson, 'Maternal Abandonment', 104.
47. Richardson, 'Marriage and Coronation', 308.
48. Vincent, 'John's Jezebel', 178.
49. *The History of William Marshal*, 63.
50. Vincent, 'John's Jezebel', 182.
51. Vincent, 'John's Jezebel', 185.
52. Vincent, 'John's Jezebel', 183.
53. Warren, *King John* , 87.
54. Wilkinson, 'Maternal Abandonment', 103.
55. Warren, *King John*, 88.
56. Quoted in Jordan, 'Isabelle D'Angoulême', 829.
57. 'Letter from Eleanor of Aquitaine (1200)', *Epistolae* (2014).
58. Turner, *King John*, 23.
59. Nicholas Vincent, 'King John: Medieval Monster', *History Extra* (August 2019), para. 15.
60. Morris, *King John*, 137.
61. Geaman, 'Queen's Gold', 21-22.
62. Geaman, 'Queen's Gold', 19.
63. Vincent, 'John's Jezebel', 197.
64. Wilkinson, 'Maternal Abandonment', 108; Magna Carta clause 61.

Chapter 5: Life After John

1. *Historical Currency Converter*, http://www.historicalstatistics.org/Currency converter.html.
2. Warren, *King John*, 139.
3. Warren, *King John*, 139.
4. Vincent, 'John's Jezebel', 196 n. 114.
5. Warren, *King John*, 71.
6. Lloyd, *The Maligned Monarch*, 83.
7. Patterson, 'Editorial Introduction', 6.
8. Patterson, 'Editorial Introduction', 7.
9. *ACOG* para 1.
10. Quoted in Bennett Connolly, *Ladies of the Magna Carta*, Kindle location 2943.
11. Warren, *King John*, 182-183.
12. Rhoda L. Friedrichs, 'The Remarriage of Elite Widows in the Later Middle Ages', *Florilegium*, 23/1 (2006), 75.

13. Friedrichs, The Remarriage of Elite Widows', 75.
14. Vincent, 'John's Jezebel', 198.
15. *The History of William Marshal*, 186.
16. 'Letter from Isabel of Angoulême (1220)'.
17. 'Letter from Isabel of Angoulême (1220)'.
18. 'Letter from Isabel of Angoulême (1220)'.
19. 'Letter from Isabel of Angoulême (1220)'.
20. Sharon Bennett Connolly, 'Medieval She-Wolves: Part Two," *History …
    The Interesting Bits* (February 2020), para. 13.
21. Warren, *King John*, 89.
22. Warren, *King John*, 90.

Chapter 6: Changing Roles
 1. Vincent, 'John's Jezebel', 204.
 2. *The History of William Marshal*, 152.
 3. *The History of William Marshal*, 153.
 4. *The History of William Marshal*, 183.
 5. Quoted in Jordan 'Isabelle D'Angoulême', 829.

Chapter 7: Representation in Literature
 1. Quoted in Warren, *King John*, 15.
 2. Philip Lindsay, *The Devil and King John* (Endeavour Media, 1951), Kindle
    location 676.
 3. Lindsay, *The Devil and King John*, Kindle location 729.
 4. Lindsay, *The Devil and King John*, Kindle location, 2087.
 5. Lindsay, *The Devil and King John*, Kindle location 2113.
 6. Jean Plaidy, *The Prince of Darkness* (Arrow Books, 1978), 86.
 7. Sharon Kay Penman, *Here Be Dragons* (St. Martin's Press, 1985), 121.
 8. Elizabeth Chadwick, *The Scarlet Lion* (Source Books, 2006), 61.
 9. Lindsay, *The Devil and King John*, Kindle location 861.
10. Lindsay, *The Devil and King John*, Kindle location 1989.
11. Lindsay, *The Devil and King John*, Kindle location 2513-2526.
12. Lindsay, *The Devil and King John*, Kindle location 3425-3430.
13. Plaidy, *Prince of Darkness*, 16.
14. Plaidy, *Prince of Darkness*, 16.
15. Plaidy, *Prince of Darkness*, 29.
16. Plaidy, *Prince of Darkness*, 81.
17. Plaidy, *Prince of Darkness*, 121-122.
18. Plaidy, *Prince of Darkness*, 287-288.
19. Plaidy, *Prince of Darkness*, 315.
20. Penman, *Here Be Dragons*, 257-258.
21. Chadwick, *The Scarlet Lion*, 69.
22. Chadwick, *The Scarlet Lion*, 168.
23. Lindsay, *The Devil and King John*, Kindle location, 2550.
24. Lindsay, *The Devil and King John*, Kindle location 2421.

25. Lindsay, *The Devil and King John*, Kindle location 2504-2508.
26. Plaidy, *Prince of Darkness*, 83.
27. Plaidy, *Prince of Darkness*, 112.
28. Penman, *Here Be Dragons*, 50.
29. Penman, *Here Be Dragons*, 165-166.
30. Chadwick, *The Scarlet Lion*, 56.
31. Chadwick, *The Scarlet Lion*, 63-64.
32. Lindsay, *The Devil and King John*, Kindle location, 6854-6917.
33. Lindsay, *The Devil and King John*, Kindle location 2559-2564.
34. Lindsay, *The Devil and King John*, Kindle location 2583.
35. Lindsay, *The Devil and King John*, Kindle location 557.
36. Lindsay, *The Devil and King John*, Kindle location 1400.
37. Plaidy, *Prince of Darkness*, 115.
38. Plaidy, *Prince of Darkness*, 116.
39. Plaidy, *Prince of Darkness*, 249-250.
40. Lindsay, *The Devil and King John*, Kindle location 2684-2689.
41. Lindsay, *The Devil and King John*, Kindle location 2968.
42. Plaidy, *Prince of Darkness*, 91.
43. Plaidy, *Prince of Darkness*, 95.
44. Plaidy, *Prince of Darkness*, 101.
45. Penman, *Here Be Dragons*, 121-122.
46. Penman, *Here Be Dragons*, 123.
47. Lindsay, *The Devil and King John*, Kindle 3462.
48. Plaidy, *Prince of Darkness*, 87-88.
49. Penman, *Here Be Dragons*, 509.
50. Penman, *Here Be Dragons*, 509.
51. Chadwick, *The Scarlet Lion*, 204.
52. Plaidy, *Prince of Darkness*, 329.
53. Plaidy, *Prince of Darkness*, 369.
54. Lindsay, *The Devil and King John*, Kindle location 1526.
55. Lindsay, *The Devil and King John*, Kindle location 2279.
56. Lindsay, *The Devil and King John*, Kindle location 3067-3072.
57. Lindsay, *The Devil and King John*, Kindle location 638.
58. Plaidy, *Prince of Darkness*, 242.
59. Plaidy, *Prince of Darkness*, 244.
60. Plaidy, *Prince of Darkness*, 314.
61. Quoted in Warren, *King John*, 275.
62. Penman, *Here Be Dragons*, 370-371.
63. Chadwick, *The Scarlet Lion*, 49.

Bibliography

'Abelard's Answer to Héloïse'. *Peter Abelard (1079–1142) and Heloise D'Argenteuil (1090?/1100?–-1164): Abelard's Answer to Heloise.* Edited by C.D. Warner, et al. (The Library of the World's Best Literature, 1993), www.bartleby.com/library/prose/5.html

Adler, Gillian. 'Female Intercession and the Shaping of Male Heroism in the *Roman d'Enéas* and *Le Chevalier Au Lion*'. *Medieval Feminist Forum*, 49/2 (2014), pp. 70–87

Ancient, Medieval, and Early Modern Manuscripts. 'The Death of King John'. *Medieval Manuscripts Blog*, n.d., blogs.bl.uk/digitisedmanuscripts/2014/10/the-death-of-king-john.html

Andrews, J.F. *Lost Heirs of the Medieval Crown: The Kings and Queens Who Never Were* (Pen & Swords Books, 2019)

Ashley, Maurice. *The Life and Times of King John* (Book Club Associates, 1973)

Bak, János M. 'Roles and Functions of Queens in Árpádian and Angevin Hungary (1000–1386 A.D.)'. In *Medieval Queenship*, edited by John Carmi Parsons (Sutton, 1998), pp. 13–24

Baswell, Christopher. 'Heloise'. In *The Cambridge Companion to Medieval Women's Writing*, edited by Carolyn Dinshaw and David Wallace (Cambridge University Press, 2003), pp. 161–171

Boethius. *The Consolation of Philosophy.* Translated by Richard Green (Martino Publishing, 2011)

Bordo, Susan. *The Creation of Anne Boleyn* (Mariner Books, 2013)

Bovey, Alixe. 'Women in Medieval Society'. The British Library, 17 Jan. 2014, www.bl.uk/the-middle-ages/articles/women-in-medieval-society

Brewer, Jessica. 'Etheldreda: Queen, Abbess, Saint'. *The Medieval Magazine*, 3/4 (March 2017), 31–36

Bromilow, John K. 'Church Monuments Society'. *Isabelle of Angoulême – Church Monuments Society*, 2010, churchmonumentssociety.org/monument-of-the-month/isabelle-of-angouleme-at-fontevraud-abbey

Brown, Rebecca Starr. 'King John's First Marriage'. *From Normandy to Windsor, Putting the British Monarchy in Context*, 5 Oct 2018, https://rebeccastarrbrown.com/2018/10/05/king-johns-first-marriage/

Brown, Rebecca Starr. 'A Legacy of Destruction: King John and Isabella of Angouleme'. *From Normandy to Windsor, Putting the British Monarchy in Context*, June 7, 2017, https://rebeccastarrbrown.com/2017/06/07/a-legacy-of-destruction-king-john-isabella-of-angouleme/

Brundage, James A. *Law, Sex, and Christian Society in Medieval Europe* (University of Chicago Press, 1987)

Burgess, Glyn S. and Keith Busby, eds. 'Introduction'. *The Lais of Marie de France* (Penguin Books, 2003), pp. 7–36

Burns, E. Jane. 'Courtly Love: Who Needs It? Recent Feminist Work in the Medieval French Tradition'. *Signs: Journal of Women in Culture and Society*, 27/1 (2001), pp. 23–47

Butler, Sara M. "'I will never consent to be wedded with you!": Coerced Marriage in the Courts of Medieval England'. *Canadian Journal of History* (2004), pp. 247–270

Bynum, Caroline Walker. *Jesus as Mother: Studies in the Spirituality of the High Middle Ages* (University of California Press, 1982)

Chadwick, Elizabeth. *The Scarlet Lion* (Sourcebooks, 2006)

Challoner, Richard. *The Holy Bible: Translated from the Latin Vulgate: Douay-Rheims translation* (Tan Books and Publishers, 2000)

Chibnall, Marjorie. 'The Empress Matilda and Her Sons'. In *Medieval Mothering*, edited by John Carmi Parsons (Garland Publishing, 1996), pp. 279–294

Clark, Christine G. 'Women's Rights in Early England'. *BYU Law Review*, 207/1 (March 1995), pp. 206–236

Connolly, Sharon Bennett. *Ladies of Magna Carta: Women of Influence in Thirteenth Century England* (Pen and Sword History, 2020)

Cormack, Margaret. 'Introduction: Approaches to Childbirth in the Middle Ages'. *Journal of the History of Sexuality*, 21/2 (2012), pp. 201–207

Cotes, Alison. "'All of Them Saints of God …'". *Social Alternatives*, 7/ 3 (1988), pp. 8–12

Crosby, Everett U. 'Children of the Middle Ages'. Review of *Medieval Children* by Nicholas Orme. *The Virginia Quarterly Review*, 78/4 (Autumn 2002), pp. 766–773

Cybulskie, Daniele. 'Infertility in the Middle Ages'. *Medievalists.net*, 2020, https://www.medievalists.net/2016/03/infertility-in-the-middle-ages/

Cybulskie, Danièle. *Life in Medieval Europe: Fact and Fiction* (Pen & Sword Books, 2019)

Cybulskie, Danièle. 'Royalit: What Did Medieval Kings Read?' *Medievalists.net*, 14 Apr. 2018, www.medievalists.net/2016/04/royalit-what-did-medieval-kings-read/

Dağ, Zeynep Özcan and Berna Dilbaz. 'Impact of Obesity on Infertility in Women'. *Journal of the Turkish-German Gynecological Association*, 16/2 (2015), pp. 111–117

Dawkins, Richard. *Outgrowing God* (Random House, 2019)

Diceto, Ralph of. *Radulfi De Diceto Londoniensis Opera Historica*. Edited by William Stubbs, vol. 1 (Her Majesty's Stationery Office, 1876)

Dresner, Samuel H. 'Barren Rachel'. *Judaism*, 40/4 (Fall, 1991), p. 442

Duranta, Berfu. 'Throne of Wisdom Sculptures'. *Khan Academy*, www.khanacademy.org/humanities/medieval-world/romanesque-art/beginners-guide-romanesque/a/throne-of-wisdom

d'Avray, David. *Papacy, Monarchy and Marriage 860–1600* (Cambridge University Press, 2015)

Eleanor of Aquitaine. 'A Letter from Eleanor of Aquitaine (1200)'. *Epistolae* (2014), epistolae.ctl.columbia.edu/letter/900.html

Elliott, Dyan. 'Marriage'. In *The Cambridge Companion to Medieval Women's Writing*, edited by Carolyn Dinshaw and David Wallace (Cambridge University Press, 2003), pp. 40–57

Erbguth, F.J. 'Historical Notes on Botulism, Clostridium botulinum, and the Idea of the Therapeutic Use of the Toxin'. *NCBI.NLM.NIH.gov*, 19 March 2004, https://www.ncbi.nlm.nih.gov/pubmed/15027048

Ferrante, Joan M. 'Male Fantasy and Female Reality in Courtly Literature'. *Women's Studies*, 11/1–2 (1984), pp. 67–97

FitzGerald, Brian D. 'Medieval Theories of Education: Hugh of St. Victor and John of Salisbury'. *Oxford Review of Education*, 36/5 (October 2010), pp. 575–588

Fowler, Rebekah M. 'Caritas Begins at Home: Virtue and Domesticity in Chrétien's *Yvain*'. *Arthuriana*, 27/1 (2017), pp. 43–72

Friedrichs, Rhoda L. 'The Remarriage of Elite Widows in the Later Middle Ages'. *Florilegium*, 23/1 (2006), pp. 69–83

Friehs, Julia Teresa. 'What Did People Read in the Middle Ages? Courtly and Middle-Class Reading Matter'. *Die Welt Der Habsburger*, www.habsburger.net/en/chapter/what-did-people-read-middle-ages-courtly-and-middle-class-reading-matter

Frijhoff, Willem. 'Historian's Discovery of Childhood'. *Paedagogica Historica*, 48/1 (February 2012), pp. 11–29

Geaman, Kristen. 'Anne of Bohemia and Her Struggle to Conceive'. *Social History of Medicine*, 29/2 (May 2016), pp. 224–244, https://doi.org/10.1093/shm/hku072

Geaman, Kristen. 'Beyond Good Queen Anne: Anne of Bohemia, Patronage and Politics'. In *Medieval Elite Women and the Exercise of Power, 1100–1400*, edited by Heather J. Tanner (Palgrave Macmillan, 2019), pp. 67–90

Geaman, Kristen. 'Queen's Gold and Intercession: The Case of Eleanor of Aquitaine'. *Medieval Feminist Forum*, 46/2 (2010), pp. 10–33

Gildas. 'On the Ruin of Britain'. *Gutenberg*, 1 Mar. 2020, www.gutenberg.org/cache/epub/1949/pg1949-images.html

Gordon, Edward E. *Centuries of Tutoring: A Perspective on Childhood Education* (PhD Dissertation, Loyola University, 1988)

Gratian. *The Decretum*. Translated by John T. Noonan (Catholic University of America, 1967), https://web.archive.org/web/20160117042750/http://faculty.cua.edu/pennington/Canon%20Law/marriagelaw.htm

Green, Monica (ed. and trans.). *The The Trotula* (University of Pennsylvania Press, 2001)

Green, Richard. 'Introduction'. In Boethius's *The Consolation of Philosophy*, translated by Richard Green (Martino Publishing, 2011)

Guillelmi de Conchis's Dragmaticon. Translated by Italo Ronca (University of Notre Dame Press, 1997)

Harris, Carolyn. 'How Medieval Kings and Queens Raised Their Children: An Interview with Carolyn Harris'. Medievalists.net, 8 June 2017, https://www. medievalists.net/2017/06/medieval-kings-queens-raised-children-interview-carolyn-harris/

Harris, Carolyn. 'King John and Magna Carta in Popular Culture'. *Magna Carta 2015 Canada*, 7 Dec. 2013, https://www.magnacartacanada.ca/king-john-and-magna-carta-in-popular-culture/

Harvey, Katherine. 'Episcopal Virginity in Medieval England'. *Journal of the History of Sexuality*, 26/2 (May, 2017), pp. 273–293

'Having a Baby After Age 35: How Aging Affects Fertility and Pregnancy'. *American College of Obstetricians and Gynecologists* (2020), www.acog.org/patient-resources/faqs/pregnancy/having-a-baby-after-age-35-how-aging-affects-fertility-and-pregnancy

Haseldine, Julian P. 'Friendship Networks in Medieval Europe: New Models of a Political Relationship'. *AMITY: The Journal of Friendship Studies* 1 (2013), pp. 69–88

Herm, Gerhard. *The Celts*, (St. Martin's Press, 1975)

Historical Currency Conversions, futureboy.us/fsp/dollar.fsp?quantity=80

The History of William Marshal. Translated by Nigel Bryant (Boydell, 2016)

Hume, Kathryn. 'The Metamorphoses of Empire in the Arthurian Tradition'. *Criticism*, 59/4, 2017, pp. 619–637

Huneycutt, Lois L. 'Intercession and the High-Medieval Queen: The Esther Topos'. In *Power of the Weak: Studies on Medieval Women*, edited by Jennifer Carpenter and Sally-Beth MacLean (University of Illinois Press, 1995), pp. 126–146

Hurtig, Dolliann Margaret. '"I Do, I Do": Medieval Models of Marriage and Choice of Partners in Marie de France's 'Le Fraisne'. *The Romanic Review*, 92/4 (2001), pp. 363–379

Isabel of Angoulême. 'A Letter from Isabel of Angoulême (1218–19)'. *Epistolae* (2014), https://epistolae.ctl.columbia.edu/letter/24162.html

Isabel of Angoulême. 'A Letter from Isabel of Angoulême (1220)'. *Epistolae* (2014), https://epistolae.ctl.columbia.edu/letter/457.html

Jeffrey, David Lyle. 'Courtly Love and Christian Marriage: Chrétien De Troyes, Chaucer, and Henry VIII'. *Christianity & Literature*, 59/3 (2010), pp. 515–530

John of Salisbury. *The Metalogicon of John of Salisbury: A Twelfth-century Defense of the Verbal and Logical Arts of the Trivium*. Translated by D. McGarry. (University of California, 1962 [1159])

Jones, Dan. *The Plantagenets: The Warrior Kings and Queens Who Made England* (Viking Penguin Books, 2014)

Jones, Peter Murray and Lea T. Olsan. 'Performative Rituals for Conception and Childbirth in England, 900–1500'. *Bulletin of the History of Medicine*, 89/3 (Fall 2015), pp. 406–433, https://www.ncbi.nlm.nih.gov/pmc/articles/PMC4696514/

Jordan, William Chester. 'Isabelle D'Angoulême, By the Grace of God, Queen'. *Revue Belge De Philologie Et D'histoire*, 69/4 (1991), pp. 821–852

Karras, Ruth Mazo. 'Invisible Women'. *Medieval Feminist Forum* 39 (2005), pp. 15–21

Keene, Catherine. 'Read Her like a Book: Female Patronage as *Imitatio Mariae*'. *Magistra*, 24/1 (Summer 2018), pp. 8–38

Kelleher, Marie A. 'What Do We Mean by "Women and Power"?' *Medieval Feminist Forum*, 51/ 2 (2015), pp. 104–115

Kibler, William W. 'Introduction'. In Chrétien de Troyes, *Arthurian Romances* (Penguin Books, 1991), pp. 1–22

Kuefler, Mathew S. '"A Wyred Existence": Attitudes Towards Children in Anglo-Saxon England'. *Journal of Social History*, 24/4 (Summer, 1991), pp. 823–834

Lacaze, P.L. 'On Suffering: Lessons from Boethius'. *The Postil Magazine*, 1 July 2017, www.thepostil.com/on-suffering-some-boethian-insights/

'A Letter from Isabel of Angoulême (1220)'. Translated by Joan Ferrante, *Epistolae*, epistolae.ctl.columbia.edu/letter/457.html

Lewis, Katherine J. 'Model Girls? Virgin-Martyrs and the Training of Young Women in Late Medieval England'. In *Young Medieval Women*, edited by Katherine J. Lewis, Menuge Noël James, and Kim M. Phillips (St. Martins Press, 1999), pp. 25–46

Lewis, Mary, Fiona Shapland, and Rebecca Watts. 'On the Threshold of Adulthood: A New Approach for the Use of Maturation Indicators to Assess Puberty in Adolescents from Medieval England'. *American Journal of Human Biology*, 28 (2016), pp. 48–56

Lindsay, Philip. *The Devil and King John* (Endeavour Media, 1951), Kindle ed.

Lloyd, Alan. *The Maligned Monarch* (Doubleday, 1972)

MacLehose, William F. 'Nurturing Danger: High Medieval Medicine and the Problem(s) of the Child'. In *Medieval Mothering*, edited by John Carmi Parsons (Garland Publishing, 1996), pp. 3–24

Magdeburg, Mechthild von. *The Flowing Light of the Godhead*. Edited by Frank Tobin (Paulist Press, 1998)

'The Magna Carta Project'. *Magna Carta Project – Original Charters of King John*, 2015, magnacarta.cmp.uea.ac.uk/read/original_charters

'Maternal Mortality in 2000–2017'. *WHO.int*, n.d., https://www.who.int/gho/maternal_health/countries/gbr.pdf?ua=1

McLynn, Frank. *Lionheart and Lackland: King Richard, King John and the Wars of Conquest* (Vintage Books, 2006)

'Medieval Women's Letters'. Translated by Joan Ferrante, *Epistolae*, epistolae.ctl.columbia.edu/

Molchan, Greg. 'Anna and the King(s): Marriage Alliances, Ethnicity, and Succession in the *Historia Regum Britanniae*'. *Arthuriana*, 24/1 (2014), pp. 25–48

Monmouth, Geoffrey of. *The History of the Kings of Britain*. Translated by Lewis Thorpe (Penguin, 1973)

Morris, Marc. *King John: Treachery and Tyranny in Medieval England: The Road to Magna Carta* (Pegasus Books, 2015)

Murray, Jacqueline. 'Thinking about Gender: The Diversity of Medieval Perspectives'. In *Power of the Weak: Studies on Medieval Women*, edited by Jennifer Carpenter and Sally-Beth MacLean (University of Illinois Press, 1995), pp. 1–26

Murray, K. Sarah-Jane. 'Marie De France, Ethicist: Questioning Courtly Love in *Laüstic*'. *Modern Philology*, 109/1 (2011), pp. 1–16

Nam, Jong Kuk. 'Social Perception of Infertility and Its Treatment in Late Medieval Italy: Margherita Datini, an Italian Merchant's Wife'. *Korean Journal of Medical History*, 25/3 (December, 2016), pp. 519–556

Nennius. *Historia Brittonum (The History of the Britons)*. Fordham University Medieval Sourcebook, 2 Jan 2020, https://sourcebooks.fordham.edu/source/nennius.asp

Newman, Barbara. *Sister of Wisdom: St. Hildegard's Theology of the Feminine* (University of California Press, 1997)

Norton, Elizabeth. *She-Wolves: The Notorious Queens of Medieval England* (The History Press, 2010), Kindle ed.

Orme, Nicholas. *Medieval Children* (Yale University Press, 2001)

Otten, Willemien. 'Christianity's Content: (Neo)Platonism in the Middle Ages, Its Theoretical and Theological Appeal'. *Numen* 63 (2016), pp. 245–270

Oxford English Dictionary. "Neoplatonism, n." *OED Online*, Oxford University Press, March 2021, www.oed.com/view/Entry/126068

Painter, Sydney. *The Reign of King John* (Arno Press, 1979)

Paris, Matthew. 'Matthæi Parisiensis, Monachi Sancti Albani, *Chronica Majora*: Matthew Paris, Roger : Free Download, Borrow, and Streaming'. *Internet Archive* (January, 1876), archive.org/details/matthiparisiens00unkngoog/page/n19/mode/2up

Parsons, John Carmi. 'Introduction: Family, Sex, and Power: The Rhythms of Medieval Queenship'. In *Medieval Queenship*, edited by John Carmi Parsons (Sutton, 1994), pp. 1–11

Parsons, John Carmi. 'The Queen's Intercession in Thirteenth-Century England'. In *Power of the Weak: Studies on Medieval Women*, edited by Jennifer Carpenter and Sally-Beth MacLean (University of Illinois Press, 1995), pp. 147–177

Parsons, John Carmi, editor. *Medieval Queenship* (Sutton, 1994)

Patterson, Robert B., ed. 'Editorial Introduction'. *Earldom of Gloucester Charters* (Clarendon Press, 1973)

Penman, Sharon Kay. *Here Be Dragons* (St. Martin's Press, 1985)

Phillips, Kim M. 'Maidenhood as the Perfect Age of Woman's Life'. In *Young Medieval Women*, edited by Katherine J. Lewis, Noel James Mengue, and Kim M. Phillips (St. Martin's Press, 1999), pp. 1–24

Plaidy, Jean. *The Prince of Darkness* (Arrow Books, 1978)

Potkay, Monica Brzezinski. 'The Parable of the Sower and Obscurity in the Prologue to Marie De France's Lais'. *Christianity & Literature*, 57/3 (2008), pp. 355–378

Potkay, Monica Brzezinski and Regula Meyer Evitt. *Minding the Body: Women and Literature in the Middle Ages, 800–1500* (Twayne's Women and Literature Series, 1997)

Price, Richard. 'King John's Letters'. *Facebook*, 2015, m.facebook.com/groups/9 87891884664480/?ref=group_header

Raabe, Pamela. 'Chrétien's Lancelot and the Sublimity of Adultery'. *University of Toronto Quarterly* 57/2 (1988), pp. 259–269

Radle, Gabriel. 'Bishops Blessing the Bridal Bedchamber in the Early Middle Ages: Reconsidering the Western Evidence'. *Medium Ævum*, 86/2 (2018), pp. 219–238

'Reproductive Health'. *CDC.gov*, 4 Feb 2020, https://www.cdc.gov/reproductivehealth/maternal-mortality/pregnancy-mortality-surveillance-system.htm

Richards, Jeffrey. *Sex, Dissidence and Damnation: Minority Groups in the Middle Ages* (Barnes and Noble Books, 1990)

Richardson, H.G. 'The Marriage and Coronation of Isabelle of Angoulême'. *The English Historical Review*, 61/241 (Sept. 1946), pp. 289–314

Riches, Sam and Miriam Gill. 'Saints in Medieval Society'. *Pilgrims and Pilgrimage*, www.york.ac.uk/projects/pilgrimage/content/med_saint.html

St. Jerome. *Against Jovianus* (Aeterna Press, 2016), Kindle ed.

Salih, Sarah. 'Saints and Sanctity in Medieval England'. *The British Library* (4 January, 2018), www.bl.uk/medieval-literature/articles/saints-and-sanctity-in-medieval-england#

Salih, Sarah. 'Sex and Spouses: Marriage, Pleasure and Consummation' (Brown University Decameron Web, 31 Jan. 2011), www.brown.edu/Departments/Italian_Studies/dweb/society/sex/sex-spouses.php

Shadis, Miriam. 'Berenguela of Castile's Political Motherhood: The Management of Sexuality, Marriage, and Succession'. In *Medieval Mothering*, edited by John Carmi Parsons, (Garland Publishing, 1996), pp. 335–358

Shapland, Fiona, Mary Lewis, and Rebecca Watts. 'Lives and Deaths of Young Medieval Women'. *Medieval Archaeology*, 59 (2015), pp. 272–289

Slitt, Rebecca. 'The Boundaries of Women's Power: Gender and the Discourse of Political Friendship in Twelfth-Century England'. *Gender & History*, 24/1 (2012), pp. 1–17

Smith, Lesley. 'Medieval Marriage and Superstitions'. *Journal of Family Planning and Reproductive Health Care*, 38/1 (November, 2011), pp. 60–62

Stafford, Pauline. 'The Portrayal of Royal Women in England, Mid-Tenth to Mid-Twelfth Centuries'. In *Medieval Queenship*, edited by John Carmi Parsons (Sutton, 1998), pp. 143–167

Stapleton, Rachel F. 'Motherly Devotion and Fatherly Obligation: Eleanor of Aquitaine's Letters to Pope Celestine III'. *Medieval Feminist Forum*, 48/1 (2012), pp. 97–121

Stoertz, Fiona Harris. 'Young Women in France and England, 1050–1300'. *Journal of Women's History*, 12/4 (Winter, 2001), pp. 22–46

Thorpe, Lewis. 'Introduction'. In Geoffrey of Monmouth *The History of the Kings of Britain* (Penguin Books, 1966). pp. 9–37

Turner, Ralph. *King John: England's Evil King?* (The History Press, 1994)

Vauchez, André. *Sainthood in the Later Middle Ages* (Cambridge University Press, 1997)

Verini, Alexandra. 'Medieval Models of Female Friendship in Christine de Pizan's *The Book of the City of Ladies* and Margery Kempe's *The Book of Margery Kempe*'. *Feminist Studies*, 2016, 42/2, pp. 365–391

Vincent, Nicholas. 'The Great Lost Library of England's Medieval Kings?: Royal Use and Ownership of Books, 1066–1272'. In *1000 Years of Royal Books and Manuscripts*, edited by Kathleen Doyle and Scot McKendrick (British Library, 2013), pp. 73–112

Vincent, Nicholas. 'Isabella of Angoulême: John's Jezebel'. In *King John: New Interpretations*, edited by S.D. Church (Boydell, 1999), pp. 165–219

Vincent, Nicholas. 'King John: The Making of a Medieval Monster'. *HistoryExtra* (12 August 2019), www.historyextra.com/period/medieval/king-john-evil-ireland-monster-nicholas-vincent-magna-carta/

Warren, W.L. *King John* (University of California Press, 1961)

Wilkinson, Louise. 'Isabella of Gloucester'. *Magna Carta Trust 800th Anniversary*, 16 Dec. 2014, magnacarta800th.com/schools/biographies/women-of-magna-carta/isabella-of-gloucester/#_edn1

Wilkinson, Louise J. 'Maternal Abandonment and Surrogate Caregivers: Isabella of Angoulême and her Children by King John'. In *Virtuous or Villainess? The Image of the Royal Mother from the Early Medieval to the Early Modern Era*, edited by Carey Fleiner and Elena Woodacre (Palgrave Macmillan, 2016), pp. 101–124

Wilkinson, Louise. 'Medieval Queenship in England: A Changing Dynamic?' *The Historian* (Autumn 2013), pp. 6–11

Willette, Dorothy. 'The Enduring Symbolism of Doves'. *Biblical Archaeology Society*, 5 January 2020, www.biblicalarchaeology.org/daily/ancient-cultures/daily-life-and-practice/the-enduring-symbolism-of-doves/

Wulf, Charlotte A.T. 'The Coronation of Arthur and Guenevere in Geoffrey of Monmouth's *Historia Regum Britanniae*, Wace's *Roman De Brut*, and Lawman's *Brut*'. *Reading La3amon's Brut* (January 2013), pp. 229–251